Supervising in the Human Services

Supervising in the Human Services

The Politics of Practice

Stephen Holloway
George Brager

THE FREE PRESS
A Division of Macmillan, Inc.
NEW YORK

Collier Macmillan Publishers
LONDON

The Free Press
A Division of Macmillan, Inc.
866 Third Avenue, New York, N. Y. 10022

Collier Macmillan Canada, Inc.

Printed in the United States of America

printing numbers
1 2 3 4 5 6 7 8 9 10

Library of Congress Cataloging-in-Publication Data

Holloway, Stephen.
    Supervising in the human services: the politics of practice/
Stephen Holloway, George Brager.
        p.   cm.
        ISBN 0-02-914810-3
        1. Social work administration—United States.   2. Human services—
United States—Management.   3. Supervision of social workers.
I. Brager, George.   II. Title.
HV95.H563   1989
361'.0068'3—dc19
                                                      88-16475
                                                        CIP

For
MURRAY and BETTY HOLLOWAY
and
LENORE BRAGER

Contents

Contents

Acknowledgments

We wish to acknowledge our gratitude to Alex Gitterman, our colleague at the Columbia University School of Social Work. Alex read and critiqued the entire volume, offering invaluable suggestions. If we have been successful in rooting our ideas about supervision in the "real world" of practice, we owe much of that success to him.

Thanks are also in order to Laura Wolff, our editor at The Free Press, and to our students at Columbia who read several draft chapters. It will not be news to most academics that students are hard taskmasters, and ours were no exception. We found their comments on early drafts to be exceedingly helpful in the further development of our ideas.

Finally, we acknowledge our debt to the staff members of Columbia University Community Services, a multifaceted University-based project of services, training, and curriculum development in the field of homelessness. Their good-natured reaction to our supervisory experimentation is much appreciated, and their contributions to our practice wisdom has been immeasurable.

Organizational Practice and Supervisory Politics

This book is about supervisory practice in the human services. It emphasizes the critical influence of organizational context on supervision, a subject that has been largely neglected in the supervisory literature. Our perspective has two major foci. One relates to the organization's structure, its hierarchy, and division of labor. In this regard, we note particularly the consequences for practice of the supervisor's location in the middle of the hierarchy, mediating the often distant worlds of the line worker and administrator. A second focus relates to the political nature of organizational life and how "small p" politics—the attempts to muster power to influence decision making in one's favor—is an inherent aspect of effective supervision. This chapter deals with theory relevant to the above and makes the case for the impact of the middle role and a political perspective on supervisory transactions.

How one practices within any agency is shaped by the organization's structure and processes. This is the case at whatever the worker's hierarchical level, whether practitioner, supervisor, or top manager, and for whatever the type of setting, whether a business or human services organization or one that is publicly or privately managed. Organizational influences are sometimes clear and direct; for example, when a specific policy or procedure is designed to attract one type of client or to exclude another. Sometimes, these influences are subtle and indirect, so that organizational participants may be unaware of the organization's effects on their own or their client's behavior. For example, in a classic study of a mental hospital, there was the serendipitous finding that although the patients were apparently unaware of the staff's relations with each other,

1

tensions among staff were highly correlated with patient acting out (Stanton and Schwartz, 1954).

As important, how one *perceives* organizational structure and process
strongly influences the interventions one chooses. Essentially, it is the
meaning that we ascribe to events rather than the events themselves that
shape our responses to them, however near to or far from reality the
ascription of meaning may be. It follows that one's frame of reference or
theoretical perspective regarding how organizations function is also a
significant factor in practice, because they color one's interpretations of
what occurs. Consider the worker who bemoans the fact that his agency is
too rife with politics, a widely shared complaint among human service
workers. What is ordinarily meant by this assertion is that decisions are
not made on objective professional grounds but are the result of the
interests and influence of particular actors. There are at least two assumptions in that statement that have relevance for practice. The complaint
presupposes that politics is relatively unique to the worker's agency rather
than inevitable in organizational life. It also betrays a pejorative attitude
toward engaging in politics, as if politics and professionalism were incompatible. The worker is thus likely to eschew playing the political game or
to play it with discomfort, thereby limiting his ability to advance desirable
programs or values. Conversely, workers who view agency politics as a
natural component of organizational life and who understand its elements are in a more favorable position to promote their strongly held
beliefs.

The influence of one's assumptions on practice is considerable,
whether the assumptions are explicit or implicit, poorly formulated or
well developed. The worker's reaction to the political nature of his agency
was probably spontaneous and ad hoc, and it is unlikely that he considered the practice implications of his remark. Indeed, the comment might
well have been prompted by his failure to advance some interest of his
and could have served as an ex post facto rationale to justify a defeat. Or it
may have sprung from a more fundamental value position that political
behavior is inconsistent with openness. But regardless of the antecedents,
unless workers can identify the assumptions underlying their points of
view, they will experience difficulty in fully taking charge of how they use
themselves organizationally. To maximize supervisory effectiveness,
workers must have greater professional self consciousness than implicit
assumptions permit, as well as a set of precepts to guide their practice
choices.

It is in this spirit that we make our own assumptions in regard to aspects
of organization and management theory clear, because they serve as the

grounding for the practice prescriptions that follow in later chapters. Four emphases in organizational thinking are sketched: (1) the structuralist perspective, with particular attention to the supervisor's location in the middle of the agency hierarchy, (2) politics as a predominant feature of organizational life (3) the human relations approach, and (4) the rationalist view of organizational decision making. Although in some formulations all four compete as a singular means of understanding organizational phenomena, they are not by any means mutually exclusive. Elements of both human relations and rational decision-making perspectives are important to practice and are, in part, incorporated into the approach to supervision developed in this book. Our emphasis is not evenhanded, however, because we view structural and political perspectives as primary.

Agency Structure as a Factor in Supervisory Practice

Organizational structure—by which we mean organizational activities that occur with patterned regularity—strongly influences the behavior of an agency's participants and, as such, importantly shapes supervisory interventions. The most obvious dimension of structure—and the most important as well—is the organization's hierarchy of authority. Hierarchy refers to the varying levels in an agency that define the extent of a person's responsibility and fix his or her accountability. Three levels of hierarchy are ordinarily identified. There is an upper level that has primary responsibility for dealing with the external environment. It must also garner the necessary resources to conduct the organization's business, and it is the level to whom persons of lower ranks in the organization are ultimately accountable. A second is the middle level that oversees the ongoing and daily operations of the enterprise and also the third group, a line level that is involved in the major output of the organization. The latter, in service agencies, consists of those staff who maintain contact with the recipients of the agency's service. As we shall see, persons located at different places in the chain of command are privy to different, potentially contradictory views about organizational issues. Their concerns and stake in organizational events are, therefore, different and potentially conflicting as well.

The pressure a supervisory position generates as a consequence of its location in the organization's structure is profound. The dilemma of Sara Widdoes may be useful to illustrate the point. Sara has been the supervisor of a satellite service unit operated by her agency, a community mental health center, for two years. There are four such satellite service units. Along with the supervisors of the other units, Sara reports to the director of clinical services, who in turn reports to the executive director. Having worked in the agency for several years, Sara feels that she took her job with her eyes open, but she also finds that being effective in the role is more difficult than she initially imagined. The previous supervisor was viewed by staff as rigid and clinically conservative. They voiced resentment at her close supervision, her unwillingness to extend staff responsibilities, and her reluctance to involve them in making unit decisions of the conduct of unit affairs.

Sara assumed the position with the understanding that staff morale was so low that major changes were in order, and the clinical director encouraged her to involve the staff in unit problem solving. Eventually, she instituted weekly staff meetings and gave her staff a larger role in recommending policy. When a new staff member was to be hired, she asked her staff to develop the selection criteria and engaged their participation in the interview process. She instituted a new system for intake and case disposition which had the effect of distributing caseloads more equitably and shortening the intake process for clients.

Since Sara has taken over the unit, the agency has faced an increasingly bleak fiscal picture. Several grants have not been renewed; administrative concerns with productivity have increased, and extra resources have been impossible to obtain. The administration has instituted several cost-cutting measures, including encouraging staff to move away from long-term work with clients to crisis, short-term interventions, work with groups, and other service activities that the administration considered to be more cost-effective. They have also instituted a management information system designed to collect further data on the nature and impact of services being delivered. These administrative initiatives have been met with staff resentment and resistance.

Sometimes Sara feels that her job is impossible. Despite her successful efforts to improve unit systems and involve staff in the administration of the unit, they seem as dissatisfied as ever. They appear to feel that she is not an effective advocate for their views and interests with the administration. They complain that the administration does not understand how penny wise, pound foolish the cost-cutting measures are, nor does the administration "really care" about the negative consequences these measures have for clients. They argue that the increased paper work imposed by the new information system takes them away from delivering service. "These," they say, "are the significant decisions in the agency, and they are also the ones in which we *never* have a say." If Sara does not closely control discussion, staff meetings seem inevitably to degenerate into gripe sessions, with the staff complaining that current agency policy virtually prevents them from providing effective service.

On the other hand, Sara's boss seems to be constantly pressing her in regard to one or another issue with respect to her staff. He indicates that staff compliance with the procedures of the new information system is unsatisfactory. He maintains that the staff is also resisting efforts to move into more cost-effective forms of service. He sometimes accuses Sara of overidentification with her staff which, he says, prevents her from being sufficiently "tough" and thus effective with them.

And then there are the other unit supervisors. Sara finds that her relations with them are fraught with unspoken conflict. They are not open about problems they are experiencing in their units, presenting a much better picture than Sara knows to be the case. She feels that they are constantly competing to "look good" in the eyes of the clinical director, often at her expense or that of other colleagues. There is continuous maneuvering and submerged conflict in efforts to protect "turf" and obtain additional resources. Information is not shared, and when it is necessary to cooperate around a difficult case or problem, it often requires substantial effort.

Although the details of Sara's situation are unique, the requirement that she function in the middle, managing relations between line staff and the agency's administration, is a general characteristic of the supervisory role. It is true, of course, that all organizational actors function in the middle to some extent. Line practitioners experience sharp contrast between the needs of their clients, the requirements of agency policy, and the strictures of their supervisors. Executives also face pressures from program and administrative staff, on the one hand, and from the board of directors, funding sources, and community groups on the other. Yet nowhere in the organization is the experience of being in the middle likely to be more acute than for the line supervisor who is at the center of conflicting demands and expectations from direct service workers below and the organization's administration above. Although, as in Sara's case, other structural factors contribute to supervisory dilemmas as well, the most important are those related to the differential perspectives, priorities, and commitments that result from the structure of organizational authority.

Linking Executives and Line Workers

The disparate concerns of executives and direct service workers translate into demands on the supervisor who serves as linkage between the levels.

Executives of human service agencies are responsible for the maintenance of the organization and the accomplishment of its goals. They
must garner the resources necessary for its survival, assure its fiscal stability, and promote support for it from relevant publics. To fulfill these
responsibilities, executives have relationships with oversight entities,
funding sources, and other politically important components of the organization's set. The executives' perspectives and priorities are shaped by
these requirements. They must, for example, receive information that is
diverse and that stems from multiple sources, as much originating from
outside the agency as from within. Their constituencies and reference
groups generate significantly different demands and require responsiveness of a different order than the reference groups of line staff. And
the criteria by which these bodies, and indeed the executives themselves,
define successful performance are also different. The concerns of executives regarding the agency's reputation and its goals and finances, as well
as the differential approach of top level staff to day-to-day operations,
impinge on line workers and thus highlight common supervisory pressure
points.

Executives are highly attentive to oversight bodies such as the boards of
directors of voluntary organizations or public officials in the case of
government agencies. Because oversight entities are, in turn, responsive
to others (e.g., influential people in the community, funding sources,
legislators, and program review groups), the executive's attentiveness extends to these powerful others as well. The reputation of the agency stems
in considerable measure from whether the agency *appears* to these constituencies to be engaged in "good works," and the reputation of the
executive is similarly influenced by agency appearances. We use the word
appear because the actual performance of human service organizations is
largely or at least partially invisible, and the executive's concern is with
how things look as well as with how they are. In any case, because the
well-being of both the agency and the executive stems from the executive's relationships with those powerful groups, the effectiveness of his or
her relationships with them is a significant executive priority.

Oversight bodies require evidence that the agency is accomplishing its
goals and meeting appropriate standards or regulations. Depending on
the agency and the outside demands on it, measures for evaluating agency effectiveness vary, extending all the way from anecdotes about client
service to systematic program evaluation. With advances in communications technology, however, internal management and data-collection systems have become widely used sources of evaluation and accountability.
Increasingly, information must be generated that details the specifics of

service delivered and the particulars of clients receiving the services. For public agencies or voluntary agencies that contract with the public sector, state and local regulations regarding service quality and standards often require keeping detailed information, as does eligibility determination and verification. (For one particularly dramatic example: following modifications in child welfare legislation in 1978 in New York state, all contract agencies receiving reimbursement for foster care and adoption were required to submit a case record that entailed collecting nine pages of data at intake for every client, as well as extensive recording during the course of service!) In sum, the collection of considerable data, either for the purpose of evaluating the agency's program or to meet oversight requirements, is a matter of some priority to executives.

The burdens of the task fall on direct service workers who are, after all, the only members of the organization with firsthand knowledge of the specifics of service character and impact. For them, however, priorities ordinarily flow from their responsibility for providing the service, and their concerns do or should reflect a service commitment. But extensive data collection deflects from direct work with their clients and is often time-consuming and thus onerous. Data collection may threaten quality service in other ways as well. Service provision regulations frequently constrain workers from providing the kind or extent of service that in their professional judgment is necessary to ensure client well-being, and in addition, clients with legitimate needs may be ineligible for service by agency or legislative mandate. Workers often try to bend the rules, but the effort entails considerably more risk when a systematic information system is in place. Further, collecting data may reveal inadequate practitioner performance, as in the case of an inordinate number of client no-shows in comparison with other workers.

In brief, the executive's need for data and the worker's need to provide it often operate at cross-purposes. The executive's means of mediating this conflict is the supervisor, for it is the supervisor who is asked to see to it that requisite procedures are followed. Gaining staff cooperation and dealing with staff resistance becomes the supervisor's task to manage.

The executive's priority regarding external relations causes similar structural strains. The care and feeding of these relations consume major amounts of executive time; studies have shown that approximately 40 to 60 percent of an executive's time is devoted to activities outside the organization (Patti, 1983). A consequence is that many internal issues emanating from or affecting the interests of lower-level staff are postponed or set aside. When the clarification of procedures, policy recommendations, and sanctions for program activities, or expenditures sit on the executive's desk, staff impatience, and sometimes resentment, is a likely outcome. Often too, the staff come to feel that executives are insufficiently concerned about or do not understand staff and client needs.

Furthermore, executives are necessarily responsive and sometimes perhaps more responsive to the ideas and values of other than staff and client constituencies. Organizational survival and well-being require an executive's attention to the powerful groups in the environment. But boards of directors and similar bodies frequently do not share the service ethic of agency professionals, including even the executive's. Nevertheless, the executive must often accommodate or compromise in regard to the positions of these superordinate bodies, thus appearing to lower-line workers as not quite principled.

Once again, the supervisor is caught in the structural middle. She is the one who ordinarily presses the executive for the needed clarification or acceptance of a recommendation while she must simultaneously cope with the staff's reactions to undue delay. And in the case of conflicting positions, she is faced with the dilemma of taking sides or not taking sides without risking her appearance of loyalty to either group.

Perhaps no subject causes greater consternation along hierarchical lines than issues relating to agency finances. It is not uncommon, for example, to hear the complaint that executives are concerned only about the budget and have little concern about the service mission of the organization. Executives, for their part, decry the unreasonableness of staff complaints. "If they cared more for their clients," a hard-working executive might be heard to say, "staff would be willing to invest more of their time and energy in their work." It is in exactly this kind of bind that Sara Widdoes found herself.

Even in periods of relative prosperity, resources are finite, and the executive's responsibility for the ultimate allocation of funds creates supervisory tensions. In the scramble for a "fair share," the supervisor is again faced with conflicting requirements. She must represent staff interests to the executive even as she seeks to gain executive approbation. How she fares with the executive in acquiring resources for her unit in comparison to her colleagues' success in other units is likely to have a significant impact on her staff's perceptions of her competence. At the same time, the fiscal needs of the organization may call for the staff to submit extended or complex recording or require special efforts from them to "market" the agency. At the least, executives will expect supervisors to obtain staff compliance to these requirements; at best, they will also expect the supervisor to educate staff so that they understand and accept the requirements as well.

In the final analysis, executives press to reduce organizational unpredictability, and one important means of doing so is directly or indirectly to control staff behavior. Staffs, for their part, seek autonomy and look to expand their decision-making domains, frequently at the expense of an executive dictum. Although the supervisor is the instrument of executive control, she must also serve as an advocate for her staff. Spanning these worlds is a critical function of the role, and it is likely that both executive and staff will pressure the supervisor to align herself with them. Thus the clinical director in our case example who accused Sara of overidentification with her staff and the staff who evidenced their dissatisfaction with agency decision making were both essentially exerting pressure on Sara to line up with them. Indeed, it is not farfetched to speculate that if the person in the middle appears to be more responsive to the persons at one level, those at the other level will increase their pressure accordingly. Obviously, the higher ranking group is favored in this contest, although the outcome is by no means fixed.

Supervisors, as middle persons, can align themselves with the higher ranks or lower ones. If they act as if they are extensions of either of these ranks, however, to all intents and purposes they have joined that rank. They thus trade some of the confusion that comes from being in the middle for lesser effectiveness in performing their supervisory role. Other accommodations are possible for those in this middle position as well. They may attempt to be equally responsive to the tops and the bottoms. Conversely, they may try to withdraw from both, creating subtle buffers around themselves to discourage intrusion by either group (Oshrey, 1980). Another accommodation is to join in coalition with colleagues in similar roles, thus trying to garner greater freedom of action for themselves. Or they may move from one to another of these various accommodations. Whatever the choice, how they deal with the middle position is highly relevant in practice, and in subsequent chapters we explore some of the means for managing the actors who are on the different rungs of the organizational ladder.

Hierarchy, however, is not the sole structural factor that affects supervisory performance. Two other structural dimensions are worth brief note here. One has to do with role differentiation or the division of tasks among participants according to their function or area of specialization. As knowledge has expanded, so too has the need for in-depth expertise in ever-growing content areas, and this has resulted in an explosion of subspecialties within professions (e.g., surgery, pediatrics, gynecology, to name but three of the numerous medical specialties). Furthermore, human problems have been found to be intractable to single-pronged interventions. People's needs are interdependent, as are the conditions that give rise to them. A comprehensive approach, blanketing diverse professions, subspecialties, and areas of expertise, is necessary for effective performance.

But if specialization of task and function is a structural necessity, it also engenders problems. Organizations are composed of a set of interdependent parts, each of which contributes to and receives something from the whole. Because the behavior of any part of the system has consequences for the other parts, a high degree of interdependence, combined with a high degree of specialization, generates contradictory pressures for organizational members in general and its supervisory staff in particular. Take, for example, a team in a pyschiatric center. It is not unusual for a social worker, psychologist, nurse, and occupational therapist to work with the same patient and for them to be ultimately responsible to different department heads. If the problems of coordination between them were not enough to cause difficulty, the varying norms, perspectives, and stakes of the different professions have the potential for inducing considerable tension among them.

An understanding of the potential consequences of role specialization on individual and unit behavior is an important assessment tool. From a structural perspective, one would ask, for example, whether conflict between a psychologist and a social worker in a public school had to do with who they are as individuals or with their respective roles, for example, is there overlap in their tasks that generate issues of territoriality? Or is one of them underutilized and the other overloaded? Clearly, remedics flow from how one answers those questions. Greater specificity of the psychologist's and social worker's responsibilities and/or a reallocation of their assignments could solve or mitigate the problem if it is a structural one. Or if these or other structural remedies are unavailable, tensions can nevertheless be less personalized if the parties understand them as inherent in an organizations's structure.

Finally, a third dimension of structure worth noting is the rules and procedures that serve to regulate organizational behavior. Rules serve a number of critical functions for organizations—among them, to coordinate diverse tasks without time-wasting interaction, to standardize staff action so as to assure consistency, to reduce the inefficiency required to make decisions anew in instances of recurring events, and to ensure behavior in conformance with the organization's mission. Rules may be unstated understandings or be written; they may be pervasive or limited to routine or standard matters. One way of characterizing organizational structure is by the extent of formalization of the agency's rule system. Not surprisingly perhaps, it has been found that agencies in a hostile environment are more likely to protect themselves by elaborating rules and developing formal structures than those in benign environments (Rose, 1955). Whatever its causes, however, rules have different impact on different actors and organizational subunits. Because they are control devices, rules generate tension among participants, especially professionals who may perceive self or peer direction rather than the organization as the legitimate authority. Nowhere in the hierarchy is the tension greater than among the organization's supervisory staff.

Although individual and unit problems may have other than structural antecedents, effective practice in our view requires that they receive major consideration in one's choice of intervention. Structural elements are too often overlooked—perhaps because their impact is indirect and therefore less visible or perhaps because workers in the human services fields place disproportionate emphasis on individual personality as a prime explanatory variable. A number of empirical studies conclude, however, that structural variables account for more attitude variance on the part of organizational members than do personality factors. (Berger and Cummings, 1979). Whatever the reason for the neglect, scrutiny of how one's place in the hierarchy, role and function, organizational rules and procedures, and the like impinge on one or a unit of practitioners provides an important guideline to practice. Although there are a number of reasons why this is so, none is more compelling that the fact that agency structure mediates how organizational resources are distributed, and it is the distribution of resources that undergirds organizational politics.

Political Perspectives

Politics has long been a neglected component in the study of organizational functioning (Pettigrew, 1972), and it is only recently that political considerations have found their way into social work thought. In his definitive contribution to the supervisory literature in social work, Kadushin, (1976, pp. 65–67) does identify some political tasks. He and others comment on the problem of the supervisor serving as an administrative buffer "absorbing crisis," "cooptation," "obtaining compliance," and "utilizing rewards and sanctions." Nonetheless, the centrality of politics to effect supervisory practice has received scant attention.

We suggested earlier that politics is a natural and inevitable phenomenon in organizational life. The case for its inevitability starts with the assumption that the allocation of resources constitutes a primary set of organizational decisions. Resources may be concrete, such as staff, money, or goods, or they may be intangibles, such as values, prestige, and influence. In either case, the allocation takes place under conditions of scarcity. That means simply that "everyone cannot get everything he wants, given the diverse things people want and the amounts in which people want them." (Lerner, 1976, p. 24). Further, resources are critical to the well-being, and therefore to the self-interests, of the organization's participants. The more resources one has, the more control one has over one's operations. This is the case from both economic and political vantage points. A larger budget provides leeway to accommodate various programs and service claims. And an increase in staff or budget makes for greater impact on the organization as a whole, enhancing the ability to influence organizational policy.

Although Sara Widdoes, in our case example, would probably not have conceptualized it this way, a significant part of her difficulty had to do with the allocation of resources. She was apparently unable to garner the necessary influence from either the clinical director or her staff to ensure the effective operation of her unit. Interestingly, too, the clinical director felt that he, through Sara, did not have sufficient influence to get the staff to perform as he wished, and the staff, in turn, were dissatisfied with the limited extent of their own influence on the agency's program. In addition to influence, another resource we may assume Sara sought was the respect or esteem of both staff and superiors, once again with apparently limited success. Concrete resources were also at issue. Thus the agency could not or would not allocate the requisite funds to her unit. Further, the competition with her colleagues in charge of other units was related to the scramble of the units for funds.

It is, as we have said, through the organization's hierarchical or vertical levels that authority and other resources are allocated. Horizontally, there are the various individuals and subunits representing differing functions or disciplines, each of which receives varying amounts of the organization's resources. Tensions that stem from vertical patterning have been noted in the discussion of the middle role of the supervisor, but tensions are also generated as a result of agency specialization as well. These occur because individuals and units with disparate roles and functions, like those on differing hierarchical levels, are also privy to different information, hold varying responsibilities, have diverse stakes in organizational actions, and thus have dissimilar perspectives and positions. Horizontal tensions are also created by the fact that resources are allocated unequally, and each subunit's share of influence and organizational approval is not the same. As a matter of fact, organizations have been described as a coalition of varying suborganizations, each with their own dynamics and their own particular set of interest, many of which are incompatible with larger organization interests. Further, in addition to the organization's official subunits, there are also "illegitimate" factions and cliques that frequently play an important role, along with some units that are independent of the organization such as unions (Caplow, 1976, p. 5).

These various individuals and groups need one another to pursue their independent aims. It is this interdependence as well as their separateness, the need to cooperate as well as their penchant to compete, that creates political behavior. If they did not need to share the same organizational space, they would disengage completely from one another, and if they did not desire to protect or expand their resources, they would not strive to influence each other's or the organization's positions.

For these reasons, organizations have multiple and conflicting goals as well as some common purposes. As might be expected, the predominant goals are those of the dominant members of the subgroups or coalitions that make up the organization, and these shift depending in good measure on shifts in influence among the parties. In a pluralist system, in which subgroups with contending interests vie to increase their control over the system, conflict is inevitable. Compromise is also inherent, and some degree of collegiality will be maintained because the subgroups are interdependent.

When a number of individuals and/or interest groups are involved and all cannot get exactly what they want, a decision-making process ensues in which each party is likely to try to influence the other. Lerner (1976, p. 25) describes the process as follows:

> At the outset the process of discussion [may be] aimed at understanding, but [it is] invariably aimed at crystallizing opinion on the next action. We presume that it becomes more intense, probably more heated, and in any case protracted as group attention to the unresolved problem continues. Of course the higher the perceived stakes given the values of the participants, the greater the fervor in haggling. For those who want their attempts at persuading a counterpart to have more chance of success than yelling or intriguing alone might allow, the prospect of making concessions is always available.

In this view, "haggling, pressing, and persuading" characterize the process as one engages in political decision making. Or to put it differently, the major interventions that are used in reaching a decision among parties who are both cooperating and contending are persuasion, maneuvering, bargaining, and mobilizing support, with the ultimate goal being to reach a negotiated settlement. If the political approach to organizations starts with the allocation of resources as a central feature (i.e., who gets what), then the attempt to influence others is the critical aspect of the political process between people (i.e., how they get it).

The attempt to affect organizational goals and methods by political processes is more or less encouraged by an organization's structure. Centralized organizations, in which essential decisions are made by an elite few, are less likely candidates for political struggle than decentralized ones. This is so because trying to influence is less frequent when decisions are tightly controlled at the top. People tend not to play when there is no chance of winning the game. Nevertheless, even strong-minded executives allow for some staff maneuverability if they are wise. Otherwise they risk the covert undermining of their decisions. And superiors who rely only on their authority, and do not use other sources of power as well, are likely to be outflanked by politically savvy subordinates.

Similarly, incentives to influence decision making are less likely in highly formalized organizations with fixed rules and routinized procedures than in other organizations. Conversely, influence attempts rise when decisions have not been fully programmed and there is organizational room for maneuver. Paradoxically, the more democratic the organization, the greater the staff's participation in governance; the more diffuse the decision-making structure, the larger the incentives to "play politics." This perhaps explains why faculty politics are endemic in universities: they have numbers of decision-making centers; decisions are often the outcome of peer give-and-take in which many players participate; and decisions by fiat are ordinarily eschewed even by administrators who could legitimately make them. The incentive to try to influence others is thus heightened.

Although politics is an inevitable phenomenon in all organizations, nowhere is its presence more striking than in "people-processing" organizations such as human services agencies. This is so, for one, because the relationship between cause and effect is unclear when people are the "raw material" of the process. The lack of predictability that is inherent in work with people encourages political behavior. With uncertainty regarding the connections between interventions and outcome, there is greater room and license for the values and interests of the participants to come into play and greater likelihood that the values and interests of some of the parties will collide. The fact that social work is a value-laden profession increases that prospect. The ideological commitments of the participants to the service enterprise—as well as the natural tendency of people to rationalize self-interest in value terms and with a moral overlay—adds both the incentive and justification for political engagement.

Finally, the concept of power as a motive force in organizational life is also critical in the political perspective. Influencing others, after all, requires power. Although power is viewed pejoratively by many people, Salancik and Pfeffer (1977, pp. 3–21) argue that far from its being a dirty word, it is "one of the few mechanisms available for aligning the organization with its own reality." Their argument, in summary, is that the institutionalized forms of authority ("authority, legitimization, centralized control, regulations . . . management information systems") tend to buffer the organization from reality and obscure the demands of its environment. Fortunately, however, power is also acquired by the individuals and subunits most able to cope with the organizations's environmentally impelled problems and uncertainties. These individuals and units widely influence organizational decision making and thus align the organization with the realities it faces. As demands on the organization begin to shift, so too do the bases for power, and those with capabilities relevant to coping with the new situational context acquire power in turn, realigning the organization again. Because the current holders of power seek to hold onto it, the fit between the organization and the environment is never quite exact. But to the extent that environmental demands shape which participants are most powerful, organizational decision making falls into line with organizational needs.

Whether the power of particular participants is organizationally useful is less our concern than is an understanding of its centrality to organizational functioning. Managing power, or enhancing one's resources for influencing, is viewed by many social workers as illegitimate. But the acquisition and exercise of power is integral to the supervisory role and is thus an absolutely essential element of effective supervisory practice. Much of what follows in this book reflects this point of view.

To summarize the points that have been made regarding a political perspective: Through structure and other means, organizations allocate resources of significance to their participants. Resources are always in short supply and are unequally distributed among the individuals and subunits that make up the organization. These individuals and units inevitably have competing perspectives, goals, and interests that engender some degree of organizational conflict. A process takes place in which the parties attempt to influence one another and issues are negotiated and compromised. Power is an essential component of this process and thus important for supervisors to understand and manage. Nevertheless, although human services agencies are among the most likely of all types of organizations to be the setting for political maneuvering, too little attention has been paid to the subject of politics in social work.

Underscoring the importance of politics is a study of clinicians who became supervisors (Patti et al., 1979). These neophyte supervisors did not identify the technical aspects of their new positions as most problematic for them, nor were they apparently concerned about handling general interpersonal issues. The two areas they identified as most difficult were (1) the assumption and exercise of authority and (2) understanding the political aspects of administration.

Human Relations and Rationalist Orientations

Although we hold that effective supervision relies primarily on integrating structural and political views of organizational life, it is useful to draw on the insights provided by other work as well, particularly human relations and rationalist theories.

The Human Relations Approach

Human relations theorists have focused on the relationship between the individual and the organization—on the ways in which individuals help or hinder organizational effectiveness and the ways in which organizations advance or impede human satisfaction. These theorists assume that when organizations are unresponsive to human needs, the organizations are likely to be ineffective and, conversely, that when people derive rewards and meaning from their participation, both they and the organization benefit (Bowman and Deal, 1984). This perspective tends to ignore structure as a source of organizational problems. It concentrates on people— their needs, feelings, and skills—as the critical variable required for organizational problem solving.

This approach encompasses two major themes. The first emphasizes human needs and motivation. Various theories of personality have provided important underpinnings, but one theory, developed by Abraham Maslow, has been particularly influential in the development of human relations thought in management practice. Maslow has suggested a hierarchy of need in which lower-level needs (food, water, security, sex) must be satisfied before higher-level needs (belonging, esteem, self-actualization) can be met (Maslow, 1950). It is a short distance from Maslow's theory to prescribing that organizations should meet the higher-order and self-development needs of its workforce, and espousing such stratagems as job enrichment. Job enrichment entails making jobs more intrinsically motivating by designing them to include more autonomy, feedback, and challenge in the tasks and responsibilities a worker carries out. (Hertzberg, 1966). Participatory management, management by objectives, and laboratory training are similar to the above in that all of them are rationalized in some measure by the notion that meeting the affective needs of workers enhances motivation for effective performance.

Whether these techniques of management practice result in more effective performance is an open question. The question derives indirectly from empirical studies that do not show a consistent relationship between job satisfaction or morale and worker productivity or effectiveness, although common sense does suggest a connection (Vroom, 1964). Nevertheless, techniques that lead to a work environment that is more humane than would otherwise be the case are desirable in their own right and surely can be expected to enhance the supervisor's credibility with her staff to the extent that the staff see her as the source of such measures. Further, to say that job satisfaction is an insufficient condition for effectiveness is not to say that it cannot enhance supervisory practice in combination with other factors.

A second theme in the human relations approach focuses on interpersonal dynamics and stresses the importance of interpersonal relations between managers and their workers as well as relations within work groups. Significant interest has been shown in managerial style, and many of its dimensions have been debated and studied by theorists. One dimension that has received considerable attention is employee-centered versus task-centered orientations to supervision. Conclusions regarding the effectiveness of the respective styles have varied with the theorist or researcher, but it may not be too much to claim that supervisors who are both sensitive to their staff *and* goal-directed appear to get the most effective performance from their workers. Interestingly, studies show that social work supervisors are more socially than task oriented (Cohen and Rhodes, 1977), more highly oriented to workers than to organizational objectives (Granvold, 1977).

Not surprisingly, human relations researchers have found evidence suggesting that supervisors who are controlling, competitive, or self-protective are less effective than other supervisors. More interestingly, perhaps, is that the same managers who evidence these characteristics see themselves as open to new ideas, concerned for others, and democratic (Argyris and Schon, 1974). The disparity indicates the importance of one tenet of social work education: the need for practitioners to develop sufficient self-awareness to be able to choose professionally responsible interventions over personal predilections.

The human relations approach emphasizes an important variable that is overlooked by structuralists, namely, the impact people have on organizational functioning. As such its insights are helpful in elaborating our political-structural perspective. It is, after all, the interpretations people make about organizational events, not simply the events themselves, that determine their reactions to those events. Some workers see an agency's supervisory structure—for example, close supervision—as aiding them, whereas others react to the same behavior as a hindrance. Although one's role in the organization and other structural factors powerfully shape the meanings an actor ascribes to an event, his or her interpretations also stem from a variety of other factors. Individuals fill multiple roles (worker, professional associate, parent, friend, etc.) and occupy multiple statuses. Thus the drug counselor who is also an ex-addict may have a different definition of the same organizational problem and espouse a different solution than the drug counselor who has never been an addict, although both hold the status of drug counselor. Social class, ethnicity, and culture are also important sources of an actor's definition of events. Past and present life experiences, both inside and outside the organization, generate values, goals, and expectations among organizational participants as well (Silverman, 1971), and these in turn influence how people interpret organizational happenings.

In this conceptualization, one function of the supervisory role is the manipulation of meanings that workers ascribe to organizational behavior, programs, rules, and procedures so as to induce worker compliance. We do not mean by this to suggest that the attempt to induce particular worker interpretations necessarily calls for covert or ethically ambiguous measures. Many of the commonly accepted myths, traditions, and ceremonies of organizations function to encourage organizationally "proper" attitudes. After all, it is through proffering emotional—and other—support that supervisors often win workers over to a particular point of view. Although human relations theorists perhaps would conceptualize the issue differently, their approach calls attention to this dynamic by concentrating on the attitudes and feelings of the organization's participants.

Basically, the centrality of motivation and interaction in human relations theory makes its significance for the study of supervisory practice obvious. This approach, with its focus on meeting human needs and its emphasis on the importance of interpersonal competence, is very much within the social work tradition. Human relations precepts have informed much of the supervision literature in social work, emphasizing as it does aspects of practice focused on supervisory interventions related to engaging the supervisee. Subjects such as developing the supervisory relationship; conducting the supervisory conference; and guiding, supporting, and evaluating workers have all been formed by insights from the human relations perspective. We draw on these contributions throughout this book, most particularly in Chapters 4 and 5.

We should note, however, that the emphasis in the social work literature on these dyadic interactions of supervisor and worker, though important, have tended to neglect the contextual issues that significantly shape supervisor-supervisee interaction. It may be that this emphasis stems from a clinical model of practice—for it has been noted that there is in social work "a recurring and unfortunate tendency" to view the supervisor-worker relationship as analogous to the worker-client relationship (Miller, 1982). Whatever its genesis, however, the neglect of organizational context as a practical matter is a limitation of supervisory theory in social work.

There have been a number of criticisms of the human relations approach. Its neglect of structural factors is one we have already suggested. Further, its assumption that individual needs and organizational imperatives can be integrated is undoubtedly optimistic. There are common interests that are shared by the participants of organizations at varying hierarchical levels—the provision of quality services, to cite one example. But as we have seen, there are inevitable strains as well, built in by the structure of organizations.

A related—and highly significant limitation in our view—is that the human relations theorists do not take organizational politics into account. Power is barely mentioned in their lexicon, as if it were not a barrier to increasing the integration of individuals and organizations. And politics, if it is referred to at all, is seen as a problem to be overcome rather than as an inevitable concomitant of organizational life.

The Rationalist View

In the rationalist view, organizations are rational instruments created for the purpose of efficiently pursuing common goals. This approach emphasizes the substantive knowledge, technical know-how, and analytic processes that are required to reach an organization's goal. It does not so much attempt to describe how organizations function as to prescribe the ways in which decisions should be made; more precisely, it is a decision-making theory.

The details of rational decision theory do not concern us here. Classically, the rational model represents a purely quantitative approach to decision making, in which numerical values are attached to objectives and alternative courses of action. Variations in knowledge are then factored in, and the payoff of maximum utility for the decision maker is identified. (Harrison, 1981). Contemporary variations on the theory call for less reliance on numbers alone and prescribe a limited rather than "complete" search—or only until a "good enough" outcome rather than an optimum one is reached.

Broadly speaking, the rational perspective may be said to highlight reasoned analysis or planning as critical to effective practice, along with the availability of sophisticated technical means to collect and process information. As in planning, problems must be identified; various solutions specified and weighed; goals precisely defined; alternate means systematically considered; and comprehensive information gathered throughout the process. In this way, the most rational outcome (i.e., the alternative that ranks highest in achieving the desired ends of the decision maker) will result.

Although a decision theory, the rational model carries implicit assumptions about organizations. As already suggested, it assumes that organizations exist to achieve goals. It also assumes that these goals are set by legitimate authorities and can be more-or-less specified. This perspective stresses rationality as a complete virtue rather than a partial logic, and thus it presumes relative certainty and predictability (Bolman and Deal, 1984). Implicitly, too, there is a sense of organizational oneness, the presumption that relative agreement exists among participants about the problem as identified, the goal as chosen, and the means as good enough.

But as we have implied in our discussion of politics, goal setting is complex and may serve a number of purposes. (Westerlund and Sjostrand, 1979). Organizational decisions regarding an agency's goal are ordinarily the result of a process in which multiple authorities such as funders, managers, advocates, community members, and professionals have negotiated the goal and compromised. The goal, therefore, may or may not be fixed and may represent a mix of ideas and values, sometimes conflicting ones. The occurence of disagreement or conflict may be acknowledged by rationalist theorists, but the implications of conflict for how organizational decisions are actually made has largely been ignored.

There is the further problem of establishing precise goals in human services organizations. Typically, their goals are lofty and unattainable— not because social welfare managers are "soft headed" or technically inept, as some rationalist writings and public criticism might suggest, but because setting high-minded purposes is necessary to gain support from an environment in which service values are precarious. Human service agencies are thus caught in a double bind. For example, the demand for accountability and businesslike methods is in part a response to the fact that welfare programs typically promise more than they attain. The anomaly is that the officials who most loudly decry welfare failure and call most zealously for accountability are those ones most likely not to vote funds for programs that lack grandiose mission statements.

Even considering its limitations, a rationalist orientation contributes to effective supervisory practice when it is integrated with other approaches. The perspective emphasizes specificity and clarity, substantive knowledge, and sophisticated data collection and analysis—all of which are requirements of effective supervisory problem solving. Indeed, it is the interplay of substantive knowledge, reasoned analysis, and political acumen that thoughtful supervisors integrate in their practice. Furthermore, rational theorists have identified or developed a number of technical components that are helpful for supervisory use: techniques for task and job analysis, systems of unit planning, performance appraisal, and the like.

Perhaps most important for our current purposes, rational theory calls attention to the process of planning. The precepts of planning can be used, interestingly enough, for political ends as well as for the purposes defined by rational theorists. Thus managers are counseled to specify by priority their primary goals, to collect available data on factors that may facilitate or impede goal achievement, to identify and evaluate alternate strategies, and to select the alternatives assessed as appropriate to meet desired ends. Although the particular goals, types of data and methods of collection differ in political problem solving from the more technical ones that typify writings on organizational planning and rational decision making, there are similarities in the process. The same precepts can be employed by Sara Widdoes, for example, as she faces the political dilemmas of supervising her unit. In broad terms she might identify three primary areas of difficulty. With her staff she experiences insufficient credibility and influence to shape their expectations and to guide their practice in a fashion that all find mutually acceptable. Similarly, with her boss Sara feels insufficient influence to shape expectations and to elicit support for her direction of the unit. With her peers—other supervisors in the agency—Sara finds her ability to induce cooperative interactions frustrated and ineffective. Sara's problems can be formulated into a set of specific goals which lend themselves to rational and systematic pursuit.

These goals largely focus on the enhancement of Sara's influence with various constituencies, and the practice she must employ is a core concern of this volume.

Since the technology propounded by rational theorists has received much recent currency, another qualification is worth noting. Hasenfeld, for example, asserts that "a great service to the field will be made if we come to acknowledge the fact that social welfare administrators need to have in-depth knowledge of the most sophisticated management tools" (Hasenfeld, 1980). On the face of it, this is hardly an arguable assertion. The implication that the major deficit in the field is its ignorance of management technology is unfortunate, however, for it suggests that inadequate knowledge rather than inadequate support for services is the more significant social welfare limitation. And to generate support for services requires in-depth political skill.

Paradoxically, the case can be made that knowledge of sophisticated technology is as necessary for generating an agency image of effectiveness (and therefore necessary to gain support for the agency's program) as much as it is for the knowledge that the tools produce. Thus, Landau and Stout (1979) suggest that there is no evidence that PPBS, PERT, zero-based budgeting, and other technical innovations of the federal government have improved federal decision making. Nevertheless, this lack of success has not diminished the appeal of these management control systems. The authors conclude that this is so because the systems are in fact used more for political than substantive purposes.

In sum, both the human relations and rational perspectives contribute to our understanding of supervisory practice, but standing alone, both are flawed. A single-minded focus on either effective interpersonal relations or the rational aspects of organizational behavior and decision making seriously distorts the reality of organizational life. Neglecting the significance of structure or overlooking politics as an organizational imperative does the practitioner a disservice, because both have a critical impact on the supervisory process and the supervisor's interventions.

We conclude this chapter by returning to Sara Widdoes' dilemma. Caught in the unique buffer position between top administration and her staff, Sara finds herself confronting discontinuities of priority and interest. She feels ill-equipped to find solutions that are responsive to the conflicting expectations she encounters. And no wonder! This is the arena of organizational politics for which neither her professional training nor the literature on supervision has sufficiently prepared her.

Becoming effective in her role requires skill in *organizational practice.* Sara must transcend the technology of supervision as ordinarily defined in its narrower sense. She needs to increase her influence with her staff so that she is able to obtain their cooperation and compliance with new policies and procedures. She needs to know the practice steps of *how* this is done. She also needs to increase staff loyalty to her role as unit leader so that when staff disagree with her direction in substance, they will nevertheless respond out of respect for her in her role. She needs assistance in the specifics of *how* this is done. Sara also needs to increase her influence with her bosses, for, in part, her ability to gain the loyalty of her staff is a function of their perception of her effectiveness with higher-ups. She needs to understand the specifics of *how* to accomplish this enhancement of her influence. It is important that she learn to be effective in the political give-and-take with other supervisors at her own level. She needs to understand the characteristics of conflict at this level and the specifics of *how* she can negotiate or maneuver to promote the interests of her unit and its clients.

The *how* of these areas of organizational practice are the substance of this book.

Supervisory Beginnings

Our focus in this chapter is on beginnings—the assumption of the supervisory role by the newly appointed worker. We first explore factors having to do with the new supervisor's socialization into the role, noting particularly issues stemming from the fact that social work supervisors typically move up from the clinical ranks. A major aspect of that role taking, and the most worrisome aspect for neophytes, is the assumption of authority, and we next look at some of the bases that make its exercise more or less difficult for the new supervisor. Finally, major attention is devoted to the identification of the practice tasks required for the supervisor to "take hold," with a review of the steps that lead to establishing credibility in the supervisory role.

Transition from Clinician to Supervisor

The majority of social service administrators have been trained as clinicians. They become supervisors or managers after having first been direct service providers (Macarov, 1977). Persuasive arguments can be made to support the practice. Among them is the fact that there is a multiplicity of often-competing political and economic interests that impact on a social agency, and because of this, the service ethic is a relatively unprotected and precarious value. For it to remain a compelling force in an agency's operation, it must constitute a critical commitment of the agency's administration. Professionals who have been trained as clinicians and have firsthand experience in observing the importance of agency services to clients are much more likely to represent that service ethic than the executive who is solely an administrative technician. Furthermore, a major function of leadership is to articulate an organization's values, goals, and methods so as to strengthen internal commitments and to enhance external support. This, too, is hardly a technician's task, and the more the executive appreciates the problems and complexities at the service delivery level, the more effectively he will perform these functions. But whether one believes that direct service training and experience is requisite preparation for administrators or whether one holds that management concentrations in schools of social work offer the appropriate balance among value orientation, service know-how, and technical ability, for the foreseeable future a considerable number of supervisory and managerial positions will continue to be filled by those moving up the ranks from the direct service line.

The transition into the supervisory role can be considered both from the perspective of the generic issues associated with socialization into any new position and also from the perspective of the unique circumstances of the shift from a direct service to a supervisory role. In each case there are transitional and situational problems posed by the shift that must be recognized and addressed. The more significant issues related to the transition are identified below.

Whenever one moves into a new position in an organization, a certain degree of anxiety and strain is to be expected. One source of anxiety is the unfamiliar and unknown set of actors with whom the newcomer must interact. If the change of position is within the same agency, the anxiety stems from the concern that the new role demands may place substantial stress on old relationships. The comfort of established relations and peer support often are left behind and are replaced by the loneliness and isolation that frequently accompanies the assumption of supervisory authority.

Anxieties stemming from the ambiguities of a new setting and/or new role are also likely. Irrespective of how competent one felt in the former role or the extent to which she had been viewed as able to assume her new responsibilities, the fledgling supervisor experiences some degree of uncertainty. In her new role the supervisor must understand the organizational culture of those in authority (Weick, 1964), as well as manage the meanings of her new role for those to be supervised. Exactly what is expected of her, the extent and the limits of her authority, and the nuances of role behavior that if not attended to will offend or discredit are concerns that remain ambiguous for her. Who has the responsibility to make a particular decision (the new supervisor or her boss), who must be consulted prior to making the decision, and who should be informed afterward may be both unknown and a matter of significant political sensitivity. Even as simple a matter as asking a question, and of whom, sometimes constitutes a significant risk—perceived or real. Finally, and perhaps obviously, there is anxiety about possessing the requisite knowledge and skill to perform the tasks required by the new position.

How individuals cope with these strains, of course, varies with the person and the situation, but there are discernible patterns. A number of empirical studies demonstrate that newcomers tend to be preoccupied with psychological safety, that is, getting established in and accepted by the organization and feeling secure in their new situation (Kahn et al, 1964; Hall and Nougaim, 1968). Newcomers also face the issue of developing a role identity (in the present case as supervisor) that will be suitable from the standpoints of both the newcomer and relevant others (superiors, peers, subordinates) (Katz, 1980). The search for security and identity is manifest in a number of ways. Because one's sense of self is in part interactive and affected by the views of others, someone new to a position tends to seek reassurance and acceptance from colleagues. The focus, therefore, is frequently more social than task oriented, which is probably useful for the newcomers, if not necessarily for the organization or for the creativity of the newcomer as supervisor. As we might expect, studies show that those who adopt collectively held values are likely to be perceived more positively and to receive more favorable evaluations than those who do not (Katz, 1980).

Another common adaptation to insecurity on a new job is to fall back on past experience. The segmented character of all organizations encourages tunnel vision, or the ignoring of broader agency concerns which are not immediately relevant to one's limited responsibilities (Bennis, 1971). The result is that practitioners who have been indifferent to system-wide dynamics are likely to continue to ignore these factors and to devote a disproportionate amount of time providing direct services in their supervisory roles (Patti and Austin, 1977). This might include the supervisor's continuing to carry a significant caseload, which interferes with her ability to fulfill the administrative responsibilities related to the new role.

The need for psychological safety also suggests that some of the components of the job of the supervisor that have traditionally been defined as positive in the literature may be less so for workers new to a position. For example, assignments that entail a diversity of tasks, call for *high* achievement, and permit considerable latitude are ordinarily viewed as professionally satisfying. Yet they are likely to pose difficulty for supervisors who have not yet established their identity in the new role. For newcomers, high amounts of initial autonomy are ordinarily experienced as disturbing

(Katz, 1978). Rather, newcomers who are in a position to influence their assignments seek assignments that entail significant interaction with others to aid them in the transition.

The problems inherent in the move into a new position are compounded when the shift is from a direct service to an administrative role. Sarri (1973) speaks of the "trained incapacity" of clinicians for administration, and others have warned against a tendency to "casework the help." Several inherent discontinuities between the roles of clinician and supervisor have been identified. Among them are sharp differences in the use of authority, decision-making style, perspectives on relationship and effective performance, and relations to colleagues which are common to the clinical versus the administrative position. (Patti and Austin, 1977; Austin, 1981; Patti, 1983).

As a clinician, one's authority or basis of legitimation stems from demonstrated competence in the effective provision of service to clients. In contrast, as a supervisor, legitimation is a function of the role or position. There are occasions when the supervisor is required to use the authority of the position to insist on compliance by the staff. With the exception of mandated services, this use of authority would be unusual in the clinician-client relationship. Secondly, the way decisions are made in the two roles differ sharply. The direct service worker approaches his or her cases with a commitment to working for optimal solutions with the client. To the extent that agency or other factors operate to compromise this commitment, the worker attempts to resist such influences. But the supervisor engages in such a wide span of activities that it is ordinarily impossible to engage supervisees and administrative or developmental tasks with optimal outcomes in mind. Rather, the supervisor is responsive to a decision-making style that settles for only adequate or satisfactory rather than optimum solutions (Simon, 1976). This may constitute a frustrating and disillusioning experience for the new supervisor.

As a clinician, one's training in graduate school for work with clients, though goal focused, tends to stress a concern with interpersonal process. If after significant time with a client toward a behavioral outcome the goal is not reached, the worker, understandably frustrated, may still assess the effort to have reflected learning on the client's part and a deepening of their relationship. As such, he might well judge the time well spent. The supervisor, on the other hand, is under pressure to deliver "results." Relationships with workers that do not result in desired outcomes, or work of staff that does not produce specified consequences for clients, tend to be judged unsuccessful regardless of the quality of the interaction that has characterized the process.

As one moves into a supervisory position, it becomes clear that the mode of engaging colleagues differs sharply in that role. Although obviously not always the case, relationships between line workers tend to be characterized by the sharing of resources and information in a cooperative effort to maximize services for clients and ease difficulties encountered by individual workers. As a supervisor, however, one is likely to be in a boundary-spanning role, linking one's own unit to other units. The result is that colleagues often tend to be competitors for funding, management support, and turf. Similarly, the supervisor soon discovers that her success with supervisees in part is a function of the ability to advance their interests over those of similar staff in other units. These factors result in relationships with colleagues that are at least as competitive as they are cooperative, open, or supportive.

Still other differences can be identified. Direct service workers are socialized to be responsive, to guide their practice in large measure by cues they pick up from the client. Decisions regarding the directions of treatment as well as the limits of work are usually viewed as the client's to make and the worker's to facilitate or explore. But supervision, to be effective, requires a proactive posture. The taking of initiative, setting of direction and priority, and exercise of autonomy in judgment and decision are central to effective practice. Assertion is important for effective service provision, but it is an essential and central element in organizational practice (Gitterman, 1982).

Finally, the view and definition of self that is typically developed in the course of one's training as a clinician frequently constitutes another source of difficulty in making the transition into the supervisory role. Although clinical training in social work has increasingly utilized a social systems perspective in addition to individual psychological models to explain the circumstances and behavior of clients, psychological theories predominate in aiding social work students to understand their personal and professional self. The conscious use of self is an important component of clinical practice and a significant objective in social work training. This is as it should be, because workers must be aware of their needs and motives—and manage these—when they come in conflict with those of clients. Unfortunately, in social work training the concept of self has focused primarily on the personality of the worker rather than the self that is shaped by role and organizational position. We noted earlier that substantial research suggests that the most powerful predictors of behavior in organizations are associated with organizational structure as opposed to psychological predispositions. Nevertheless, the clinically trained worker tends to utilize individual psychological explanations to understand both his own behavior in the agency as well as that of others. If the concept of self were extended to include aspects of performance that result from tensions in the role or turf, as well as other organizational interests, the transition from clinician to supervisor might be smoother. Appreciating such distinctions, workers would be less prone to define structural issues in psychological terms and more likely to incorporate a systemic perspective along with an individualistic one.

Supervisory Authority

One of the most complex as well as subtle attributes of the bureaucratic form has to do with the fact and implications of *authority*. This concept refers to the prerogatives of a specified position—the organizationally sanctioned right by virtue of role to initiate action, make decisions, allocate organizational resources, and determine outcomes for others. In theory, the staff accept the legitimacy of a superior's exercise of these prerogatives and feel obliged to comply with supervisory decision. Bacharach and Lawler (1980, pp. 28–29) note that "the unique aspect of authority is that subordinates acquiesce without question and are willing to (1) suspend any intellectual or moral judgments about the appropriateness of the superior's directives, or (2) act as if they subscribed to the judgment of the superior even if, in fact, they personally find the directive distasteful." Authority implies "unquestioning obedience from subordinates" in regard to organizationally relevant issues.

But such unquestioning obedience may or may not be forthcoming. It is the area of major worry for supervisors who have just ascended to their new position. Their concern about exercising authority may in part have roots in attitudes toward power. Ambivalence stemming from negative attitudes regarding power, on the one hand, and the attractiveness that many people feel in its exercise, on the other, may be one source of discomfort. Another source may be that there is an assumption of superiority in one person's having the right to tell another person what to do. The new supervisor who, if anxious, feels in no way superior may well experience embarrassment in making such an implicit claim. Finally, there is the uncertainty that neophytes must feel about whether they "can pull it off." They are, after all, inexperienced in the uses of authority, and intuitively, a new supervisor must know that authority is only one source of power. She is expected to gain compliance, although she may not yet have the opportunity to develop any additional resources for influencing others. Because she is dependent on how her staff respond to her, they hold a lien on her success as a supervisor that may feel awesome to her. This concern is further intensified if she also does not *feel* herself to be more knowledgeable than they.

If staff do, in fact, resist the authority of a new role occupant, it can constitute a problem of potentially long-range significance. Acceptance of authority is a developmental phenomenon; hence persistent indifference or resistance to supervisory authority is likely to erode further this authority over time. In other words, rather than being self-correcting with time, situations in which workers resist supervisory authority are likely to worsen unless the supervisor initiates remedial measures.

Supervisory authority is a much more uneven and less potent source of power in the human services than it is in the corporate world. This is so for several reasons. First, there are significant differences in the use of rewards and sanctions in the two sectors. Within the managerial levels of the corporation, the rewards and sanctions of promotion, salary increment, and termination are less constrained by regulations such as in civil service and by the existence of professional norms and associations. This enables a corporate manager to exercise fuller use of available incentives and disincentives in support of his or her authority. Also, there is less ambiguity and ambivalence regarding the values associated with the distribution of rewards and sanctions in the corporate sector than in the human services. Corporate norms tend to be based on the distributive principle of equity—people are rewarded on the basis of what they have earned, with the measures typically being hierarchical loyalty, competence, and productivity. But in the human services, professional and organizational values frequently not only support the distributive principle of equity, but the often-competing principle of equality. For example, if a supervisor has a fixed amount of money to distribute to members of a work unit for salary increments, equity would dictate that the allocation be made on the basis of the supervisor's assessment of the varying degrees of staff loyalty, competence, and productivity. Equality, on the other hand, would dictate that each unit member, regardless of differences in performance, should receive equal amounts of the increment pool. Allocations on the basis of equality are much more common in the human services than in the corporate world. Partly as a consequence of these factors, rule conformity, the presence of norms supporting respect for the organization's hierarchy, and the acceptance of the authority of a superordinate are more common in the corporate world than in the human services.

The high proportion of professional staff is another factor that operates to lessen the significance of supervisory authority in the human services compared with other organizations. A major tenet of the notion of profession is that knowledge, expertise, and norms of conduct are defined by one's professional affiliation. To a significant degree this constitutes for the lower-ranking professional a parallel source of authority, along with that of the superiors who represent the authority of the organization.

Finally, the multiplicity and often contradictory character of organizational goals to which we have already referred frequently operate to undercut hierarchical authority. Goal ambiguity and the frequent absence of identifiable measures of goal achievement tend to foster an independent sense of direction on the part of organizational members. The imprecision or "softness" of much of the technology in the human services further diminishes organizational authority. When technology is precise, as is the case with manufacturing procedures, for example, less ambiguity surrounds the specific means of reaching a goal or the degree to which it has been attained. In turn, this results in less potential controversy regarding the appropriateness of supervisory directives and less justification for independent judgment on the part of the subordinate. But when uncertainty is associated with the relationship between selected service procedures and desirable outcomes for clients, the staff feel more justified in questioning supervisory directives regarding such issues.

Nevertheless, even though supervisors are by no means necessarily accorded the requisite authority by human services staff, we suspect that persons new to supervision worry about the matter more than is really necessary. The expectations inherent in any role set constitute a potent lever for encouraging appropriate behavior. In the role set of staff and supervisor, compliance is expected and is therefore most likely to occur. Erroneously, a neophyte supervisor often thinks that she can count only on herself. Of course, if the new supervisor, because of nervousness, makes the mistake of acting as if noncompliant behavior is a possibility, she will have encouraged it. All other things being equal, however, the widely held expectations of how staff and supervisors are supposed to behave toward one another provides considerable support for supervisors to establish their authority in the role. Further, incumbents to new positions ordinarily have a honeymoon period, during which time their acts are more likely to be interpreted benignly and their authority is most likely to be accepted.

There are, of course, special circumstances that serve to encourage or deter the supervisor's assumption of authority. Three conditions are worth noting in this regard. One relates to the style and character of the person who preceded the supervisor in the job; another has to do with whether the supervisor was promoted from within or recruited from outside the organization; the third concerns whether the supervisor's background characteristics—age, ethnicity or gender—are similar to those in the setting or make her different along one or more of these dimensions.

A number of dimensions of a former supervisor's performance can influence staff reactions to the new one, but one of these is primary: the relationship of the predecessor to the staff. This is especially the case if the relationship has been in some way special. If the previous supervisor was viewed as particularly competent, responsive to the staff, and open to their points of view, the new one may be perceived as less than adequate or a threat to the staff's continued influence. On the other hand, if the former supervisor was seen as anti-staff, the appointment of a new person provides the staff with the opportunity to extend their influence. The new supervisor is fortunate if the relationship was negative, because winning them over should be a relatively simple matter. On the other hand, if the earlier relationship was positive, the new supervisor will have to be more circumspect in regard to any changes she might otherwise wish to make.

In either instance, the staff may engage in an implicit power negotiation with the newcomer. Their bargaining chip is their acceptance of or resistance to the new supervisor's authority. What they often seek in return are prerogatives or privileges they believe the supervisor has the discretion to dispense. We return to this matter of implicit trading in Chapter 8.

Because a promotion or lack of it is an event of considerable importance in an organization, the new supervisor's status as an insider or outsider before her appointment can potentially generate strong feelings. Among friends, of course, there will be pleasure in her promotion, although there could also be ambivalence on their part. For one, they may feel a sense of loss or concern about the relationship now that she is no longer a peer. For another, the friend who is left behind may be left with the need to rationalize why she was not considered for the job.

If the promotion is internal and there are staff members who are less than friendly to the new supervisor, the issue of being passed over assumes greater interpersonal significance. More important, however, is the resistance to an appointment that is generated by agency and professional rivalries, because this kind of resistance has a group basis and is reflective of organizational structure. This occurs, for example, when a new supervisor's relations have been with different factions in the organization or if she is recruited from a unit that some staff view as competitive or from a group that represents a differing specialization. In such an instance, these staff members are likely to believe that the appointment somehow diminishes their significance or the significance of their unit, and the selection process itself may come under attack. The executive will be accused of making the appointment for personal rather than professional reasons or on ideological rather than substantive grounds. If neither of these arguments are vaguely credible, the attack may go to the character of the appointee, the executive, or both. Thus one sometimes hears the complaint that so-and-so was hired because she could be controlled, a statement that questions the integrity of both parties. The complaint is all the more potent because there are occasions when it is, in fact, true. But it is often falsely used to delegitimate the appointment and to gain converts who will withhold affirmation of the supervisor's authority.

Although the challenge is of a very different order, both friends and enemies pose some risk to the authority of the newcomer. Supervisory interventions to reduce the risk vary, depending on the instance, and in a following section of this chapter we suggest the beginnings of an approach to the matter.

Outsiders carry less baggage with them into a new position. The supervisor recruited from outside generally has an advantage in not being associated with the person she replaced. If her predecessor was inadequate or unresponsive to staff concerns, the newcomer will be welcomed and has the opportunity to look good in comparison. When an insider replaces an inadequate or unresponsive predecessor, on the other hand, she cannot reap the same benefit if she is perceived as the predecessor's friend or owes her loyalty. The same holds true if the predecessor was competent (Caplow, 1976, pp. 12–13). An outsider, as a stranger, may be free to put her own imprint on the job, whereas the insider's position is more difficult. If she adopts the predecessor's style, she will appear to be imitative, and if she changes policies that have been working well, she will appear imprudent.

The outsider's lesser baggage is sometimes a mixed blessing, however, because staff's reaction to their new supervisor may be influenced by factors that are beyond her control. The existence of a favored candidate among the current staff has the potential for creating an undercurrent of ill-feeling, for example; so, too, does dissatisfaction with the search process; also, any negative attitudes toward the executive may rub off onto the executive's choice. The new supervisor does not have the insider's advantages of knowing with whom or what she is dealing. She must take the time to learn the play and the players before she can intervene, and if there is trouble, the necessity may be to act without sufficient understanding of agency and unit norms or culture.

Issues of age, ethnicity, and gender may also be significant as the new supervisor assumes the authority of her role. Often, these variables are among the formal selection criteria for a supervisory position. A common example is the case of a predominantly white agency serving a mixed client group that seeks a minority supervisor so that its staff will better represent the client mix. Also, the advent of affirmative action has increased the likelihood that a search for women and persons of diverse ethnicity is routinely incorporated in the recruitment procedures of human services agencies.

Reactions to the appointment of someone who differs from the majority of staff in the setting vary greatly, depending on setting, actors, and circumstances. When there is consensus in the agency that selecting someone of a specified ethnicity or gender is desirable, the new supervisor's difference from the majority constitutes an asset. In the same way that skills or expertise in a needed area lend one initial credibility, so too meeting a desired criterion of difference holds the potential for enhancing one's value. In such a case, the minority supervisor has an advantage in establishing supervisory authority.

In a formerly homogeneous setting, the appointment of a minority supervisor may cause initial discomfort. It would probably be inaccurate to characterize this discomfort as prejudice, or at least necessarily so, because a staff's lack of experience with persons of differing backgrounds can engender initial feelings of apprehension regarding their new colleague that dissipate with experience. Often well-meaning staff members heighten the discomfort by being excessive in their welcome or overly solicitous in orienting a minority person, inadvertently highlighting the tension they are feeling in the situation. This initial discomfort probably holds little special relevance for establishing supervisory authority pro or con as long as it is successfully overcome. When the efforts on each side are well intended—even if inept—the discomfort is usually transcended and relationships ultimately develop as they would normally without issues of difference to further complicate them.

In other instances, there may be explicit or covert dissension regarding the desirability of hiring a minority group supervisor. Sources of such disagreement have multiple origins and are often difficult to verify. Unfortunately, the source is sometimes a categorical preference to avoid difference—racism, sexism, ageism, or homophobia—though the holders of these feelings may or may not be consciously aware of them. Conflicts between class equity and individual equality are also sometimes the source of disagreements regarding the appropriateness of including criteria of difference in the recruitment of a candidate. We refer here to the classic complaint by some majority members that on a case-by-case basis majority candidates are disadvantaged when minorities are given selection priority, even though minorities have historically been disadvantaged in hiring procedures. Such sentiments can translate into covert resentment of a supervisor who was selected through a successful affirmative-action search.

In agencies in which the staff mix already reflects diversity, reactions to the new supervisor are likely to be influenced by the politics of the setting. In organizations in which factionalism is not an issue, sentiments regarding a particular selection are less likely to be predicated on the candidate's difference. When subgroups vie for the selection of a supervisor reflecting their particular background, however, the stage is set for lingering resentments between subgroups and potential resentment against the successful minority candidate. More often than otherwise, the struggle is covert. An example of this occurred in an agency that was heterogeneous regarding race, gender, and sexual preference, and a powerful faction of the staff included several gay men. Others in this coalition were not gay, and there were also gays in the agency who were not identified with the faction. During the recruitment of a new supervisor, some staff members unsuccessfully attempted to block the appointment of a male candidate whom they assumed to be gay. While publicly using arguments against the candidate unrelated to his presumed sexual orientation, privately they admitted among themselves that it would be unwise to hire another gay man. "It would further empower an already too powerful coalition," they argued, "and besides it doesn't look good in the community having so many gays on staff." Fears that minorities of whatever persuasion will band together and compromise the interests of other groups and/or the majority are all too common. That such assumptions clearly reflect prejudice in no way alters their potency or the potential difficulty for the minority supervisor entering the agency.

Establishing Role Legitimacy

If, as we have suggested, the acceptance of authority is a developmental phenomenon, a primary goal as one assumes supervisory responsibility is claiming the authority of the role. The practice of taking charge or beginning to legitimate oneself as a supervisor varies according to the individual, the specifics of the succession, and the organization. Three initial steps may be noted, however, each of which directly or indirectly aids in legitimating supervisory authority: a public expression of confidence by the executive for the newcomer's having been selected, adopting a posture with subordinates that connotes one's acknowledgment of the authority and function of the role, and establishing a base through initial contacts for developing relations with peers and superiors.

Anointing

The way the organization's representatives pass the reins of power and confirm the new supervisor's appointment can symbolize the importance the organization attaches to the organizational role, the confidence of upper-level staff in the appointment they have made, and the extent to which these superiors are prepared to support the supervisor in her new role.

Ceremonies add meaning to the ambiguities and confusions of organizational life. Symbols, myths, and the rituals of "state occasions" such as an annual meeting, a commemoration, or the granting of an award are all intended to convey a message that some set of organizational actors wants some audience to hear. The messages sometimes have little to do with substance but are anyway important in representing an organization's culture, values, or behaviors.

Sayles refers to the process of passing authority from one to another person as *anointing*, observing that status in organizations to a significant degree is transferable (Sayles, 1979, p. 40). Ideally, the process occurs in both written and face-to-face forms. An official announcement of a new appointment is forwarded by the executive to all staff members in the affected unit as well as organizational peers and others with whom the new supervisor will work. The communication might include the following components: (1) an expression of executive pleasure at the choice of the new supervisor and a reference to the search process having been an extensive one, if applicable; (2) brief reference to the credentials that qualify the new supervisor for the position; (3) an expression of executive confidence that staff will help orient the new supervisor in her position and accord her their support.

Executives understand the symbolic significance of anointing the newcomer in this way and ordinarily extend themselves to communicate their support. In the press of day-to-day managerial responsibilities, however, the gesture may be forgotten. If so, the supervisor can suggest that the appointment be announced—and she may even go so far, if she is an insider, as offering to draft the memorandum herself.

The memorandum serves a political purpose. More than a mere announcement, it is an attempt on the executive's part to encourage staff acceptance of the supervisor's authority. As such, the details of the wording reflect specific agency circumstances. If there is little controversy surrounding the appointment, the message can cover the areas noted in a relatively cut-and-dried fashion. But if there have been either overt or covert issues in regard to the appointment, the message of the memorandum might well contain counterarguments without appearing as if it is trying to make a case. For example, if the appointment has been criticized because the new supervisor's expertise in a particular area is viewed by some as inadequate (e.g., her clinical experience is sparse), the memorandum should make reference to her credentials in clinical work. Or if the appointment is intended to move the agency in new directions (i.e., there is executive interest in added emphasis on staff development activities), the new supervisor's attainments in staff training should be noted. Nevertheless, neither by special pleading nor by implication should the memorandum lend credence to the existence of any staff dissatisfaction with the appointment.

In addition to formal announcements, the executive anoints the new supervisor through face-to-face and informal means. The new supervisor's first meeting with her staff can be facilitated by the presence of the executive, for instance. He introduces her to the staff or officially announces the appointment at the meeting, expresses his confidence in the supervisor, requests the staff's support, and perhaps makes reference to the day's meeting agenda. Having sanctioned the new supervisor and her initial activity—the conduct of the upcoming staff meeting—the executive has in effect transferred authority and can leave the meeting as the supervisor commences her new role.

The Honeymoon Period

Supervisors must decide how to deal with the honeymoon period that newcomers to a position are often granted. (A reasonable estimate of its length is three to six months.) Their choice is whether to take advantage of the time to introduce policy and procedural changes that might be more difficult to manage once the honeymoon is over or whether instead to simply settle in and get their bearings.

The personality of the new supervisor often determines the choice. Risk-taking practitioners are more likely than others to seize the moment and seek to innovate. Similarly, persons for whom it is important to place their mark on a job will be predisposed to seek change quickly. The studies referred to earlier regarding the tendency of newcomers to be preoccupied with psychological safety and security, however, suggest that a majority are likely to move in slowly. And in most cases, this is probably the right choice.

The newcomer's personality should not, of course, determine the decision; rather, considerations that relate to job and agency should rule. How the predecessor was viewed and whether the newcomer is an insider or outsider are once again significant variables.

Obviously, the insider is favored in this regard—she has a better line on the predecessor's deficits as well as greater knowledge about the system itself. Nevertheless, even an outside replacement can gain sufficient information in a reasonably short time to intervene, if the predecessor's inadequacy was widely acknowledged. She can then garner immediate applause at no expense by changing unpopular practices. For instance, if the predecessor had a penchant for forms and other bureaucratic paraphernalia, the newcomer might score by emphasizing informal communication, reducing form filling and yet not upset essential procedures. An instance such as this, and perhaps a limited number of other special circumstances, are among the few in which immediate action appears desirable. Another example is when the supervisor was specifically hired to solve a problem or effect a change. She must then visibly plan and implement the new initiative in order to meet the executive's, and perhaps even the staff's, expectations.

Clearly, when a predecessor is viewed as able, the advantages of the honeymoon period will have to be foresworn. The outsider will simply not have time to gather enough information on which to base significant changes without risking the disruption of working procedures or the antagonism of the participants. Nor is the insider well favored in this situation either. If she has been endorsed by her predecessor, she is expected to be loyal, which means that no significant change is possible until a decent interval has passed. (The supervisor must, in addition, resist a quite usual temptation of people new to their jobs, namely, being critical of the person they replaced.) And if the unit has been functioning well, proposing an early change makes it look as if the change is for its own sake, to meet the needs of the supervisor rather than the unit.

Prudence suggests that under most circumstances the new supervisor should decide to follow established procedures and forego the advantages of the honeymoon as a time for change. The outsider, particularly, needs to devote significant effort to accumulating information about the organization—for her most creative idea will only be as good as its fit with the organizational circumstances in which it will be embedded. One principle in promoting change suggests the importance of "doing one's homework." That means, of course, learning as much about an issue as one reasonably can: why the problem exists, and what the forces that favor change, the barriers to it, and the attitudes of relevant participants on the various sides of the matter are. It is usually critical to know with whom one may be contending and the sources of contention in order to neutralize opposition effectively. It takes time to become this familiar with a unit and its issues, and even more time to get to know the actors well enough to judge whose feedback is candid and accurate and whose judgment may be valued.

Even the insider, as a new supervisor, must collect information about the unit or the changes she might seek before she can be certain about their appropriateness. In her new role the perspectives she held as a worker or as a member of a different unit will be modified, for, as we have said, as one becomes privy to more and different information as one moves up the hierarchy, more factors must be taken into account in decision making, and the often-potent reasons why some policies remain in force, seemingly against all rationality, become apparent. In these circumstances, she might with justification want to move slowly. Furthermore, the attempt to introduce changes before one's authority is established and supervisory power solidified carries the risk that one may not yet have sufficient control over unit personnel and procedures to be successful in its implementation.

In any event, as the new supervisor begins the job, she needs to decide whether she will take the risk and use the advantage of the honeymoon period to seek changes, whether she will forego the opportunity and "lie low" awhile, or whether she should try, as we would suggest, to balance these extremes by cautious risking. She need not directly share her approach with staff, nor need it be a fixed or final determination. But it is useful to have in mind as she engages the workers in her unit.

Shaping Expectations

The decision regarding the honeymoon period is not made independently of the supervisor's beginning process of getting to know and be known by the workers in her unit. She initiates a series of meetings, preferably one-on-one but minimally in small subgroups, that have three ends in mind. One is for her to learn more about the staff—their attitudes about the program or the agency, how they view their jobs, and its problems, the issues they believe require priority attention, and some sense of who they are as people. A second purpose is to share some general perspectives in regard to services—to articulate a platform, so to speak, against which the unit's future work can be measured. Finally, the overriding purpose of these discussions is to shape staff expectations regarding the supervisor's role so as to enhance their responsiveness to her authority. In sum, the discussions mark the start of a contracting process in which supervisor and workers ultimately agree on the terms of their working together.

Because the initial understandings of supervisor and workers may be implicit, a caution is in order. The expectation of people who meet one another for the first time is that they will behave pleasantly. Goffman (1967) has observed that persons adopt parts similar to actors in a play, displaying expressions that convey the impressions they want to make in any particular public encounter. For persons who expect to have a strong need for one another, as do supervisors and staff, the parts call for *special* pleasantness during their initial interaction. Of course, it is possible to be *too* pleasant; that is, for one or another party to overact and therefore to be less credible in their role. Nonetheless, both supervisors and workers have a strong incentive to reassure themselves and each other regarding any issue that they anticipate might bring trouble. Because authority relations often cause subtle or not-so-subtle discomfort, the subject becomes a prime candidate for such reassurance. Although not directly stated, the supervisor's implied reassurance could go something like this: "I intend to be one of the guys; I'll be considerate of your needs and I expect you'll be considerate of mine." The workers, for their part, could endorse that message or initiate one of their own. They might, for example, affirm that the supervisor is a good guy or understanding or flexible if laissez-faire leadership practices are satisfactory to her. Behind the broad smiles, then, an implicit contract is being forged in which the supervisor trades away the prerogatives of her position for subordinate affection. Her ability to carry out her responsibilities thus becomes disproportionately dependent on the preferences of her subordinates.

We are not suggesting that the supervisor should directly state that she expects staff to comply with her directives. Quite the reverse. As the norm of compliance is widely understood to apply in supervisor-supervisee relations, direct reference is unnecessary unless the supervisee's behavior threatens to violate the norm. Short of that, a direct reference will suggest uncertainty on the supervisor's part. People who make a point of underlining their authority give the impression of being overly concerned that their directives will be ignored (in itself an invitation to ignore them), or they seem uncomfortable with being in a position of authority at all. As we point out below, one supervisory task is to build a habit of compliance on the part of the workers, and this must be done incrementally. At the other end of the continuum, an excess of modesty on a new supervisor's part about her expectations or expertise is also to be avoided.

The special attainments of a person who behaves modestly must be absolutely clear for the modesty to appear to be a virtue. Otherwise, modest behavior risks being seen as an accurate reflection of someone with modest ability. For example, in hoping to coopt a teacher in his planning for a child, a school social worker might suggest that the teacher knew the child considerably better than he. The comment would only serve his purpose, however, if the teacher had a generally high opinion of the school social worker's understanding of children. Otherwise, his "modesty" about his lack of knowledge might only confirm for the teacher that his help was limited.

As the supervisor explores the workers' points of view, she also shares her own opinions. Her intent is to indicate (or leave the impression) that she is eager to have staff input, wants their cooperation and help, and will give serious consideration to their views in making decisions. At the same time, there are a number of reasons why she also makes her own positions known. The free sharing of one's ideas is suggestive of assertion and independent judgment; and in the event that the workers have any question about it, her avowal of professional issues implies strength and thus potentially strong leadership.

A new supervisor should articulate a platform—a general and informal statement of how she thinks the future work should be measured. Depending on what appears natural under different circumstances, she may make her points incrementally over a period of weeks or may use an appropriate occasion for a one-time exposition of her basic views. The platform helps give workers the sense of what is important to the supervisor *before they act*. In that way, they can act accordingly if they choose. It is, as a matter of fact, one way of asserting supervisory authority with grace. If, during this process, the supervisor makes visible to staff her early grasp of issues, her knowledge about services, and her awareness of the complexities of the agency's function, then she will have generated a respect that further legitimates her authority.

If, in the beginning phase the supervisor hears facts or opinions about the unit's functioning or the staff performance, of either a positive or negative nature, she would do well to make this known to the unit. If the information is laudatory, there is no issue; the supervisor then shares in the unit's pride in a good performance. If the data is negative, she may handle it directly, although it is important that her directness not be accusatory, or she may wish to make use of it without direct reference to having heard the criticism. For example, if she had been told that the children in the unit's care were treated insensitively, she might speak about children's needs or a caring environment rather than raising the question of insensitivity directly. When staff are aware that derogatory information has been told to the supervisor, however, she must discuss it with them, even if it is uncomfortable for her to confront negatives so early in the game. Avoidance at that point will seem like weakness. When sharing negative data, it must be clear that she is seeking clarification rather than that she has yet accepted the criticism as accurate.

Whether the supervisor and worker deal directly with the supervisory relationship in their first sessions is an open question. Direct discussion on how the two plan to work together is usually prescribed, and one norm of supervision in social work relates to openness between supervisor and supervisee. The latter is expected to reveal his work-related concerns and identify impediments in his performance. The supervisor, in turn, is expected to use this information to foster the supervisee's growth and not to abuse the trust. (Levy, 1979). Because the contributions to supervisory literature have been largely made by educators, it may be that advice such as the above follows a model of the teacher-student relationship. Clearly, however, changes in context require changes in professional prescriptions.

When a staff is experienced, the supervisor must presume that they are aware of how social work supervision works. Supervisory practice does entail individual variation, of course, but it also follows familiar patterns. For example, supervision is now generally viewed as integrating educational and administrative objectives and fulfilling the needs of organizational accountability, as well as facilitating professional development. (Gitterman and Miller, 1977). The supervisor is seen as responsible for encouraging free exchange and the acceptance of difference, and workers are expected to express their questions and register their disagreements, if any, but then to go along. To review commonly known material with someone may imply a lack of trust in that person's knowledge or understanding and thus seem patronizing. One might also expect a difference in orientation in a supervisory relationship when a worker is new to both agency and supervisor than when the supervisor is the one who is unfamiliar with the setting or the staff. In the former instance, it is the worker who is likely to feel insecure (and therefore receptive to help); in the latter instance, the insecurity is likely to be the supervisor's (who may therefore be uncertain about her helpfulness).

A conversation about how two people will work together and with what degrees of freedom is a potentially intimate conversation. Its content in part is—or should be—shaped by the attitudes and feelings of the parties. For example, how closely supervised the worker will be should depend on his competence and his attitudes regarding close supervision. But attitudes and feelings are likely to be unclear at this early stage of the contact and may be well hidden. The risk, then, is that a conversation about supervision will ensue that is either overly general or largely unreal.

Building a Habit of Cooperation

Staff compliance with supervisory directives is, as we have suggested, supported by organizational norms and the structure of roles within the agency. Even so, some orders may be ignored, and for the supervisor who is beginning, there is a helpful guideline regarding the giving of orders that decreases this possibility. Sayles (1979) has noted that staff develop a "habit of compliance" with supervisory directives through a process whereby the supervisor gradually increases the demands that her directives place on staff members over time.

Directives that are not implemented have the effect of compromising the authority of the supervisor. It is irrelevant whether the noncompliance stems from indifference, disagreement, or defiance; the result is the same. Once an order has been disregarded, the likelihood that the circumstance will repeat itself is encouraged by pattern and symbol. The task of the supervisor in this regard, therefore, is to devise a system whereby over time staff members are predisposed to implement supervisory instructions irrespective of their degree of difficulty.

The supervisor begins by making requests of staff members on matters in which there is reason to expect that cooperation will be forthcoming. For example, during the supervisor's orientation period, she may indicate that she is planning a series of meetings that she expects all staff to attend—a rather mild directive, but one that nevertheless reflects her authority. Areas of controversy or tension are, wherever possible, avoided in these early stages, and directives are issued sparingly. The principle requires that the supervisor anticipate potential staff reaction before she makes a demand. Although the specifics of the following example are idiosyncratic, the fact that supervisors do not sufficiently anticipate staff reactions to their directives is probably not unusual. One of the workers in a unit complained to a supervisor, who was new to her position, that another worker had not cooperated in a joint venture for which both were responsible. Without considering how the worker might react, the supervisor indicated that she would handle the matter but wanted the worker to outline the complaint in a memorandum. The worker's response was terse, "I won't put that in writing!" Not only had the supervisor prematurely tried to solve the problem, as clinicians frequently do, but she should have assumed that her demand would have occasioned tension and thus resistance. In not anticipating the worker's reaction or even exploring a potential reaction before making the request, she effectively undercut her authority with him.

As workers become more comfortable with the supervisor, and as the supervisor gets to know her staff better, the frequency of order-giving can be increased and the demands that such orders place on staff enlarged. With the habit of cooperating with supervisory requests established, the supervisor has, in effect, trained her staff to comply with her directives and established a normative structure that supports worker cooperation.

Even with time and training, however, workers will not follow all directives all the time, and the wise supervisor will refrain from issuing directives that are likely to be resisted. (Miller, 1982). As Miller notes, the supervisor "who wishes to expand the areas of compliance and assent must attend to the subordinates' behavior at the marginal areas of assent, i.e., activities that must be carried out under equivocal or demanding circumstances" (p. 353). The ability to obtain compliance at the margins is one important indicator of supervisory effectiveness.

Relationship Building with Friends and Foes

Although we discuss exchange theory in the next chapter, it needs a brief reference here (Blau, 1969). Put oversimply, exchange relations refers to the interactions between parties that involve the exchange of resources or favors that lead to feelings of obligation and social commitment. In other words, supervisors can engender worker obligation through acts of special consideration, as in turn can workers in regard to their supervisors. Much of what takes place between people in organizations can be conceptualized in exchange terms—but for now we are interested only in the case of the practitioner from the inside who moves up the ranks from clinician to supervisor. Earlier, we noted that her authority might be challenged by both friend and foe. Here, we look at the practice implications of a prior relationship between supervisor and supervisee.

The supervisor who has been promoted from within will have to build new relationships and renegotiate old ones. When she shares a collegial history and close relations with those she now supervises, there is likely to be some tension on both sides. The supervisors's new role inexorably introduces a major political dimension into the relationship equation. For better or for worse, she is now the *boss*; whether either party articulates that fact, it is omnipresent and likely to be felt by both. It is essential, therefore, that the supervisor take on the implications of her new status.

Prior to the new appointment, exchange relations between the two have been largely expressive (though probably not as completely so as the parties often believe). In their new roles, instrumental factors emerge. On the supervisor's part, the worker-friend is a source of information that might not otherwise be communicated to her and a source of advice from someone who knows the system. The friend can be used to test new ideas without official commitment to the ideas or without the risk of embarrassment or lowered esteem on the supervisor's part. Further the supervisor can count on the friend in private councils or public meetings to support the supervisor's initiatives with other workers, or if in disagreement, to deal with their differences as a friend, sometimes privately and never excessively.

The worker-friend reaps benefits as well. In return for the information he has supplied, the supervisor must share some material that workers are ordinarily not told, thereby contributing the satisfaction to the worker of having an in. His views also receive a special hearing from the supervisor, and there may in addition be private arrangements (or the potential for them) that serve the worker well. Special assignments, permission to attend conferences, and the like are examples.

But there are disadvantages for both as well. However discreetly they handle their relationship, they are subject to the accusation of playing favorites; indeed, the accusation drives some supervisors to so bend over backward to appear evenhanded that their friends suffer as a consequence. Unfortunately, there are supervisors—either because they are concerned about evenhandedness or because they want to woo the opposition—who are most considerate of or forthcoming with the least cooperative members of their staff. Essentially, such a supervisor makes the mistake of rewarding organizationally bad behavior.

There is a more significant disadvantage to the worker-friend and supervisor. Their genuine feelings for one another and their history of cooperation and trust may be jeopardized. For the worker, the initial issue might be, "Will the new position go to her head?" For the supervisor, there may be two concerns. If she is insecure in her role, she may worry about whether she will be called on to exercise authority in regard to her friend and whether she can do it in light of their friendship. If she is insecure in her relations, she may be concerned about whether the other's identification as a worker will create separateness from her because of her administrative position. If they overcome these difficulties, the two are likely to face a further hurdle. When the instrumental nature of their interaction heightens, as it is likely to do with time, it can call the friendship into question. Both sides may worry about being used.

If the parties can confront the dilemma with sincerity, they may be effective in reshaping the friendship to fit the tensions which the change in role has imposed. When this is not successful, however, the supervisor (or worker) may have to decide between the benefits of the friendship versus the costs of maintaining a primarily affective relationship within a structure that is unresponsive to such relations. Or she may have to decide whether to take political advantage of the relationship, even if there has been strain or if the friendship is otherwise at risk. The choices are determined by one's values: the importance that the persons accord affective relations versus the importance to them of the organization's or their own instrumental interests. It has held that in a contest between affection and self-interest, the former will give way (Alinsky, 1971). We opt for the former as the primary value, but we recognize the potency of the latter as an influence on behavior.

Because our interest here is in beginnings, however, we are somewhat ahead of ourselves. It is, of course, well to anticipate the issues that one is likely to confront subsequently, for they then can be handled in a partial or less formidable manifestation. At the start, it is appropriate for the supervisor to take responsibility for managing the transition. Because she is the one who was promoted, she has to show that the position has not gone to her head. Furthermore, workers run the risk of appearing to curry special favors if they move out too quickly to make a connection with a new supervisor.

Finally there is the question of favoritism. The opprobrium of that accusation falls primarily and disproportionately on the supervisor; she grants the so-called favors. The worker's association with the supervisor costs him nothing unless the supervisor is disliked. As a matter of fact, it is likely to be a benefit, because the worker's access to her suggest to other participants that he is influential. Here, too, it is the supervisor who takes the initiative and offers assurances. In short, it is she who throughout the beginning phase must demonstrate her loyalty and commitment to her friends by maintaining those relations with them.

The newly promoted supervisor must also move out to those workers who were unfriendly to her prior to the promotion. Each may be leery of the other: the worker because he wonders if his unfriendliness will be held against him; the supervisor because she sees a potential foe. But unfriendly workers may now be embarrassed that they were not more prescient, and a gesture from the new supervisor puts a potentially uncomfortable matter to rest. In addition, the supervisor garners considerable good will by extending herself to persons who do not expect to be particularly well treated. Although the supervisor's behavior is a consequence of her role (her wish to gain the cooperation of *all* the unit's workers), others perceive her act in personal terms and view the new supervisor more favorably as a result.

When the opposition to the newly promoted supervisor is based on factional differences rather than on individual grounds, friendly gestures are likely to be insufficient. Two additional approaches might be pursued. One is the early identification of members of the faction who can be separated from the rest of the group and the attempt made to win them over either through "stroking" or perhaps be giving concessions on matters of importance to them. If they have followers, so much the better— for the purpose is the withering away of the faction. The long-range strategy, short of reducing the number of staff with allegiance to a dissident group, is to put the faction in disarray. The second approach, to aid in reaching this end, is to isolate members of the faction from the rest of the staff. But this comes later in the game. In the beginning, the new supervisor's goal is to assess the cohesiveness of the dissidents and to pry away those members whom she can salvage as cooperative. As suggested before, however, care must be taken not to continue to reward those participants whose noncompliance or negative effects remain fixed and consistent.

The Special Case of the Minority Supervisor

As suggested earlier, the minority supervisor may or may not face reactions, particular to her minority status. The staff may be neutral about her, in which case her task in beginning is little different from other neophytes. Or she may be viewed more positively than would a majority supervisor, thus easing her transition to the supervisory role. Because the past experiences of minority supervisors as blacks, Hispanics, women, or gays shape expectations regarding how people will respond to them, it is important that they are open to assessing the current circumstances without preformed bias. If they perceive a problem where none exists and act accordingly, they may well risk unnecessary difficulties for themselves and others. On the other hand, when tensions do exist, it is better that they be identified rather than denied and that some informed hunches are developed regarding their source.

In cases in which initial discomfort exists but is not rooted in deeply felt prejudice, we may expect that both supervisor and supervisees will look for ways of easing their initial anxieties. Nevertheless, because it is in her interests, as well as the fact that she is the boss and thus responsible, the supervisor should initiate the effort if necessary.

To span the presumed difference between them, the supervisor engages in what might be termed a *bridging* activity. Bridging communications are those that lead people to feel that someone else appreciates their experiences and accepts who they are despite the differences between them. An example is the situation in which a young professional assumes responsibility for a unit of seasoned but untrained staff. One can readily imagine how the news of such an appointment might be received by an entrenched staff. In such an instance it is incumbent upon the new supervisor to find ways to communicate her respect for her staff's experience and her interest in their perspectives. She does this by asking questions, referring to observations previously made (hence demonstrating that she not only heard but incorporated communications from the staff), and relating her own views in terms that acknowledge the staff's frame of reference. She thus begins to communicate her respect and the fact that the seeming difference is not as significant as might have been anticipated. Bridging is effective in transcending initial tensions, however, only when stronger prejudices or subgroup politics are not at issue.

Even so, if more basic problems exist in the agency, they probably should not be engaged early upon entry into the setting. One reason is that quite often these problems are not as serious as they initially appear. Some of the negative sentiments that give rise to such problems may be based on assumptions of future jeopardy for members of the majority or other subgroups. When the fears do not become a reality, they fade with the passage of time. In our earlier example, the male candidate whom some opposed on the ground that he might be homosexual did in fact turn out to be so. But within a few months it became clear that he had little affinity for the coalition that his opponents were afraid he would join, and his sexual orientation became a nonissue. He was not only readily accepted as a staff member but became friendly with some staff who had initially resisted his being hired.

There are other reasons for the new supervisor to move cautiously in directly engaging problems associated with a minority status. These matters typically call forth wellsprings of feeling and have the potential for serious division between people. Effectiveness at engaging emotionally laden issues requires thoroughly understanding the feelings and perceptions of the involved parties and is far better dealt with when the actors have a shared history and some degree of relationship.

The possibility that prejudice or subgroup politics is involved, of course, compounds the supervisor's difficulty in assuming her new role.

During the beginning phase, she has recourse only to two further means of handling the problem. One is to demonstrate her own openness and lack of bias. The task is to find ways to disabuse staff of the notion that she is entering with a fixed agenda regarding issues of difference or that she will engage in activities that are prejudicial to other agency subgroups. Essentially, she models the behavior that she desires from her staff.

If her minority status does appear to be an issue for others, the supervisor must begin to collect specific evidence. Ultimately, the issue may have to be confronted, and this cannot be done effectively without sufficient hard data. Our prescription is admittedly a difficult one. We suggest that the supervisor monitor the setting for negative information while she positively communicates her own lack of bias. Sometimes this behavior will ameliorate the uncertainties that feed prejudice. But even if this does not occur, the supervisor is positioned to confront prejudiced behavior with specific data while at the same time having demonstrated that she has not behaved similarly. These circumstances restructure a situation that might once have been politically ambiguous but now clearly favors the supervisor.

Contacts with Superiors and Peers

There is a correlation between one's influence in an organization and authority as a supervisor and the network of associations one has developed. The reasons for this are obvious enough. The more extensive one's network, the greater the potential for obtaining support with respect to one or another organizational initiative. Similarly, the wider one's contacts, the more access one has to organizational information and the more likely it is that one can accurately measure the "truth" regarding relevant organizational events and patterns. Finally, because power in organizations is affected by the impressions that others form about an actor, the more one is *observed* to possess and engage in a wide network of associations, the more she is differentiated from peers with more circumscribed associations. The consequence of such a contrast is to increase the supervisor's appearance of influence.

Consequently, the sooner the supervisor becomes significant in the flow of information within the agency, particularly between components of the organization and her staff, the sooner will her authority be legitimated in practice as well as in theory. This suggests her need to build and extend a network of working relationships throughout the organization. During the initial period in her new position, she must seek opportunities to make contact with superiors and peers. The foci of the contacts are threefold: to obtain information; to learn and affect the expectations that these others have for how she will perform her role; and to develop links that facilitate access to them in the future.

Orientation discussions between the supervisor and an executive are an important means of legitimate contact, providing the content and interaction from which effective links can be built between them. But the supervisor needs to maintain a delicate balance regarding the number of contacts she seeks with high-ranking participants. Sometimes practitioners initiate contacts that do not appear legitimate or substantive to superiors or that seem excessive in the context of an executive's limited time. Thus these practitioners come to be perceived as overly dependent or insufficiently resourceful, or they may be perceived as too self-promoting, expending excessive energy to be noticed. We note parenthetically that executives are unlikely to be judgmental about self-promotion per se. Self-promotion, after all, is to be expected in a relationship in which the party's well-being is dependent on the other's evaluation. It is only when the promotion is obvious, and thus ineffective, that it is of concern.

Some supervisors, on the other hand, tend to minimize their contacts with the executive on the principle that if they have fewer conversations, they will have greater autonomy in performing their jobs. With the increase in autonomy, they have to settle for less executive help, protection, and influence in decision making. Caplow (1976, p. 33) has argued that faced with this choice, most subordinates choose autonomy and minimize interaction with their superiors.

If so, it is an unfortunate accommodation to superior-subordinate relations. Close association with the boss brings the supervisor more benefits than the cost to her of close supervision. Research suggests, as a matter of fact, that influence without formal authority (such as is the case when a supervisor attempts to influence an executive) is gained through behaviors that establish individual prominence (House and Baetz, 1979). Furthermore, the supervisor's effectiveness with her own staff is affected by the degree of access and influence she has with her superior.

The wise supervisor should want to know the executive's priorities with regard to supervisory responsibilities (e.g., supervisory conferences, departmental staff meetings, data collection, program development, and employee evaluation). She should also want to discover which accountability measures the executive deems important and which are less so (e.g., the timely preparation of reports, submission of case records, responses to memos). Some of the information about executive preferences and attitudes can be gained informally from contacts with peers, but the supervisor needs also to assess the executive's positions herself, independently from the agency grapevine. The more accurate the supervisor's reading of the executive's values, professional stance, and administrative preferences, the more she can make the executive's priorities her own, or the more she can *seem* to make them her own, which serves her purpose just as well.

Adhering closely to executive priorities may feel costly to a supervisor who has her own priorities and who may disagree with some of his. Once again, a delicate balance is required. She must find the fulcrum that allows her to respond to the executive's definition of need while simultaneously representing and pursuing her own judgments as well. More often than not, the two are not mutually exclusive, but it does take time and a process to work them out.

The cornerstone of increased influence with one's boss is one's track record in fulfilling executive expectations and priorities. It is necessary early in the relationship to demonstrate one's effectiveness in this regard before one develops the credibility and influence to begin to attempt changing his expectations. If the supervisor does not share the executive's priorities or some of his views, she may have to register her difference with him, albeit gently, if the disagreement is important to her. But it is not likely early in her tenure that she will be able to change these views. It is only when she has demonstrated her competence *to him* that she has created a resource for exchange and can seriously hope to influence him. At the least, he will owe her some gratitude for a job well done; at the most, he will be dependent on her continuing contributions to the agency.

It is not unusual, as a matter of fact, for conscientious and creative supervisors to exact a price for their work. And the price is often assertion in pressing for new directions in the agency program or in the components of their jobs. Executives may expect this price and feel that it is a small one to pay for effective performance. Some may even view the supervisor's assertion as an added benefit. Those executives who are able and secure know that an assertive supervisor who represents her unit determinedly with him will represent agency interests to others with the same determination.

The beginning supervisor, as she learns to know the agency's upper-ranking personnel, may assess whether her boss or some other superior might be counted on to sponsor her. It has been suggested that new employees at various hierarchical levels might do well to seek out an organizational mentor, actors who bet on the talent they perceive in newcomers and are willing to work closely with junior staff. (Zaleznik, 1977, p. 76). There are clearly risks in prematurely finding a higher-ranking mentor (for one thing, how that person is perceived by others). Nevertheless, having friends in high places has many advantages, not least of which is that it provides the supervisor with a whole different level of power. To be adopted as a protege requires that the supervisor find someone whose values, positions, and personality are sufficiently similar to make the exchange rewarding for both (Sanzotta, 1979).

Contacts with organizational peers such as other unit heads and specialized staff such as the fiscal officer, medical records librarian, or evaluation specialist have similar purposes to contacts with superiors: to gain information, shape expectations, and create links necessary for future access.

As with upper-ranking actors, the contacts that one makes with peers must appear natural, never contrived. The norm generally is that oldtimers will (or should) seek out newcomers rather than the reverse. The newcomer who appears too friendly in the absence of a reasonable basis may risk the other's suspicions. Particularly if the newcomer is overattentive to a peer, the latter may worry that something will be expected in exchange for the attentiveness that she may not want to profer. Although there are no inviolate rules devoid of their context, generally the supervisor's initial interaction should be task-focused and related to—or at least credibly appear to be related to—the substance of one's work. Broadening the relationship to include a social dimension follows later.

In these initial contacts, the supervisor needs in particular to learn the details of how her role interfaces with the roles of others. Of primary concern is the issue of interdependence. What are the specific ways one is dependent on others for information, and what activities must be coordinated to accomplish her responsibilities effectively? Dependence in organizations is closely associated with power and influence. If one needs information and cooperation from another, the other is in a position to require—subtly or explicitly—activity or gesture in return for the needed service. As indicated in Chapter 1, peer relations that involve two-way dependency or interdependence tend to hold the potential for both cooperative and conflictual interactions. The activities inherent in relationship development, as well as in agency problem solving, are ordinarily shared by both parties. Relationships that involve one-way dependency tend to place the burden of management of the relationship disproportionately on the dependent partner. Learning the characteristics of these relationships and attempting to work out means of interaction that will maximize cooperation and gain the resources necessary for the unit are early tasks for the new supervisor.

Another concern in these explorations is the possible impact that organizational history and the past actions of her predecessor may hold for the way organizational peers develop expectations of the new supervisor. If she learns that there is a history of cooperative relations between units at least at the outset, this becomes a priority for the new supervisor to maintain. In an important sense, the expectation on the part of the cooperative colleague that such relations will continue constitutes a kind of instant ally for the new supervisor—an organizational actor who is predisposed to support and legitimate the supervisor's authority without the supervisor's having to "start from scratch" in developing the relationship. If, on the other hand, one learns that there has been a history of difficulty or enmity, careful exploration of the extent to which there may be a legitimate conflict of interest in their roles or function or some other reason for caution in the relationship becomes an opportunity for the supervisor to develop an ally through making the commitment, if only implicitly, to start afresh.

As the first weeks in her new position pass, the recently appointed supervisor finds herself making a subtle transition from the tasks of orienting and establishing herself in the position to the tasks of managing it. There is, of course, significant overlap in these phases, and some aspects of managing the position begin on the first day, just as the orientation process may continue on, to some degree at least, for several months. We turn in the following chapters to issues related to the ongoing concerns of the role.

Extending Supervisory Influence

Much as social workers and other human services personnel may be uncomfortable with the notion, at the core of the supervisory process is a significant element of control. Control need not be viewed perjoratively, at least until one considers *what* is being controlled and *how* the control is exercised. A benign example makes this point. The supervisor whose objective is the self-discipline of her supervisee, his self-learning and development of professional autonomy, may be said to be attempting to control the outcome of the supervisory encounter. Self-discipline, after all, constitutes a demand that the supervisee behave in ways that are professionally prescribed, and self-learning can aid the worker in making judgments that the supervisor would want to have made. Even to promote professional autonomy is to recognize that effective practice requires that workers intervene in ways reflective of their own differing styles and personalities, but the ends of the intervention are expected to conform to the supervisor's goals. Essentially, even the notion of motivating people to act in a particular way implies trying to get them to do what you want them to do *on their own*. It may be argued, as a matter of fact, that the emphasis on self-discipline and self-learning stems at least in some measure from the invisibility of most client-worker interaction, and thus represents the encouragement of internal controls to meet external requirements.

How one tries to influence (or control) is also significant. For one thing, the means of intervention is often critical in effectively accomplishing a particular outcome. Self-discovery, for example, does not ordinarily result from a didactic supervisory style. Conversely, the performance of a task that requires specific information is not likely to be advanced by a supervisor's exploration of a worker's feelings. Beyond issues of effectiveness, value issues also come into play, and one's moral judgments about influence or control are shaped by supervisory means as well as by the supervisor's ends. But whatever the case or the judgments we may make, enhancing one's influence and control is central to supervision.

The supervisor's task of obtaining staff compliance may be viewed from two vantage points. The first has to do with those contacts between supervisors and staff that relate directly to helping the latter function capably in their practice roles. We take these matters up in subsequent chapters. The second is contextual—what the supervisor must do in her interactions with staff *and* other organizational actors to promote unit effectiveness. From this vantage point, her organizational performance and persona contribute importantly to her capacity to induce staff compliance and ground all of her work with staff.

As we have asserted and as research has consistently shown, supervisors who are more influential with their own superiors are also more influential with their supervisees than are their less upwardly influential colleagues. For example, in one study, managers perceived as having an in with the boss were described by subordinates as more skillful, having more information, and being more supportive than other managers (Cashman et al., 1976). It may be that these managers were able to work both levels of the hierarchy, upper and lower, with similar skill. It is likely, however, that supervisors who had clout with their superiors were also more able to gain both personal and job-related advantages for their staff and were thus more able to call on staff cooperation and compliance. The matter is reciprocal. When a supervisor has clout with a boss, she increases her influence with staff. And when staff cooperation is assured, in part as a result of supervisory influence with the boss, the supervisor's influence with the boss is also extended.

Similarly, supervisors who can manage their peers well can garner resources for their units that generate subordinate obligations as well. However much a unit's success may be beyond her control, the evaluations of the supervisor by staff and superiors will enhance her unit's success or the success of its program. When she can affect agency decision making to optomize unit effectiveness, she enhances her own position in the agency and her credibility with her staff.

Unfortunately, supervisors are often held accountable for the performance of their units without sufficient power and resources to affect outcomes. As a consequence, the most demanding aspect of the supervisory role may be the political skill necessary to develop and maintain agreements with varying constituencies—supervisees, peer, and superiors, among others—that can promote unit effectiveness (Patti, 1983, p. 58).

Social workers and other mental health professionals need to develop a political viewpoint that is analagous to their clinical way of thinking. They are attuned to incorporating clinically related knowledge into their practice. Workers listen to client problems to ascertain underlying or unstated personal concerns, make inferences about the client's feelings and behaviors, and use clinical knowledge to guide their assessments and interventions. The knowledge varies with the theoretical orientation of the practitioner, but regardless of its base, the practitioner is expected to use the knowledge to both act and monitor the action at the same time. In other words, the worker is expected to develop a clinically rooted self-consciousness.

The same ought to hold in regard to a political approach to practice, with politically related knowledge similarly incorporated into practice. In simultaneously acting and monitoring her action, the supervisor needs to be as aware of the political implications of her situation and interventions as she is the clinical implications.

The development of a political perspective starts with the integration of such concepts as power and social exchange into one's work, and we begin this chapter with a discussion of these ideas. We then discuss three organizationally related practice tasks that enlarge the supervisor's ability to garner influence with her staff.

Power and Social Exchange

It is useful to distinguish between influence, power, and authority. The terms have been used to refer to a range of interrelated processes in the literature, and shades of meaning with respect to the same term differ with various authors. Here we use the term *influence* to refer to the process of successfully directing the activity of another. The measure of influence, then, is the extend to which the target's activity conforms to the preferences of the person exercising influence. If influence is the process of regulating the activity of another, *power* in an organization can be conceptualized as the potential capacity to influence another actor—in this case, the supervisor's potential capacity to influence workers, peers, or superiors. Such influence might have to do with the values, attitudes, and/or behavior of another. Finally, as was noted in Chapter 2, *authority* refers to one's right to exert influence being formally sanctioned by the agency. Considered in this way, authority constitutes one of a number of possible foundations of supervisory power.

Bases of Power

Many writers on power have used designations noted by French and Raven (1959). They identified five different foundations of power within organizations with which supervisors have the capacity to exercise influence to the extent that they have or can develop these bases of power:

1. *Reward Power:* Believing that the supervisor controls access to a desired reward, the subordinate yields to the supervisor's influence in order to receive the reward.
2. *Coercive Power:* Believing that the supervisor controls the exercise of punishment, the subordinate yields to the supervisor's influence in order to avoid negative sanctions.
3. *Legitimate Power:* Believing that the supervisor has the right to request compliance, the subordinate yields to the supervisor's influence. This is the dimension of power based upon authority.
4. *Expert Power:* Believing that the supervisor possesses special knowledge or expertise and therefore knows what should be done, the supervisee yields to the supervisor's influence.
5. *Referent Power:* Admiring the supervisor, the supervisee yields to her influence out of a desire for approval and to emulate her example.

In practice, of course, these bases of supervisory power are mixed, and supervisees comply with the supervisor's influence attempt for multiple reasons. For example, if a supervisor recommends a course of action for a worker to take in the conduct of a particular case, his motives for following the recommendation may include a combination of factors. By virtue of the authority associated with the supervisor's position, the worker believes that such direction is legitimate—that it is appropriate for her to direct his work. The worker may also feel that as a result of her training and experience, the supervisor has expertise in such matters, and hence her advice is likely to be sound technically. Finally, the worker may have grown to respect the supervisor professionally and may wish to emulate her professional example either to please her or to approximate her professional style more closely. Thus, in the present example, it is a combination of the supervisor's legitimate, expert, and referent power that together result in the worker's cooperation with the supervisory directive.

It is likely, as a matter of fact, that there is often a multiplier effect, in that one source of power supports another. Thus the authority vested in a role can act to increase the perception of the incumbent's expertise, and the perception of expertise in turn may heighten a person's social attractiveness.

To have, or to develop, any one or a combination of the five bases of power is a necessary but insufficient condition for the exercise of influence. The supervisor may be socially attractive and an expert, her authority sanctioned by the organization, and yet not be influential with one or another set of actors. For legitimate, expert, referent, or other bases of power to act as a source of influence, other conditions must be operative as well. We cite three that are critical in the supervisor's relations with subordinates and others. They are that the subordinate or other:

1. *Perceive* the resource for power and consider it legitimate or valid.
2. *Desire* the resources (or avoidance of the sanction).
3. *Believe* that cooperation with the influence attempt is likely to result in access to the desired resource (or avoidance of the sanction), and that lack of cooperation is likely to call forth the reverse response.

We may presume that each of the three conditions was operative in the example we used. Perhaps the supervisor had been effectively "anointed" by upper-level staff as she began at the agency. Or perhaps her initial discussions with workers had served their purpose, and she had come across as knowledgeable, clinically astute, and someone to be liked and trusted. Or perhaps over time the supervisor had developed a reputation at the agency for traits such as these. The point is that it was the worker's *perception* of the supervisor as having legitimate, expert, and referent power that largely impelled him to follow her recommendation.

A worker's perception and objective reality may or may not conform with one another. Four permutations are possible. The supervisor may be perceived as knowledgeable on cases like the one in question and may in fact have the requisite expertise. Or she may be perceived as an expert although her knowledge is meager. The opposite may also be true; that is, she may not be perceived as an expert when in fact she is one. Or she may be perceived to have limited expertise, the perception reflecting the actual state of affairs. The consequences for the influence attempts of the supervisor of each of these four circumstances is profound.

Supervisors accrue additional credit if their advice is taken and turns out to be sound (i.e., actual and perceived expertise). If their advice is taken and is in error, it is likely that over time the perception of expertise will suffer. The risk of perceived expertise without the requisite knowledge or skill is that expectations are raised and there is the danger of exposure. In many cases, however, the impression of expertise (or the impression of any other characteristic) is as useful a source of influence as the characteristic itself. Between the choice of being perceived as generally knowledgeable or not, the supervisor usually opts for the perception of knowledgeability. Although there are exceptions to the rule, the desirability of passing oneself off as having resources for influencing requires attention to impression management, a subject to which we turn later in the chapter. For now, it is enough to note that supervisory practice requires concern regarding not only what it *is* but also regarding what *seems to be*.

The second condition implicit in the French and Raven typology, that the worker must desire to have or avoid the resource, highlights the interactive and reciprocal quality of influencing. The worker follows the supervisor's direction on the case because he wants to be viewed as respectful of her authority or to be effective on the case in question and/or because he desires to emulate or please the supervisor. For influencing to take place, then, requires that the rewards and/or sanctions are responsive to the worker's attitudes and feelings, particularly with regard to the supervisor.

One organizational theorist says in this regard that "opinions differ about whether it is better for a manager to be loved or feared by his subordinates, but to be loved *and* feared is best of all" (Caplow, 1976, p. 9). The statement is oversimple, of course. If influencing is interactive and if subordinates differ, the potency of love, fear, or any other feeling will vary, depending on the subordinate and the circumstances in which the supervisor and subordinate find themselves. But the statement is suggestive. To be feared requires that the supervisor be seen as active and decisive in protecting the interests of the unit, its clients, and/or the agency. To be loved, of course, requires that the supervisor be supportive to her staff and helpful with regard to task achievement.

Finally, the worker has to hold certain beliefs about the interchange with the supervisor. These include the judgment that the supervisor and others will respect his accommodation to supervisory authority, that following the supervisor's guidance in the case is more likely to result in effective practice than otherwise, that modeling himself after the supervisor will enhance his own professional self, and/or that the supervisor will think well of him for so doing.

These processes often occur without the conscious awareness of the participants. The example of a supervisor directing a worker in the conduct of a particular case is a simple interchange that might occur between supervisor and workers numerous times each week. Nonetheless, had one or another of the conditions of perception, desire, and belief been absent or at odds with the circumstances as we described them, the likelihood of worker cooperation would have been reduced. Appreciating that influence processes frequently take on a patterned or predictable quality without the awareness of the participants raises a question regarding the process by which the parties arrive at this arrangement. Thus it is not sufficient for the practitioner who is interested in extending his influence in a new role to understand the bases of power and the conditions required for its effective exercise. It is also necessary to understand how relationships evolve between supervisor and subordinate such that each party learns the rules and terms that lead to effective influencing.

The Processes of Social Exchange

The ways in which one party begins to yield to the influence of another are illuminated by concepts associated with *social exchange theory* (Blau, 1964; Hollander, 1979). The basic premise is that interactions between parties involve the exchange of benefits or favors that lead to a feeling of obligation, social commitment, and/or attractiveness. In part, the process is predicated on the observation by sociologists that a *norm of reciprocity* exists in Western culture (Gouldner, 1960). The norm operates like a social standard which suggests that when another is thoughtful or helpful, an obligation is engendered toward one's benefactor. The terms of such exchanges are broad. Benefits that may be traded include material resources, effort, and support in pursuing one's goals, as well as psychological benefits such as respect, affection, friendship, and esteem.

Let us illustrate how such a relationship could develop in a supervisory context. Penny Brown has been a unit supervisor for three months, and at her initial staff meetings, she noticed Max Casson. The latter was attentive; he asked bright questions, and his comments helped Penny to elaborate points she wished to make. Their positions on value and professional issues appeared comparable, and Max's participation connoted support for Penny's role as unit supervisor. With time, Penny began to feel that she could count on Max and was grateful to him for that.

On his side, Max's early reaction to Penny was that she would be an able supervisor, perhaps tough, but client oriented and professionally stimulating. From time to time, he sought Penny out to initiate exploration of a particular practice problem, and in sounding out Penny's positions, he found them compatible with his own. Max was pleased that Penny, in setting up a series of lunch appointments with staff members, had chosen Max to meet with first. He had no trouble sharing considerable information about the history of the unit and the perspectives of various agency staff personnel. When the executive asked Penny to develop a proposal for a specialized service, Penny asked Max to assist her. Now, if the proposal is funded, Penny intends to offer Max the position of coordinator of the service.

The relationship that developed between Penny and Max is illustrative of the mutual benefit that accrues to both parties from exchange transactions. Max's support triggered Penny's gratitude—and because she was new to the supervisory role, she needed Max's continued support. Penny responded by paying special attention to Max, who was flattered by the interest in him and his work, as would most workers. As such exchanges continued, Penny gave Max special assignments that were performed well. This increased Penny's trust in her initial judgment of Max's competence and also had the effect of enhancing Max's esteem in his own and other eyes. In sum, the feelings of the participants in the interaction became one of respect, loyalty, and mutual dependence.

Max may also have developed or been granted what has been called *negotiating latitude*. It has been observed that very early some workers are given considerable latitude from their boss in regard to how tasks are to be performed and the extent to which decisions can be made without clearance. Other workers, on the same hierarchical level and with similar responsibilities, are granted considerably less control over their role development (Dansereau, Graen, and Haga, 1975). As one might expect, the person who, like Max, is perceived as competent by his supervisor, who can be counted on to follow through on his work, whose values appear congruent with the supervisor's, and who is viewed as personally loyal is most likely to be granted latitude. In our example, Penny learns to count on one of her workers, and Max manages to develop an in with the boss. But because Penny's location is in the middle of the hierarchy, her concerns are also similar to Max's. She, too, must establish an in with *her* boss. The dynamic is the same, of course, and if Penny is as able as we have described her, she will have learned from her experience to attune to the needs and sensitivities of those on both levels, superior and subordinate.

Research suggests that superiors frequently develop the kind of close exchange relationship that took place between Penny and Max with a number of trusted subordinates. The result is a kind of two-class system within the unit: an in-group made up of those close to the superior and an out-group made up of other staff members (Yukl, 1981). This arrangement results in benefits and constraints for both parties. For the supervisor, a competent and loyal group of trusted subordinates assures that work will be accomplished in a timely and effective way without constant attention. The in-group is also useful in supporting the supervisor's position with the larger staff and thus helping to maintain staff commitment to unit goals and conformity to agency procedures. In return, the supervisor must remain attentive to the needs and interests of the group members, reinforcing the fact of their special access through sentiment and deed. She cannot be arbitrary or coercive with in-group members without endangering the relationship. Their cooperation must be won through persuasion, negotiation, and influence-sharing, and this may at times be costly with respect to both personal resources and time.

Similarly, there are costs and benefits for the in-group members. They can expect more influence in the character of their jobs, more opportunity for advancement, fewer conflicts with their boss, and a greater share of available rewards than will the out-group. On the other hand, they also must be loyal to the supervisor and supportive of her position, as well as being more committed to their jobs and responsible in their conduct. They may have to contend with the resentment of fellow workers who are not part of the in-group, and, being so closely identified with a supervisor, they also have to share the positives and negatives of the supervisor's reputation or status in the agency generally or as her reputation goes up or down.

There is a comparatively low level of mutual influence in the exchange relationship with out-group subordinates. (Yukl, 1981). Authority, in combination with coercive power and a limited degree of reward power, is the major source of supervisory influence. To satisfy the exchange, according to Yukl, workers comply only with the formally prescribed role expectations and receive only the standard benefits from the agency.

At the heart of the exchange relationship is the power that attends the dependence of another. The activities of organizations impel interdependence—thus creating a dependence on others for effective task accomplishment. Coordination of services, integration of work flow, timely and accurate sharing of information, and prompt review of initiatives are examples of the ways in which one's effectiveness on the job necessitates dependence on others. Although the occupational dependencies cited above are instrumental in character, in addition we experience strong needs or preferences in the emotional realm as well. Recognition from a supervisor for a job well done, support during a demanding or precarious period, advice or feedback concerning dilemmas one is facing on the job, respect, esteem or concern, these are all areas of emotional experience that, when met, greatly enhance the quality of work life. Whether the resources in question are instrumental or emotional—in fact, more often than not the two are closely intertwined—when we find ourselves in relationships where such resources are forthcoming, we settle in and become dependant on them. In exchange, we offer what we can in response to our understanding of the needs or desires of the other— cooperation, support, esteem, and the like. Central to the discussion of power development in organizations is the fact that in these kinds of relationships we are highly predisposed to yield to the influence of the other. Herein lies the power of dependency and the power potential implicit in the exchange relationship.

The power of an exchange relationship is typically two-way. If one is receiving benefits in such a relationship, he or she is likely to be providing them as well. The commitment and feeling of obligation that one feels toward another is most often reciprocally experienced and returned by the other. One dimension of that commitment or feeling of obligation is the predisposition for both partners to meet the requests and bend to the influence of the other; that is, they each have a degree of power over the other. Both are more powerful than organizational peers of similar cir-cumstances who have not developed such exchange relationships.

It is, of course, true that one party may have more to give in the relationship than another. If this extra giving is a one-time event, it leads the giver, in political parlance, to be one up on the person who receives the benefit. The beneficiary is then expected to return the other's quid with his or her quo. It is not unusual for a skillful actor to look for the occasion to be responsive to or perform a service for another, either to return a favor or to be in a position to exact one in the future. The bookkeeping on this is not rigid, but the obligations that are generated by these exchanges most certainly are.

Ordinarily, if one person is consistently in the position of giver, one of a number of potential accommodations will result. Slowly, the giving may be extinguished, as the actor learns that the other can or will not respond in kind. Or before that actually occurs, the other party decides not to bother the giver any further—because the former does not have the resources to balance accounts or has picked up cues that further requests for assistance or support will be frowned on. At the least, a consistent pattern on nonreciprocity requires the beneficiary of the favors to be deferential to the other party. Deference thus substitutes for other types of benefit in the exchange.

Social exchange is not, of course, restricted to vertical relationships in organizations. Exchange relations develop in much the same fashion between organizational peers as between the subordinate and superior.

Indeed, as a result of developing exchange relationships with unit directors and other peers, a supervisor can build an influence network in the agency, thus increasing access to information and cooperation that is not available to the professional who does not engage in such activity.

Trading Resources

It remains to identify more systematically what may be traded in these relationships. In the example of Penny and Max, we referred to some of the instrumental and emotional resources that generate dependency and influence. No list is complete, of course, for anything that one party has to offer that another wants is subject to a trade. It may be useful, however, to summarize briefly some of the major resources for influencing available within organizations. For readers interested in a more expanded discussion of the topic, we refer to our treatment of it elsewhere. (Brager and Holloway, 1978, pp. 92–101).

Resources fall into two categories: those that result from the structure of systems (e.g., the supervisor's position gives her authority in reference to her staff and grants upper-level administrators authority in reference to her) and those having to do with the attributes of individuals (e.g., charisma). There is often an overlap among resources that might be described as structural and those that stem primarily from the characteristics of individuals. Indeed, in some measure the potency of even individual characteristics in generating influence has to do with the location of the parties in the agency's structure. Thus, all things being equal, supervisors tend to value the gratitude and approval of executives more than the gratitude and approval of lower-ranking workers. In addition, whether the resource is a structural one or a resource that flows from personal attributes, it can be put to use only under the conditions cited earlier in this chapter: that the practitioner perceives the resource, that he desires it, and that he believes it will be forthcoming if he acts appropriately.

Organizational rank creates resources. Clearly, the higher the rank, the more rewards and punishments one has to induce cooperation from others: responsibility for hiring and firing, promotions, assignments, evaluations, references, and the like. These are, of course, the grounds for reward and coercive power. Often, the rewards and punishments that are available at the higher ranks are not allocated to the supervisory level. Supervisors must then gain the executive's confidence so that they have access to the sanctions that go with upper-rank positions (e.g., the ability to recommend hiring and firing and have the recommendation followed).

Task, subunit membership, and professional background also create resources, depending on the interests and backgrounds of those who are the potential targets of an influence attempt. Members often identify with the group to which they belong—whether the group is based on actors performing a set of similar tasks in the agency, the fact that the group or unit has an identifiable structure and common interest, or because the members of the group have a common professional identity. Supervisors who share this commonality with workers can call on group norms as regulators of behavior. Workers who violate prevailing norms may pay a high cost for doing so, not just with their supervisor. They also risk losing influence in the unit or the esteem of their colleagues. Supervisors who can use group norms and group solidarity for their own purposes have a potent resource for influencing.

Information is another source of organizational influence, because organizational decision making can hardly take place without information on which to base the decision. Information is differentially available, depending on the organization's structure. For example, an executive's influence with regard to his agency's trustees is greater in large, complex, geographically far-flung organizations because of the wider gap in organizational intelligence between him and his trustees than in smaller, less-complex organizations. At the same time, he also has less influence with his staff than executives in these smaller agencies—and for the same reason, his access to information depends on the staff more than it would in the simpler setting. To the degree that supervisors, or other upper-level staff for that matter, need information to perform *their* tasks ably, their dependency on the holders of the information is increased. In addition, participants with access to information have considerable potential for exerting influence through selecting or withholding information, providing accurate or ambiguous information, or otherwise adapting data to the purpose at hand.

A closely related and similarly determined resource has to do with the actor's location in the communication system. When supervisors control access to important others or serve as links between groups, the resource can be a potent one. Thus people who can open and close doors may have little authority but considerable influence. It is for this reason that later in this chapter we single out the supervisor's need to widen her network of associations in the agency and beyond as an important organizational task requiring a supervisor's attention.

Further, supervisors serve as links between persons and groups and are thus in a position to interpret each to the other, for example, top management to staff and the reverse. In controlling much of the flow of information, the supervisor can segregate audiences if she wishes, share information differentially, or shift its emphasis. Interests are thus made to appear similar or dissimilar almost as the supervisor's wishes and skills dictate.

Among the resources available to individuals regardless of structure are knowledge and expertise, social appeal, and tenure in the agency.

Professionals control their dependence on a given system by creating and maintaining a favorable impression of their "product" in the eyes of a salient public (Rabinovitz, 1969, p. 121). Through expertise, or apparent expertise, they accrue the prestige that enhances their opportunity to obtain compliance from relevant publics. Furthermore, to the extent that organizational decision making requires technical know-how, the expert who has know-how—or seems to have it—can make demands on organizational actors in turn. It follows that knowledge and expertise—or to put it differently, competence in the performance of one's job—is an important resource for influencing those on both the higher and lower rungs of the organizational ladder. The supervisor's ability to develop the appearance of competence is thus critical to her ability to perform effectively, and we devote the following section of the chapter to this matter.

Social appeal is another individual attribute with influence potential. The more socially attractive a person is, the more likely others are to seek her approval or recognition, and therefore the more likely that she can influence their behavior (Mechanic, 1964, pp. 145–46). Although the exact qualities that comprise social appeal are uncertain, insight into the needs, hopes, and values of others is an important quality (McClelland, 1975). Another, according to House (1977) is self-confidence or, at least, the acting ability to project the impression of self-confidence to others. In a study of a medical school, Bucher (1970) observes that the *assessed stature* of individual faculty members was an important source of their power and that the assessment of their stature was determined by their competence within the institution, their outside reputation, and by such factors of social appeal as whether or not they are "decent human beings," have "good judgment," and "pull their load."

Social appeal supports or enhances other resources for influence. As persons are seen as appealing, the rewards they have to dispense become more valued. As we inferred earlier, every individual has social rewards to dispense: gratitude, deference, recognition, approval. These rewards are effective or not, depending on both the person who dispenses the reward and on the desire or need of the recipient for it.

Finally, tenure—the length of time the supervisor has been with the organization—is another source of influence. There are a number of reasons why this is so: the identification of the long-tenured supervisor with the agency and her loyalty to it are less subject to challenge; her historical perspective may be critical to the way issues are shaped; her established place permits greater risk taking; she is likely to have developed relationships that can be called on or to have granted favors for which she can exact repayment; and she may make use of precedents with more legitimacy. Furthermore, the long-tenured member knows the agency's rules, those which circumvent other rules, and their differential application, depending on circumstances. Perhaps most important, the longer an actor has been with an organization, the more thoroughly she knows its formal and informal decision-making system and therefore how best to route an influence attempt.

Clearly, the beginning supervisor cannot count on tenure as a resource. As with all resources for influencing, however, access to persons with tenure, or as a matter of fact access to other resources as well, may be almost as good as the resource itself. Aggregating resources is, of course, the basis for the development of coalitions.

We turn now to the practice steps associated with developing and extending supervisory influence following the orientation period.

Enhancing Perceptions of Competence

Expert power is predicated on the practitioner's competence. There is probably no other single factor available to supervisors that is more reliable in legitimating their role or extending their influence that an impression of effectiveness.

Supervisory effectiveness is a function of three interdependent factors: the agency environment, the specific demands of the job, and the ways in which the supervisor deals with these contextual elements. Here, as in other circumstances, the social work precept of *person* and *situation* applies, although in the present instance the precept might be termed *supervisor* and *organization*.

Supervisory expertise is most valued when it contributes to significant agency goals. It has been observed, for example, that influence accrues to those professionals whose expertise conforms to an organization's primary mission. Thus a study of five correctional institutions revealed that psychiatric social workers were perceived as more influential in institutions with treatment goals than those with custodial goals. Teachers were seen as having a lesser amount of influence whether the institution was treatment or custodial, apparently because academic work was not central to the purpose of either institution (Zald, 1965).

On an individual level, the extent to which supervisors contribute to the goals of those they are seeking to influence determines the extent to which they are perceived as able and thus the strength of their influence. The supervisor in a hospital setting whose staff members play an important role in timely discharge planning accrues particular credit if an aim of the hospital administration is to reduce their patients' length of stay. Similarly, the social worker in a school setting who focuses on work with families with whom the principal and teachers need special help enhances her credibility with them. The practice principle is clear. The supervisor needs to search out the objectives of relevant organizational actors, and unless it is professionally contraindicated, she must seek to contribute to these ends in her work.

Another organizational factor has to do with the demands of the supervisory job. Particularly important is the diversity of tasks for which the supervisor is responsible. How she approaches the visibility, quantity, and nature of her tasks have a bearing on the degree of expertise she will be credited with by others.

Credited with are the operative words. It is, of course, unnecessary to exhort professionals to bring maximum knowledge and skill to the tasks they perform. Supervisors ordinarily function as best they can, and in what follows, we *assume* the supervisor's competence and discuss only the means of maximizing its recognition. For, as we pointed out earlier, it is only as others perceive her to be competent that the political purpose of getting others to accede to her wishes is served.

Professional interventions are often invisible, and work styles differ in the extent to which professionals act to call attention to what they do. For some, virtue is its own reward; that is, if they perform well, the satisfaction of a job well done is sufficient in itself, or they assume that their professional competence will be noticed. This may be true, but it is hardly the whole story. Attention to impressions and how to manage them is also important to those who would increase their influence in an organization. For the effective supervisor, impression management takes precedence over excessive modesty or apprehension with respect to self-assertion.

One caveat is in order. We noted earlier that blatant self-promotion is ineffective. Those whose efforts are obvious are viewed as lacking in skill, and they may even be perceived as needy, self-important, sometimes arrogant. They thus diminish their social appeal, and, even worse, they also generate an incentive for others to challenge their apparent view of their own capacities. Paradoxically, one must be concerned about creating the impression of competence while simultaneously appearing not to be invested in creating such an impression at all.

Most supervisory positions do not permit anyone in a service agency sufficient time to devote herself to the many tasks that are called for. As a result, some tasks may be completed promptly, some postponed, and some may be ignored. At times tasks are approached with care and thoughtfulness, while in other instances, the supervisor has to cut corners. Practitioners develop an implicit, and sometimes explicit, way of establishing priorities to aid them in allocating attention to the multitude of activities that go with their position.

Many supervisors will not admit to choosing those tasks that they enjoy doing most as their priority, but this is frequently the basis of the choice. Still others respond to demands as the demands are experienced without sufficient consideration to what is *most* important and to whom. Responsible professionals, however, weigh client needs most heavily. Supervisors who are politically adept operate on the principle that executive expectations must also be accorded priority. Another principle is that *tasks which show* must receive priority attention, because these too are highly significant with respect to enhancing the supervisor's image of competence. Including "what shows" among her other priorities in deciding how to allocate her time may seem like one priority too many to a harried supervisor. In fact, however, a relatively small percentage of tasks fall into the highly visible category. These are activities such as presentations to staff meetings, reports slated for distribution, and ready familiarity with new programs and proposals. Giving priority to these tasks often requires the postponement of other important activities, but supervisors who appreciate the importance of appearing informed, well-prepared, and imaginative with respect to their more visible acts must pay that price.

Managing to remain on top of routine responsibilities such as client appointments or scheduled conferences that are observed by others falls into a similar category. The person who neglects them does so at the risk of appearing uncaring or disorganized (and may even cost herself considerable time and grief in damage control). Further, to the extent that she is in control of her job, the supervisor must take on only as much work as she can accomplish well, although here as in other circumstances, a balance between competing interests must be maintained. On the one hand, a tendency to assume too great a responsibility risks placing her in a position of structured incompetence. On the other, it is important to be viewed as a team player, willing to share collective burdens with others. The important point is not so much what the supervisor decides, but that she makes her decision with a conscious eye to appearance, aware of the tension between doing something well and not doing it at all.

Another factor affecting the impression of one's competence has to do with the *nature* of the tasks that the job demands. The more innovative one's duties, the more the actor is seen as an expert, hence powerful relative to peers who engage in routine activities (Sayles, 1979). Routine activities are common (to be performed by anyone), whereas innovative tasks are special (thus requiring skill). Seeking opportunities to be responsible for innovative tasks or activities associated with planning for the future is thus another practice principle, because influence accrues in part to those who are able to contribute to the organization's control over uncertainty. The organization's future, of course, represents the dimension of uncertainty. In addition, these are activities that often contain a large measure of discretion—the ability to recommend outcomes and exercise sanctions—and thus are influence enhancing. Finally, responsibility for innovative tasks or projects has the additional advantage of providing access to key information and may also permit interaction with key individuals, both of which are sources of power (Katz, 1980).

There is usually scope for a competent supervisor to involve herself in innovative assignments that set her apart from her less-assertive peers. The assignment may be obtained as a result of negotiating latitude, or it may simply come from volunteering. Offering to research a problem area and contributing to the development of proposals for funding are examples of potentially innovative work that also carries high visibility. Executives are usually more than willing to share these types of assignments with able supervisors.

There is, finally, one other dimension to the nature of a task that connotes expertise in professional work: the extent to which the task is specialized. In an increasingly complex service enterprise, the trend toward greater specialization has been commonly observed—extending, as we noted earlier, to the organization of well-developed subspecialities within professions. In most instances, the more highly specialized the set of activities associated with a position, the more influence, status, and compensation the position is likely to bring. For example, however much logic or one's social values might dictate that it be otherwise, general medical practitioners place lower on the medical hierarchy than, say, neurosurgeons.

On a quite different scale, standard caseloads in social agencies often require special knowledge to deal with particular problems. Line staff working with a heterogeneous caseload can hardly do justice to the range of content required for effective service. Knowledge about substance abuse, domestic violence, special categories of psychiatric dysfunction, details of various entitlement programs, and the availability of specialized community resources are examples of information that no one worker is likely to have but which may be necessary for all workers to know from time to time. The supervisor who has specialized in substance abuse, entitlement programs, or the like has the ready advantage of being the person to whom others in the agency must turn when they need help in regard to a particular problem.

To develop a specialization within an agency may be simpler than at first it seems, as the following example illustrates. The supervisor of one of the services of a large voluntary hospital observed that the hospital's social service department has no formal system for those engaged in discharge planning to identify referral sources for patients who needed follow-up care such as nursing home placement, homemaker services, and supportive services. Rather, each worker developed his own sources. Workers would develop personal relationships with staff in particular agencies and tended to be sparing in the sharing of such contacts and information, feeling that they should be held in reserve to be available when needed for "their" patients. New workers in the department had to depend on the kindness of senior staff and supervisors to assist them on a case-by-case basis. To help remedy this situation, the supervisor assigned a worker to research all relevant community referral sources and develop an open referral system for the use of all staff members in her service. Within a few months the supervisor and her worker began to be viewed as experts on specialized referral sources throughout the hospital social service department. Because they offered their information freely, the staff not only became dependent on them for the provision of this information, but their frequent contacts with various providers resulted in close collaborative relationships that sometimes enabled them to obtain special consideration for unusual or particularly needful cases. In time, the efforts of this supervisor in developing a specialized area of expertise not only translated into informal power with her peers, but she also obtained formal recognition from the head of her department.

In almost any agency there is an issue, area, or problem about which a supervisor can especially educate herself. The principle holds at all levels of the hierarchy and in most organizations. Almost nothing is more reliable in setting one apart from one's peers than developing such specialized knowledge. One criterion for one's choice of area, in addition to one's interest in the subject and belief in its importance, is, as we noted earlier, its significance to the agency's goals, as defined by relevant others. Influence is also maximized to the extent that the practitioner maintains something of a monopoly in regard to the area of expertise. When the knowledge or skill is both valued and in limited supply, it is clearly more useful in exchange with others.

Research exploring managerial competence has identified a number of management traits or skills that have a statistically significant correlation with effective performance (Boyatzis, 1982). They are relevant to supervisory practice as well, and we note some of them below in discussing indirect forms of supervisory influence.

Self-Confidence

Boyatzis (1982) includes self-confidence among a group of competencies he calls a *leadership cluster*. The cluster also includes the capacity to recognize patterns in shared values and objectives and the ability to communicate these to others. The supervisor who exudes an aura of self-confidence enhances the perception of others regarding her as competent and increases the prospect of influencing them (House, 1977). Research indicates that superior managers demonstrate significantly more self-confidence than do average or poor performers, and average performers demonstrate significantly more self-confidence than do poor performers (Boyatzis, 1982, p. 102).

Self-confidence is defined as a property of practitioners who appear to know what they are doing and believe that they are doing it well. They are comfortable with making decisions and can present their position with assurance as to its correctness. They are neither arrogant nor defensive in regard to their choices. From a practice point of view, it is this relationship to decision making—and their willingness to take blame and share credit—that is particularly salient.

The fact that supervisors function in the middle and can segregate their audiences makes them prone, in structural terms, to blame upper levels to subordinates for agency deficits and to blame subordinates to executives for inadequacies in a unit's functioning. This blame represents an avoidance of responsibility and demonstrates a lack of self-assurance on the supervisor's part. In most cases it is also a practice error. It is true, of course, that agency policy frequently inhibits effective practice on the line. Nevertheless, the supervisor is expected to pursue a change in the policy or to obtain an exception to it. The staff must believe that she has effectively advocated their position rather than having "yessed" the boss if she is to place responsibility on the upper levels. At the least, it must be clear to them that, however much she agrees that modifications are necessary, the policy is not amenable to change. Even more important, staff must believe that the supervisor *really* disagrees with the policy and is not using the executive as a cover for a position she holds herself. If they suspect the latter, their resentment will be all the more palpable.

Supervisors are under scrutiny from many quarters, and staff observations of them are often shared. What, after all, is more interesting data for the organizational grapevine than the vagaries of one's boss? This in itself suggests caution in affixing responsibility to others. Further, because blaming the executive may well be perceived as faint-heartedness, it diminishes the esteem in which the supervisor is held.

The same holds for those seeking credit. One study suggests that supervisors tend to claim credit for decisions made at higher levels (Jago and Vroom, 1977). This is unfortunate because such a stance risks the appearance of obvious self-promotion. Subordinates tend in any case to evaluate their supervisors positively by successful program or policy outcomes, whatever a supervisor's role in achieving that result. Credit thus accrues without the need to stake claims to it.

It is even worse for the supervisor to blame her workers for malperformance to upper-ranking staff. Because she is accountable for their performance, an attempt to avoid responsibility will seem as though she is making excuses to the executive at the expense of her workers. Conversely, it is the better part of wisdom for supervisors to give credit to members of her staff when organizationally desirable results are achieved. Supervisors who are lacking in confidence often try to garner credit for themselves for staff achievements. As a consequence, they risk appearing ungenerous in the eyes of their superiors and are seen as unappreciative by their staff. Finding occasions when credit can be publicly shared with staff members represents good practice, because it both increases the latter's motivation to do their best and constitutes an indirect way of pointing out the unit's successful functioning.

Taking Initiative

Being proactive and being concerned about one's impact on others are included in a cluster of activities that exemplify entrepreneurship: assuming risks, having a clear image of desired outcomes, and understanding when and how to take initiative (Boyatzis, 1982, p. 60). As with self-confidence, these activities have a statistically significant correlation with effective management, with a strong and consistent trend for superior managers to be more entrepreneurial than average or poor ones.

Proactivity suggests behavior that goes beyond reacting to a situation or standing guard over the status quo (Zaleznik, 1966). It refers to the predisposition to initiate action. Thus the proactive supervisor thinks ahead, anticipates problems or opportunities and their implications, and raises issues with others rather than waiting for others to place a problem on the organizational agenda.

There are several advantages to a proactive stance on the part of supervisors. These advantages hold at whatever hierarchical level with which the supervisor is engaged. First, the more anticipatory the supervisor can be, the greater the influence she will be able to exercise. Being the first to identify a problem enables her to shape the way it is viewed and defined. Values are, in part, determined by the very choice and definition of problems, because these influence the ways in which the issues are explored and, by extension, their outcomes (Merton, 1957, p. 216). Suppose, for example, that the morale of trained social workers is low because of a preponderance of case aides in a unit. One way of formulating the question is: How can we make the trained workers accept the aides? Another is: How can we increase the number of trained staff? How the question is defined and framed will clearly have an impact on how it is answered.

Another advantage of a proactive stance is that it allows the supervisor to deal with issues or plans before they have progressed to the stage at which little or nothing can be done to alter them. With both supervisees and superiors, the supervisor is better able to avoid the trap of the fait accompli. Finally, by virtue of having anticipated and considered an issue, the supervisor is more thoroughly aware of the context and potential consequences of the issue than those who may be grappling with it for the first time. She is thus better positioned to head off an undesired action or to move a desired one forward than would otherwise be the case.

Boyatzis' research (1982, p. 78) does show, however, that there is a curvilinear relationship among managers who *define* themselves as proactive; that is, both the superior managers and the poor ones view themselves as taking initiative and instigating action more so than average managers. He has offered as explanation the possibility that certain poor managers may act more often than is appropriate (e.g., providing close supervision when loose supervision is called for), or that they act in such a way as to violate organizational norms (e.g., ignoring cherished organizational ways of doing business when they intervene). This finding suggests a need for balance in assuming initiative.

From a practice perspective, skill in striking the right balance relates to both which issues and how many are raised, along with the ways in which the supervisor raises them. For example, initiating discussion of issues that supervisees view as complex is likely to be appreciated, whereas raising matters that staff view as simple may make them feel that they are being unduly checked-up on. The supervisor must also strike an appropriate balance by limiting the number of times she raises issues for consideration with the staff. The point here is that some is *enough*. To the extent that the supervisor periodically initiates questions related to her supervisee's activities, the staff will be predisposed to anticipate and be prepared for such encounters. Because this is a key objective of the supervisor, it is not necessary to discuss all matters.

With executives, the supervisor measures the issues to be raised in the context of the agency's goals and the executive's values. Initiating action to solve problems that are perceived by upper-ranking participants as requiring solution will be appreciated, as long as the action does not violate important values or cherished beliefs. When supervisory efforts to change agency policy or procedure are likely to be controversial or may generate less-than-positive responses from superiors, the supervisor once again has to limit her initiatives. One important criterion is her assessment of the policy or program's amenability to change. She chooses only those issues that she has some chance of winning, and she does not fight every battle, for tilting at windmills is hardly a practice strategy. Because it is often not possible to have a definite reading about which issues are subject to her influence until she has begun to intervene, the supervisor must limit the occasions she tackles potentially controversial subjects. A perception by the executive of the supervisor as someone who initiates problem-solving and is willing to risk herself to advance an issue ordinarily increases his sense of her competence and adds to her influence. A perception of the supervisor as a dissident does neither.

Closely related to a supervisor's proactivity is her persistence in her approach to her 'ob. The practitioner who uses repetition and keeps "asking, talking, explaining" further legitimates her authority and enhances her ability to get others to do as she wishes (Sayles, 1979, p. 42). To validate the truth of that observation, one only has to observe the kind of informal double standard that evolves in organizations with respect to responsiveness. Those who communicate through their words and actions that they expect early movement on iniatives and press to get action are typically dealt with differently from those who are inconsistent with respect to follow-up, apologetic in requests, or overly "reasonable" in accepting inaction and delay. Those who anticipate cooperation and persist in its pursuit typically are responded to more consistently. Once again, however, balance is necessary. Zealousness must be sufficiently modulated so as not to engender unnecessary resentment.

The manner in which one initiates action or persists in seeking some outcome is also important in supervisory effectiveness. With supervisees, for example, a direct question regarding what her staff has done about an issue sometimes appears as though the supervisor distrusts their capability or conscientiousness. To suggest instead that she has been thinking about the problem or issue and would like to discuss its implications or a strategy for dealing with it seems more collaborative. Without having to say so, the supervisor's mutual exploration of details associated with the issue alerts her staff to the need to attend to it. How the supervisor wishes to come across to them, authoritative or collaborative, may vary. The important point is that the manner in which she raises the issue or initiates the action regulates the reaction of others to the initiative.

Finally, the research suggests that people who are motivated to influence others *and* are skillful in manipulating symbols of influence are effective as organizational actors (Boyatzis, 1982, p. 92). Just as the supervisor must be concerned about her visibility as a competent practitioner, so too must she give the impression of being an influential one. Once again, the appearance is almost as good as the reality—because if people believe that one has power, they will behave toward that person as if he or she does in fact possess it. Of course, if the actors with a reputation for power are called on to deliver on their purported influence and cannot deliver, their image will plummet. But skilled practitioners who have developed a reputation for influence will be careful that their reach does not exceed their grasp. In other words, they will make only those requests, demands, or offers that do not actually test their inferred influence.

It is the symbols of influence that concern us here; other means of influencing others, through persuasion, negotiation, and mobilizing support, are discussed in later chapters. The practice task in this instance is to enhance one's prestige to be able to influence other organizational participants more effectively. From this view point it may be more than vanity that impels participants to be concerned about such organizational trappings as the size of one's office or its furnishings, because these symbolize one's place in the organizational world. If, as a consequence, the participant *seems* more important to the organization, he or she *is* more important—and all other things being equal, will be more influential as well.

We cite organizational trappings only as an example; it is not by itself significant. The point, rather, is that effective supervisors must consciously attempt to develop an image of importance in the agency. False modesty is self-defeating, although skillful practice requires once again that the supervisor accrue prestige without appearing to be concerned about seeking it.

An organization's structure or process sets parameters that encourage or circumscribe one's potential success in acquiring prestige, quite apart from anything the supervisor does. Circumstances permitting, however, there are ways in which organizational actors take advantage of opportunities that present themselves. If a supervisor has the ear of her boss, for example, it is useful for other top staff, peers, and her workers to know about it. Or if the supervisor has inside information (rather than rumor), sharing that information prior to its becoming public indicates her in and, by implication, her importance. We refer here to benign information; otherwise, she risks being perceived as indiscreet or unethical. Knowing and being known by people who are important to relevant others in the organization may also be a source of prestige. For this reason some people make it a point to make comments such as "When I had lunch with so-and-so . . ." if so-and-so is a prestige figure. The fact that name dropping is viewed pejoratively suggests the risk in this tactic. Its effectiveness, as with a number of other such tactics, requires that it be very lightly made and not overdone. Furthermore, such attempts at personal enhancement are not effective in increasing one's influence among those in formal positions of authority (as in the case of the supervisor influencing her supervisees), but they are effective when formal authority is not at issue (as in the case of supervisor attempting to influence her boss or her peers) (House and Baetz, 1979).

When a service is important to an agency, people associated with the service garner some of the importance for themselves. The points made in regard to the supervisor thus apply to her unit as well. For example, when a unit is able to obtain perquisites and resources or can establish significant connections to important others within the organization, the prestige of the unit and, by extension, the unit supervisor are also enhanced. Clearly, the supervisor who represents her unit well, both within the organization and externally, adds to the unit's prestige and increases her own status in the bargain.

Representing Subordinate Interests

Establishing supervisory influence with subordinates requires effectiveness in representing their interests with others. This is in large part a consequence of organizational structure and the supervisor's role in the middle of the hierarchy. Because workers are required to use established lines of authority, the supervisor is necessarily the staff's link to the rest of the agency at large. If rules are to be modified, grievances to be handled, workers to be protected, or resources to be gained for the unit, it is the supervisor who must be the prime actor in pursuing these ends. In short, workers are dependent on the willingness and ability of the supervisor to advocate for them up the hierarchy as well as laterally.

Effective advocacy enables the supervisor to strengthen the social exchange relationship that is inherent in her position vis à vis staff, as well as others in the agency. When she is effective in redressing staff concerns, obtaining rewards, and modifying expectations regarding their activities, she engenders a sense of loyalty among her workers, increasing the likelihood that they will comply with her direction. Staff cooperation, in turn, sets the stage for the supervisor's exchanges with her superior. Having developed the impression that she is an effective leader, in charge, and able to deliver staff compliance on issues of importance to the executive, she is better positioned to ask for and get concessions from him that are of benefit to her staff. The most fortunate circumstance is when both the staff and executive together generate a climate that makes such exchanges possible. The supervisory task is to promote and maximize such a climate.

An important factor in the supervisor's ability to represent staff interests is the quality and productivity of her unit's performance. When the unit is viewed as a valuable organizational component to the executive or agency colleagues, they are more likely to accede to the supervisor's requests. To a considerable degree, the quality and productivity of the unit is in the staff's hands. The staff's communication within the agency also does much to color the perception of others about the unit. Their contributions and commitment to the agency are in good measure presumed by the nature of their interactions with others in the organization. Conversely, wholesale complaints or tales "told out of school" have negative consequences to the unit as a whole. Occasional disenchantment or dissidence by a single or few workers may create only minor damage— but if complaints are widespread or chronic, both the supervisor *and* the unit suffer. The supervisor must thus try to solve problems before they become too firmly embedded in the unit's operation, and the staff must appreciate that both their informal and official contacts in the agency influence perceptions about the unit and that these perceptions affect worker interests as well. In short, the supervisor and the staff both have a stake in the unit's image. As staff appreciate this fact, the supervisor can more readily elicit their cooperation in building the unit's reputation within the organization. Similarly, when a unit's conduct facilitates the work of other departments, it enhances the ability of the supervisor to use that dependency in soliciting the cooperation of the departmental supervisor when cooperation is necessary.

It is a principle of effective organizational practice that one not only tries to increase one's own power, but the power of friends as well. Clearly, if one has a connection or relationship with another, that other can be effective in proffering help if he or she is more influential. This point is obvious, but is often overlooked in practice. Promoting the reputation of potential collaborators, suggesting sympathetic colleagues for influence-enhancing assignments, or helping friends make useful contacts can, over time, increase the practitioner's own power in the organization, for these others can be expected to reciprocate and/or support the practitioner's position at crucial junctures. It is in the staff's interest to help maximize the supervisor's position of influence within the agency, just as it is in the supervisor's interest that her staff is perceived to be cohesive and competent. A necessary condition for this collaborative effort, of course, is that the parties trust one another. The supervisor must feel that her workers are loyal and will not undermine her, and the workers must be assured, by deeds as well as words, that the supervisor will advocate effectively on their behalf.

The staff's understanding of social exchange will encourage their cooperation with supervisory efforts to manage the process. They will also be more accepting of the need to accommodate to occasional extra work or stressful periods if they know that their efforts help the unit to win a special request or to fend off an onerous demand. With staff understanding of exchange, the supervisor has access to a powerful persuasive device. She is able to link her request for staff cooperation to a past or future benefit to them. Such a link must be real to be credible, and it is incumbent on the supervisor to make her case in the reverse as well. She must also persuade the boss that obtaining staff cooperation in a special circumstance is facilitated by their receiving desired payoffs, now or in the future.

None of this need be done directly. Indeed, it is often the case that an exchange, to be effective, must not appear to be a trade at all. A powerful norm requires that people act as a result of the substance of an issue and how the substance conforms to their values and beliefs. It is irrelevant for our purposes that the norm may be as observed in its breach as in its execution. The position must appear to be related to substance and justified on that ground—whether the motivation for taking the position is to offer a concession to a friend, to support a colleague, to undercut a competitor, to threaten some consequence, or to win on an issue. This is particularly the case in the human services, because many human service personnel hold pejorative judgments about the politics of exchange.

Even workers who are sophisticated with regard to how exchange operates may expect that the fact of a trade should remain unstated. On the other hand, workers who are unaware or unaccepting of the exchange process must be educated about its importance by the supervisor. The supervisor must do so with sensitivity, however. She may, for example, point out that this is the way particular actors in the organization respond or that the strategy is effective in a particular instance. She is not then required to generalize beyond the single person or situation unless she senses the workers' responsiveness to her point. Nor does she need to embrace the process as desirable; the argument, rather, is that exchange is inherent in organizational life and thus impossible to avoid.

A related matter that must also be handled sensitively is the underscoring of the supervisor's role at the center of significant communications between her unit and the rest of the organization. Effectiveness in buffering workers and mediating unit interests with upper-level staff, as well as with lateral units, requires that she be at the hub of unit communications. It is she who must manage the range of resources that fuel the exchange process (e.g., any special requests sought or granted). She also has to plan and administer external relations in a fashion that maximizes unit benefits and minimizes unit costs (e.g., staff willingness or reluctance to cooperate with other units or adherence to particular procedures). For her to be effective as a representative or advocate, significant communications must be located at the supervisory level. Thus supervisees must be helped to understand that the supervisor considers linkages between the unit and other components of the organization to be her prerogative. With such understanding, the staff will routinely clear such communications with the supervisor before implementing them.

Organizational "manners" prescribe that matters related to the unit or its staff be directed to the supervisor. We refer here only to significant communications, by which we mean those that are evaluative or that seek or tender assistance of an unusual nature. Participants are ordinarily aware of this protocol. An executive, for example, will not usually engage in significant interaction with the supervisor's staff unless he distrusts the information he has been receiving or questions her competence, or if there is an emergency or unusual event that requires his intervention. Similarly, workers are usually aware that significant communications with upper-ranking staff or personnel from other units is expected to take place through the supervisor. Indeed, when this rule is violated, the worker risks the interpretation of having tried to go over the supervisor's head.

The reason the matter must be handled with sensitivity is that gray areas abound. The executive may well want to reach beyond the supervisor to establish his own relations with the workers, and there is no issue of his distrusting her. The staff, too, may want, or even need, to interact with others in the agency to perform their jobs satisfactorily, and they may have not thought of circumventing the supervisor. The distinction between normal and significant communication is, in other words, not always clear. If the supervisor is overly concerned about controlling the contact, she may be viewed as overly protective with regard to her prerogatives. And when the executive or staff are, in fact, supportive of her, there is hardly an issue. In the final analysis, the question is whether these contacts undermine her authority with her supervisees or her accountability to the executive.

Nevertheless, if she has been bypassed in a significant communication, even though inadvertently, the matter is sufficiently important to be confronted. Unless there is evidence to the contrary, she ought to eschew even the suggestion of invidious interpretation. With the executive, duplication of effort and the potential for confusion may be her best argument. With the staff, it is that the unit's interests require that all their efforts be concerted and that she is in the best position to coordinate them because representing the unit is one of her important tasks.

Just as the supervisor helps the staff to understand, or experience, that they play a crucial role in her successful advocacy on their behalf, so too does she enlist the executive's aid in the effort. Just as it is in the workers' interest for the supervisor to gain influence with upper-level staff, it is in the interest of upper-level staff that she gain influence with the workers. When executives support the supervisor in engendering staff loyalty and commitment, their goals for her unit become more attainable.

To some degree, organizational procedures can serve to encourage staff responsiveness to supervisors who are mindful of the opportunity potential they provide. Executives, for example, do not usually expect that rules will always be enforced. The wise supervisor knows which rules should and can be ignored to facilitate worker morale or to promote unit goals, and she will either modify them or look the other way as they are violated. Gouldner (1954, p. 173) suggests that rules are the chips to which organizations stake supervisors to play the organizational game. Having chips to cash in allows the supervisor to express her concern for worker opinion and increases her bargaining power with them. Of course, the supervisor must know the rules that are important to enforce. Just as she garners staff loyalty by representing worker positions with upper-ranking members, she gains executive loyalty by responsibly transmitting upper-level demands downward. She can afford to modify or ignore only a limited number.

For supervisors to represent subordinate interests effectively, it is obvious that they must have access to decision makers. But sometimes executives protect themselves with staff who regulate access to them. The gatekeeper may be a secretary or administrative assistant; yet, however low in the hierarchy, he or she accrues considerable informal power. It may be—and probably is—a mistake for an executive (or a supervisor) to turn this task over to someone, because it isolates him from others in the organization. The executive may thus insulate himself from important positions and pressures that could need his attention. If there is a gatekeeper, however, the supervisor does well to view that person as someone to include in her network of associations. Short of that, she will have to devise ways to circumvent him or her to get to the executive.

Representing subordinate interests does not require that the supervisor is necessarily or always the appropriate person, or the only one, to place an item on the executive's agenda. She may decide to enlist the aid of a colleague to act on her behalf or with her. Depending on the colleague, the executive's relationship with the colleague, or the subject at issue, enlisting the help of another may increase the chances of gaining a positive decision. At the least, when an issue is in the interest of the supervisor's unit, an objective confederate adds legitimacy to her case.

Consider the example of the supervisor of a treatment unit, one of the best of three treatment units in a moderately sized multiservice family agency. The supervisor had worked out an informal arrangement with the intake supervisor that emergency and crisis cases encountered at intake would be seen immediately by unit staff, some of whom had a particular interest in short-term and crisis work. This cooperation enhanced the perception of the treatment unit as effective at its work and having special expertise in crisis intervention. The arrangement also enhanced the intake unit's ability to address the needs of clients in crisis, and thus enhanced its reputation as well.

To comply with a pending program audit by a state funding source, the executive requested that all service units review their case records over a two-week period to provide a detailed analysis of service data for the auditors. When the supervisor informed her staff, she encountered significant resistance. Workers argued that they did not have sufficient time to comply with the request and meet their service demands as well. The supervisor agreed that she would approach the executive and attempt to have the demand modified, but she could not guarantee success.

The supervisor decided to first meet with the supervisor of the intake unit to inform her of the consequences of the executive's request. She indicated that during the period of the case review, she would find it difficult to cover cases in crisis and was genuinely troubled by this. She suggested that the intake supervisor explore some backup arrangement for the period in question. The intake supervisor asked if it would help if she spoke to the executive about the problem of service disruption, and the unit supervisor indicated that she would appreciate the former's intercession. When the supervisor finally met with the executive to discuss the adverse effects of the audit on emergency services, he indicated that the intake supervisor had already expressed concern. The executive agreed to consider alternatives, and after some discussion, he decided to assign a temporary staff member to the supervisor's unit to do the required case review, thus allowing the staff to continue the service that they were currently providing.

The example is a relatively straightforward one, and the decision could, of course, have gone another way. Nevertheless, behind the simple interchange are a variety of apparent as well as possibly hidden exchanges that took place prior to and during the supervisor's meeting with the executive. There is the supervisor's implicit bargain with her staff that was developed over time. She went to bat for them, and they contributed to the positive image of the unit in the agency. The arrangement with the intake unit promoted a mutuality of unit interests, and the connection allowed the supervisor to call on her intake colleague for assistance. The executive saw both units as producing quality work; the treatment staff's commitment to the agency and its service was clear to him, and the supervisor's credibility as a loyal and able practitioner had been established. He was thus predisposed to accommodate a request from the unit if he could do so. These exchanges were interdependent, each contributing to and shaping the other. The supervisor had, in effect, developed a pool of stored credits with a number of organizational actors that she could draw on in the specific instance.

To summarize: in this chapter we have explored the relationship between effective supervision and the need to extend supervisory influence within the organization through the use of social exchange and the development of a heightened awareness of the political aspects of organizational practice, including the various resources available to the supervisor to trade in the process. Three significant means available to the supervisor to accrue influence are: enhancing the perception of the supervisor's competence, demonstrating her enterprise, and representing subordinate interests with other constituencies. With this as background, we turn our attention to extending supervisory leadership through the provision of structure and support.

Providing Structure
and Support

Influence is not only central to supervision, but to leadership as well. Although leadership has been defined in many ways, two components are inherent in all definitions: influencing others and their acceptance of the influence. (House and Baetz, 1979). It is useful to view supervision as a special case of leadership, because it permits one to draw on the extensive empirical work that has been done on that subject.

According to a major nationwide study (Strauss and Sayles, 1980, p. 80), the two characteristics of workers' jobs most closely related to overall job satisfaction are (1) having a nurturant boss (i.e., the affective dimension of supervising) and (2) receiving adequate guidance and direction (i.e., the work-related dimension). Although job satisfaction and quality performance are not necessarily correlated, the two dimensions are both clearly important supervisory ingredients. Indeed, a major line of research inquiry has been to examine the association of leader behavior with work-oriented and affectively oriented styles, on the one hand, and their impact on the exercise of influence on the other. A series of widely known behavioral studies conducted at Ohio State and the University of Michigan used these two variables, calling them "Initiating Structure" and "Consideration." The findings with respect to "initiating structure" vs. "consideration" were equivocal (Szilagyi Jr. & Wallace Jr. 1980), p. 287)—in part perhaps because the two were juxtaposed rather than seen as a mix.

It is now generally accepted that supervisory effectiveness is contingent on a variety of situational factors, as opposed to being represented by one set supervisory pattern. To say, as posited by contingency theory, that there is no single right or wrong way to intervene but that it depends on contextual elements is hardly a startling notion. From a practice point of view, however, only when the supervisor knows which interventions work in regard to what tasks and with which subordinates can she act effectively in any specific instance.

That supervisors must simultaneously consider the interdependence of a number of variables adds considerable difficulty to their role and makes the study of supervision more complex. Some order in considering the material is gained, however, by focusing on the two primary functions of supervisors: to guide the quality and quantity of the service (their task-oriented function) and to maintain a service-enhancing work climate (their affective or employee-oriented function). Much of the supervisor's work with supervisees can be thought of as the fine tuning of these dimensions of leadership. We devote this chapter to each of them in turn.

We use the term *providing structure* to represent an approach to supervision in which task accomplishment and the structuring of the subordinate's work are central. In this meaning, providing structure entails a constellation of activities that may include clarifying worker role and purpose, specifying job description, developing supervisory contracts, coordinating workers' actions and evaluating staff members. Whatever the particular set of activitites, however, the term refers to interventions in which the supervisor explicitly defines the work to be done, closely monitors the staff, and develops or oversees the procedures and policies that workers are expected to follow. High degrees of structure connote close supervision.

Support is the term we use for the affective dimension of supervision, for those behaviors that indicate trust, respect, and concern for the worker's welfare. We use support as a shorthand term, however, because the word is to some degree a misnomer. It is meant to convey the supervisor's responsiveness to the needs and feelings of supervisees in her interaction with them, rather than reflecting the outcome of their interaction. In effect, supervisees may gain more actual support from high degrees of structure than from a supervisor's expression of encouragement and understanding. It is important to keep in mind, therefore, that our use of the word support in this chapter is meant to convey only an employee-oriented approach, rather than the outcome of the supervisor's acts. In this regard, Austin identifies the elements of support as "(a) creating a feeling of approval, (b) developing personal relations, (c) providing fair treatment, and (d) enforcing rules equitably." (Austin, 1981, p. 299).

Providing Structure

Five aspects of structuring are worth particular note. The first has to do with the supervisor's clarity about unit purposes and priorities. The second deals with the relationship between the tasks, that workers are required to perform, on the one hand, and the desireability of high degrees of structure, on the other. A third practice issue in structuring relates to its impact on workers and work groups, for both influence the appropriateness of close or loose supervision in particular circumstances. A fourth concern is the means by which supervisors, as they are directive, exercise their authority most effectively. Finally, we consider the impact of agency context on the suitability of more or less structuring by supervisors.

Clarifying Unit Purposes

Various technologies have been devised to aid executives and supervisors in clarifying unit purposes, the priorities among these purposes, the expectations for unit performance of relevant constituencies, and the measures by which adequacy or success are determined. For example, there has been recent emphasis in the management literature on strategic planning, a technique entailing the analysis of the organization's external environment and its uniqueness in the field so that goals emerge from a pragmatic assessment of factors that will enable the organization to prevail (Glueck and Jauch, 1984; Rumelt, 1974). Another example, one that has produced a spate of books and articles, is *management by objectives* in which a process incorporating staff input is outlined for determining organizational and unit goals and specifying individual and group outcome measures (Raia, 1974; Patti, 1983). Supervisors are also frequently enjoined to establish performance goals that are concrete and subject to objective appraisal, "written down . . . so that all concerned know what the objectives are" (Steinmetz and Todd, 1975, p. 136). Indeed, whatever technology is used, it is usually recommended that the process be made formal and be recorded.

Within limits, there is much to recommend formalizing these efforts. Specifying unit goals and projecting unit outcomes is difficult to do—particularly in the human services, where the nature of people—the raw material of the enterprise—makes precision elusive and further, where the social objectives that constitute the organization's mission are necessarily broad. A formalized process at the least encourages discipline and makes it more difficult to avoid the rigors of analysis. Supervisors can hardly be effective in providing structure for staff if they have not determined the hierarchy of priorities among the functions, services, and staff activities for which they are responsible and the measures by which to assess the staff's performance and the unit's outcome. Among the questions a supervisor must answer, for just one example, is whether worker effectiveness is to be measured in client contact hours, placements of numbers of clients, records of service process, staff assessment of service quality, indicators of staff morale, other indicators, or some weighted combination of all.

Our aim here is less ambitious, however, than to review the technology of planning by which supervisors achieve clarity of goal, function, or outcome. It is sufficient for now to note that an ad hoc, intuitive, or existential approach is frequently inadequate; at a minimum, effectiveness requires that the supervisor have a concept or set of concepts that provide direction for collecting information and making decisions, a framework against which to assess one or another option in providing structure for the staff.

It may be a truism to say that any analysis, regardless of the problem that the analysis is intended to solve, can be only as adequate as the data used to inform the attempt. Basic to developing goals, ascribing priorities, and identifying methods, then, is the type and accuracy of the information that is brought to bear as one engages in the process. One type of clearly important knowledge relates to the substance of a particular content area of unit or agency concern. Because this varies so widely according to the service being provided, there is little to note here. A second source of knowledge is the social context within which decisions relating to the content area are made. Sensitivity to the interplay between substance and context—how each influences the other—is an essential ingredient of effective problem solving.

It is with context in mind that Yates (1985, p. 59) refers to successful managers as "political detectives" and suggests some broad areas of knowledge that require supervisory attention. Among them are the "natural history" and evolution of the program or particular problem; in other words, how we got to where we are. Past processes are potentially revealing of the potential for modifications in specific areas and also illuminate the agendas and commitments of significant organizational actors. Another element has to do with professional and agency norms—social work and other professions—and the extent to which the prospective goal or program or method conforms to or diverges from the norm. A further base of knowledge relates to agency constituencies, both within the unit or external to it, and how potential goals, priorities, and methods affect them. For example, the supervisor needs to recognize the personal or professional interests of constituents that may be supported or undermined by her choice of objective and priority. She will need to know whether sufficient expertise is available to accomplish her goal or if it can otherwise be acquired, and who among the constituents has more or less influence in regard to particular issues. We shall say more in later chapters about political intelligence as an underpinning of effective organizational practice. Our point here is that effectively providing structure requires information of both a technical and a political nature.

In any situation, supervisory or otherwise, actors who are clear about what they hope to accomplish are positioned to exert more influence than those who are less certain about their objectives. Clarity permits purposive behavior, and purposefulness maximizes the actor's potential for reaching a desired outcome. Whether it is wise to express one's aims or keep them hidden, or whether to state them clearly or ambiguously, depends on the issue and the social context. Thus a supervisor who is certain about her wish to reduce the caseload of her workers may not immediately articulate her aim to her boss because she believes he may reject the idea out of hand. Or she may state her views ambiguously to prepare him for a subsequent request or to test his reactions without having to commit herself publicly. Or she may postpone raising the matter at all until she has garnered further support from other colleagues. Her objective is clear, but her behavior is guided by her judgment of how best to advance it.

To cite the importance of clarity is not by any means to overlook the advantages of ambiguity. It is not chance, however, that the example above of the supervisor who might express herself ambiguously is an example of a lower-level participant attempting to influence a higher-level one. A clear and precise expression of one's position is ordinarily more advantageous to upper-ranking participants—it is, after all, the goals of the more powerful members of an organizational coalition that become the established goals of the organization. Defining them clearly and specifically obliges lower-ranking members to live within their constraints or else suffer the penalty of appearing to be either incapable or subversive. Ambiguity, on the other hand, broadens the options of lower-level participants, because it permits them to choose any of the meanings in an ambiguous statement to which they wish to adhere and at the same time allows them to *appear* as if they have been guided by the boss' position.

Thus, in instances in which influence is at issue, the supervisor may express herself ambiguously to the executive but would be wise to be as clear as possible in giving directives to her staff. Clarity is maximized by considering first what background information is required for the listener to understand the point. This seemingly simple rule is often overlooked, as in the case of the speaker who uses initials, assuming that the listener shares the same referent (e.g., using DSS to mean Department of Social Services), referring to a person without identifying relevant information about the person's agency or position. The implicit assumption is that when the speaker knows the initials or who the person is or other background data, it follows that the listener will also know.

Another common source of obscure communication, particularly with staff members whose professional background differ, is the use of technical terminology or jargon that serves as shorthand in one profession but has little or even a different meaning in another. Computer professionals, for example, often mystify social workers with whom they are consulting, when they refer to "booting up the system" or "linking to the main frame." They are unaware that phrases so common to them may seem a foreign language to their listeners. Similarly, the social worker who uses such diagnostic categories as "atypical bipolar disorder" or "conversion disorder" to the computer specialist is guilty of the same oversight. The ability to empathize with another—to see the world as the other does—is perhaps the most significant assurance that the supervisor's message will be clearly framed and that it will be cast in terms most acceptable to the worker as well.

Eliciting feedback narrows the margin of potential misunderstandings between a supervisor and supervisee. Feedback reduces the "noise" or distortion that takes place in much communication. To be optimally useful, the supervisor must invite feedback that deals with specific and partial reactions to her direction rather than general or total ones. Feedback that is immediate (i.e., solicited as close as possible in time to the events for which reactions are sought) also contributes to increased clarity and, further, permits adjustments in the supervisor's direction that enhances the likelihood that staff will follow it. Unfortunately, supervisors are sometimes vague with supervisees because they are not themselves clear about what they want their staff to do and the workers do not question their lack of clarity. Gross and his colleagues found, for example, that a school system's attempt to introduce open classrooms foundered on just this ground. The teachers did not function in the hoped-for ways in part because the school's administrators were imprecise about what they wanted the teachers to do, and the teachers never aired their perception of this lack of clarity with the administrators (Gross et al., 1971).

On occasion, some supervisors are only too glad not to clarify an understanding or agreement. This occurs when there is some tension in the directive, and it might appear that the supervisor does not sufficiently "trust" the worker. It occurs, too, when the supervisor is sensitive to a potentially negative reaction to the directive by the worker. Because negative interchanges cause her discomfort, she is more prepared to let things slide than to ensure that the directive is followed. She has thus appeared to herself to have fulfilled her responsibility by making the demand and relieved herself of discomfort by obscuring the message. This is not to say that obfuscation is not sometimes helpful. Unless the supervisor has a consciously identified reason for being vague, however, her concern must be with clearly communicating her intent.

Just as a supervisor might choose ambiguity in conversation with an executive, so too must she be alert to ambiguous communications initiated by workers to her, and for the same reasons. Ambiguity is one way by which a worker can meet the requirement of informing his supervisor without really telling her very much. Further, unless she listens closely to the worker's questions, requests for permission, and the like, she may grant him license to act in ways that do not reflect her preference.

Tasks and the Provision of Structure

As tasks or technology varies, so too does the need for the supervisor to provide more or less structure to ensure maximum performance. Variations include those tasks that are already structured and routine, in contrast to those that are complex and nonrepetitive. Some tasks provide direct feedback with respect to adequate performance and completion, whereas other tasks require guidance or environmental manipulation on the part of the supervisor or other persons. And some tasks are intrinsically more satisfying than others.

Highly routinized and repetitive tasks essentially provide their own structure. Similarly, there are tasks that are designed or carry with them relatively explicit feedback with respect to the appropriateness of the worker's effort. Examples are the social worker's contribution to a medical chart, an instrumented intake or discharge procedure, or record keeping of various types such as statistics on client contacts. Other tasks are so clear regarding the appropriateness of an intervention or the degree to which a professional standard is operative that the worker's room for choice is severely constrained. In regard to these tasks, it is usually unnecessary for the supervisor to provide additional structure unless there is evidence that the worker is unresponsive to the structure provided by the task itself.

By and large, social worker positions contain some mix of routine tasks and tasks that are ambiguous or complex. Often, however, the mix will fall more heavily in one direction or the other. For example, child welfare workers assert that accountability regulations promulgated by the child welfare system require them to spend approximately 30 to 35 percent of their time in filling out standardized forms. In contrast, the work in other agencies may primarily involve such activities as managing a varied and complex caseload, conducting in-service training seminars in areas of the worker's expertise, or shaping new program directions—all tasks that are nonroutine and have uncertain requirements and demands.

In the former case, where the position contains an inordinate amount of structured tasks, the reduced need for supervisory structure may not hold. The distinction here is between supervisory direction with respect to particular tasks that are largely self-regulating (a low structure condition) and the supervisory direction required in those situations in which a disproportionate share of routinized work may create worker boredom, apathy, anger, or frustration. Studies of workers who find their work intrinsically dissatisfying are suggestive in this regard. When worker tasks are by and large dissatisfying, high supervisory structure increases the workers' negative feelings. But more importantly, it also enhances their performance (Fleishman, 1973). Structure in such cases may therefore be necessary, even if resented. It may be the case that with regard to routine and repetitive work, the relationship between high or low worker morale, on the one hand, and worker performance, on the other, is minimal.

What has been said about routinized tasks and those that are intrinsically dissatisfying applies to the highly bureaucratic organization as well. Organizations that must cope with a hostile environment, as do many public service and welfare agencies, try to protect themselves from external criticism by elaborate accountability mechanisms. The aim is to standardize the practice and ensure that workers follow standardized procedures to minimize unpredictability and any basis for attack. This dynamic can occur even though the service is complex and the practice requires individualization. It is in settings such as these that the supervisor's location between upper management and line staff is most problematic. She must balance the agency's need for self-protection with the clients' need for effective service when the two conflict, as they frequently will. In such a case, she will have to decide which agency procedures can be overlooked and which service needs should be pursued regardless of the risks.

An organization, in elaborating procedures, codifying rules, detailing systems, and formally delineating areas of responsibility, constitutes a source of structure that is independent of the supervisor. Her attempt to impose structure would seem at the very least redundant (House et al., 1971). At the most, it would be resented as overkill.

Indeed, when much of the worker's responsibilities are standardized or repetitive, the supervisor's efforts should be to reduce excess routine—either through intercession with higher-ups or by redesigning unit responsibilities so that purely routine tasks are assigned to less-skilled personnel. Also helpful would be assigning to workers ad hoc tasks that might capture their interest or permitting them released time for training and development. To the extent that these interventions are possible, they constitute examples of maximally supportive uses of structure. Expressions of support—in the form of understanding and sympathy—are appropriate in the face of routinized tasks that risk deadening a worker's creativity and sense of professionalism. At the least, they constitute an extrinsic reward that supervisors can profer to make up for intrinsically uninteresting work. But they are not a substitute for the responsibility of the supervisor to marshall as effectively as possible whatever organizational forces are potentially available to deal with the basic problem.

Conversely, when workers are highly satisfied with the tasks they perform or with significant aspects of their work overall, the need for supervisory direction is considerably reduced. The bases for a worker's satisfaction with his tasks vary, of course, depending on the worker's characteristics. Two workers performing the same set of tasks may have widely divergent reactions such as stimulation on the part of one and anxiety on the part of the other. Clearly, then, there is less need for the supervisor to guide the first worker while proferring more direction to the second. Although worker variability must be taken into account, by and large the following characteristics of tasks tend to be viewed favorably by most trained professionals: (1) the task calls on a variety of skills, (2) it can be performed reasonably autonomously, (3) it is seen as important to do or significant in some respect, (4) the task is readily identifiable as the worker's own, and (5) it is work that provides internal feedback so that self-correction by the worker is possible. Hackman and Lawler (1971) have found that workers tend to be self-motivating when these conditions are present. In that event, the supervisor may provide technical support, but otherwise limits herself to interventions cued by the worker. This is one of those situations in which the supervisor accomplishes more by doing less.

A related characteristic of a task that guides the degree of supervisory intercession is its challenge. Many tasks are sufficiently challenging to workers so that beyond providing general direction and technical help as indicated, the supervisor need not concern herself with structuring task specifics or providing special support. Challenging tasks are typically experienced as sufficiently compelling by staff so that close supervision would not only be unnecessary but would be felt as constraining.

This generalization also has to be qualified by the character of the individual worker. For one thing, if the supervisor anticipates that the worker may have difficulty in performing the task, she must be ready to intervene. In that case, it would be well if, as she made the assignment, she tried to minimize potential defensiveness in the event that she subsequently has to intercede. A statement along the following lines might serve that purpose: "This is a difficult task and one I'm interested in too, so I'd like us to stay in close touch on it."

In addition, the challenge of a task rests in the eye of the beholder. What may be challenging to some workers may be experienced as too little challenge or too much to others. With too little challenge, a worker is likely to be dissatisfied, and extrinsic satisfactions must be found to substitute for intrinsic ones; an understanding supervisor and friendship ties with peers are among the more usual of work-related extrinsic benefits that may be available. When the task is too challenging, workers will also seek or accept close supervisory direction. Tolerance for structure tends to increase as the pressures of a task increase. Kerr and his colleagues (1974) have noted that pressure can take the form of task demands, time urgency, interunit stress, or physical danger, and they have cited consistent findings to support the proposition that structure is welcomed in such instances. There is also evidence that high structure under conditions of pressure improves performance as well.

Visibility is another characteristic of a task that should be noted. The more visible the task, the less the need for structure. Structure serves an accountability function in part, and the supervisor who can observe a worker in action has a lesser need for formal monitoring mechanisms. Thus individual services, at least those conducted in the privacy of workers' offices, are more apt to call for formal process reporting, regular supervisory conference, and similar structures than tasks that are more generally observable such as group and community services. Because the latter services are in themselves informal, there is a propensity for their oversight to be informal as well. Furthermore, the norm in social work supervision requiring a worker to share with and trust the supervisor, while the supervisor returns the trust with respect and support, probably has something to do with the invisibility of the service. To monitor or help with respect to individual interventions, the supervisor must count heavily on information elicited from the worker. In short, it is likely that casework services demand more structure than other social work services.

One final characteristic of a task should be noted: the amount and source of information required to perform the task effectively. It is perhaps obvious that in any circumstance when there is a significant discrepancy between the amount of information available to the supervisor and workers, the provision of greater structure by the supervisor is necessary. The point is applicable to all information that has a bearing on worker activity. One area of discrepancy in information between higher and lower levels is worth underscoring, however, because it is pervasive. It relates to political matters. As has been noted, upper-level staff are ultimately responsible for sensing the external environment and shaping the organization's response to it. Line workers are ordinarily not privy to data regarding outsiders whose view of the organization is important to its maintenance, and line workers may also be unaware of external factors that critically impinge on the agency's health. Top executives count on supervisors to transmit information of this kind to the staff so that the latter will act in a politically sensitive manner.

Workers and Work Groups

Evidence suggests that the reaction of workers to supervisory structure is curvilinear and that both too little and too much are experienced negatively (Strauss and Sayles, 1980, p. 77). Too little and too much are relative matters, and we have already suggested that the tasks workers perform constitute a significant variable in how they respond to supervisory intercession. Individual workers also vary significantly with respect to their need for and response to structure. Although shaping one's interventions to the needs of a particular person and situation is a point that hardly needs underscoring for social work supervisors, brief mention of some supervisee characteristics may be worth noting in this regard. One relevant factor, of course, is the psychological makeup of the subordinate (e.g., how dependent or independent, how easily frustrated or cool, how defensive or self-critical). Other factors that come into play are the subordinate's experience, ability, and commitment.

Directive supervision is obviously more appropriate for workers whose ability to perform their jobs adequately is less clear than for more competent workers. If the worker's lesser competence stems from lack of experience or training, his limitations are more likely to be accepted and viewed nonjudgmentally by both the worker and supervisor than would otherwise be the case, and the supervisor's direction may well be sought or at least welcomed. Newly hired workers tend to fall into this category, for they may understandably be unclear about the specific goals, priorities, procedures, and expectations of the particular agency. According to one study, for example, high structure in supervision is positively correlated with worker satisfaction among new and untrained employees, whereas high structure is negatively perceived by more experienced staff. (Katz, 1978). Thus supervisory attentiveness to the "tools" and resources that the newcomer or inexperienced worker requires is important at the start and for probably at least a few months beyond the initial orientation period.

Because many social workers are disposed to an affective style of supervision, they may be insufficiently concerned about providing sufficient structure. Even in the case of the new worker, for example, some social work supervisors provide specific direction largely so that the neophyte can feel comfortable in beginning. They do this more to indicate supervisory concern than to guide his accomplishing a task, or worse, they neglect structuring behavior altogether in favor of friendliness and consideration. When this leaves the worker insufficiently clear about what to do or what is expected, frustrations arise and morale plummets. Indeed, the supervisor's friendliness may even be suspect, because excessive friendliness that is not based on a relationship that has had time to develop may hardly appear to be friendliness at all. This is not to say that the supervisor should not be empathetic and accessible, of course, for she wants the supervisee to consider her a caring person. Rather, it is to suggest that supervisors should initially focus more on job-related matters than interpersonal ones. It is, after all, through job-related content that the supervisor and supervisee develop a relationship.

As the worker increases in familiarity with the job and demonstrates competence in carrying it out, the supervisor must then assess the extent to which it may be time to begin backing off from some degree of structure and recognizing worker effectiveness with increased autonomy. The time period and degree of variability regarding appropriate structure among different workers fluctuates, of course, depending on their prior experience, training, talent as practitioners, and such psychological factors as their achievement needs. As the supervisor begins to reduce initial degrees of close supervision, she must find means to encourage the worker to link his own job-related goals with those of the organization, as well as to provide the means necessary for the worker to accomplish these goals.

An illustration is the supervisor who routinely used special projects for staff to facilitate this process. In encouraging staff to "individualize" their efforts, she guided them to reflect on how their own particular interests such as family work, policy research, or a friendly visiting program, might also fit with the needs of the agency's older adult clients and the priorities of the unit. She worked with each staff member to identify a project that incorporated this linkage, then set about to assist the staff member in implementing the endeavor. To link staff interests to agency goals successfully is, of course, an ongoing process, but when the supervisor is successful in this effort, the need for an external structure has been substantially reduced.

If a worker is self-protective in regard to his limitations, the supervisor must provide direction in one form or another, whatever the worker's reactions. Inadequate performance that stems from lack of ability obviously requires active supervisory intercession, and the worker's potential negative reaction must be a secondary consideration. It may be mitigated, however, by the extent to which the supervisor is attuned to the worker and his feelings. It has been found, for example, that when supervisors are perceived as considerate, structure is defined as helpful, whereas the same structuring behavior is seen as restrictive under conditions of low supervisory concern for the worker as a person (Fleishman and Harris, 1962).

We have asserted that structure varies with a worker's competence— the more capable he is, the less need for direction; indeed, the more capable, the more likely that providing structure will be perceived as intrusive and resented. The point must be qualified, however, by the worker's feeling about himself, his confidence and openness. It is possible, for example, that a worker who is less than thoroughly familiar with a job will be nondefensive about mistakes and welcome supervisory correction, viewing the experience as part of the process of learning. By contrast, another worker who is exceedingly competent may evidence significant stress because his sense of himself is wanting or because he holds too high a standard for himself. In such a case, the more-able worker might need as much or more supervisory attention than the less-able one.

The work group—and most particularly, how cohesive it is—is another factor that shapes the degree to which supervisors need to intercede with individual workers. In part, the cohesion of a work unit may be the outgrowth of structural factors in the agency. Such factors, for example, as a group composed of like professionals in an interdisciplinary setting,

close geographic proximity in a unit's work, competitive functions between one unit and another, and the existence of an outside target, all
predispose cohesion within a unit. The agency's culture may further
contribute to the development of tightly knit worker groups. But the
cohesion of a work unit may result from the supervisor's intercession as
well. She can encourage in-group solidarity in numbers of ways. One
means, for example, is to highlight the unit as special to its members,
using opportunities as they arise to enhance unit identity. Another is to
conduct unit activities—and relate to unit members—so as to facilitate
positive interaction among staff. (Supervisors sometimes aim for the reverse under a divide-and-conquer theory of influencing.) But whether
unit solidarity stems from organizational elements, the supervisor's
efforts, or other factors, it serves to make supervisory structure less
necessary.

Effective work teams can perform several functions that would otherwise be the supervisor's responsibility. Orientation of new staff, technical
assistance with respect to work tasks, feedback regarding work quality,
assurance that the worker's contributions are appreciated, and enforce-
ment of relevant standards are examples of such functions. An appreciation of the positive effects of cohesive work groups—and conversely, the
negative effects of fractured work groups—partially explains the popu-
larity of organizational development activities among business firms.
Team building, a significant activity associated with the field of organizational development, is, in fact, a synonym for fostering effective work
groups.

Although cohesive work groups operate as a partial substitute for supervisory structure, they also pose a risk to the supervisor's influence. Gone
awry, the group can cause supervisors to increase rather than reduce
structure. As we have noted, group norms and sanctions can act as potent
determinants of member behavior. When the dynamics of the work
group support the supervisor, she gains an important advantage. But
when the group is not supportive, it can undercut her authority with
individual members and engender broad resistance in the unit as a whole.
This suggests the importance of supervisory attention to the processes
operating within such groups. The point is perhaps obvious, but it is
ordinarily observed more in the breach than in practice, because supervisors tend to focus more on direct and manifest factors (e.g., the re-
calitrance of an individual worker) than on indirect and latent factors
(e.g., a group's subtle support of worker resistance).

We have noted that supervisors develop exchange relations with their
staff in which the latter receive unobtrusive benefits in return for their

acquiesance to supervisory influence. Establishing such an implicit compact with the informal leaders of the work group is useful in extending the supervisor's influence with the group as a whole. This is a common technique in other contexts; for example, community organizers try to develop links with a community group's leadership to win the group's support for their effort. But the technique has not been considered in the literature on supervision, perhaps because the hierarchical pattern of supervisor-supervisee relations makes it seem untoward or unworkable. Nevertheless, an implicit compact between a supervisor and worker-leader can be effective in garnering group support, even considering an organization's authority structure. Although the compact has elements of risk and must be indirect and understood but unspecified and invisible, it is another example of exchange relations that facilitate the common enterprise.

There is a converse situation in which a member of a faction of the unit is antagonistic to the supervisor and encourages the resistance of other staff members. A number of steps are possible: attempting to woo and win the recalcitrant worker, exploring his feelings as nondefensively as possible to understand the bases for his reactions, modifying her own behavior in the context of what may appear to her to be legitimate grievances, indicating that the worker's negativity is unacceptible, and explicitly or implicitly threatening sanctions. When all else fails, the supervisor can attempt to gain influence in the work group by isolating those who, for personal, self-interest, or other reasons, are antagonistic to the supervisor or her directions. Put more precisely, it is not so much to gain influence that she does this as it is to protect herself from a possible loss of influence. We referred in Chapter 2 to the desirability of the supervisors treating confirmed enemies in this way, and although the context was different, the issue is the same. To the extent that she is able, the supervisor must try to quarantine (if she cannot win over or neutralize) those who would steer the unit in ways that contravene her authority.

Exercising Authority

It is advisable to minimize the degree of authority that must be exercised in providing structure—or at the least, to balance the exercise of authority with the requirements of the desired action. As suggested earlier, there are many occasions in which workers welcome supervisory direction, and on those occasions, there is no issue of supervisory authority. Nevertheless, few staff members appreciate closer controls than is appropriate to the work, and this is particularly the case with a staff composed of professionals. The matter has been expressed well by Caplow, who said that "the unnecessary exercise of personal authority is a kind of sabotage ceaselessly practiced by incompetent supervisors" (Caplow, 1976, p. 94).

There are gradations in how authority may be invoked, ranging from unobtrusive and impersonal forms to obvious and more personal ones. To direct staff effectively, the supervisor must be able to use a variety of these forms as circumstance dictate.

The most unobtrusive interventions are those in which structure itself is used to eliminate the necessity for the supervisor to intercede directly. Often, compliance can be achieved through the very way in which the situation has been arranged. A striking instance of structure obviating the need for supervisory intervention is reported (Whyte and Hamilton, 1964). Tension between a waitress and a cook, and the cook's resistance to taking commands from someone he considered a lower-status employee, led to upset and anger each time the waitress had to place an order. The consequence was a delay for customers in receiving their food. Remonstrations to the cook, and instructions to the waitress on how to handle him, would have been considerably less successful than the remedy that was chosen. The manager instituted a system in which orders were placed on a rotating spindle, eliminating the order-giving interaction that went counter to the ostensible status differentials between the waitress and the cook. A restructuring of work procedures thus induced cooperation and eliminated what might otherwise have required an exercise of supervisory authority.

The foregoing is an instance of a simple reordering of the communication flow required to coordinate a task. There are, of course, both more and less ambitious ways of restructuring that compel an increase or decrease in the direct assertion of authority. Entire jobs may be designed or redesigned to encourage worker compliance and limit supervisory intercession. There is a vast literature on job design, one of its important notions being that by changing the content, function, and/or relationships of a job, the supervisor can exert a strong influence on a staff member's motivation and therefore on his behavior (Oldham, 1976). The characteristics of tasks that tend to be viewed favorably by professionals, noted earlier in this chapter, are suggestive for purposes of job design.

Supervisors' freedom to design or restructure their subordinates' work varies, and those with more influence within their agencies are at an advantage in this regard. The more latitude a supervisor has in how she can redesign the work, the more she can call on unobtrusive means of influencing. The major redesign of a position or the reorganization of an entire unit (thereby modifying a worker's function and/or rearranging power relations among staff) are important ways for a supervisor to reward her staff. But the unobtrusive exercise of authority through restructuring can also be accomplished with only quite modest revisions of job content, function, or relationships, as exemplified in the waitress-cook example relating to communication flow.

An example of restructuring that may encourage worker compliance is to increase the visibility of what the worker does. For many workers, the fact that their work is observed by their supervisor or by their peers acts as an incentive to encourage behavior desired by the supervisor. Visibility may be increased in two ways. One is through heightened interaction, for example, by arranging for some tasks to be done in concert with others or building in an obligation to share information periodically to accomplish a task effectively. Thus supervisors who ask their staff to make progress reports at unit meetings are effectively enhancing the visibility of the worker's activity. Another means of heightening visibility is impersonal, through organizing systems or paper flow. A prime mechanism is the computerized information system. Computer programs uncover and distribute data that might otherwise have remained invisible. Often, the information is useful to the line worker in guiding his decision making regarding a case or particular intervention. But often, too, it is useful in disclosing worker practice to the supervisor, and in these instances the staff's awareness that their work is visible makes their anticipation of and responsiveness to the supervisor's views more likely.

A brief example highlights this point. The supervisor of a mental health clinic was dissatisfied with the operation of its intake unit. The length of time from a client's initial inquiry to the scheduling of intake appointments and from there to the client's assignment for service seemed overly protracted to her. Once the process from inquiry to assignment was programmed on the clinic's computer, a precise record was created of how long each step actually took for each client, as well as an accounting of the results accomplished by different workers. Unearthing that information and circulating it within the clinic was sufficient in itself to shorten the intake process. Thus the matter was resolved without the supervisor's having to "lean on" her staff.

Formal agency guidelines, rules, and procedures also serve to limit the personal exercise of supervisory authority. The structure in this instance is provided by the organization, and because it is impersonal, supervisor-supervisee relations are less likely to be affected. When agency rules are clear, make sense to workers, and are not perceived as excessive, they substitute for direct supervisory intercession. Even when they are less acceptable to workers, the onus for the rules is not ordinarily the supervisor's. Deflecting negative reactions to other parts of the organization is a sometimes useful way of avoiding worker hostility toward a rule or toward the direct exercise of supervisory authority.

The technique of locating responsibility one step removed from the supervisor can be invoked in a number of ways. Supervisors can, for example, use agency policy directly as a justification for their intercession, or they may even inconspicuously seek an agency rule so that they can subsequently call it forth. Sometimes, too, they can obtain license to cite *their* supervisor as the source of a potentially unpopular position. They may also ask higher-level personnel to intervene directly with the staff on matters that could cause significant upset if done infrequently—so that it does not appear that the supervisors cannot be tough minded, take responsibility or represent their staff effectively. The operative test is that the intervention does not stem from a supervisor's weakness or even appear to reflect it. The converse is true as well. Supervisory toughness or its appearance should also be avoided unless it is required by a particular set of circumstances.

It is worth noting parenthetically that agencies do not expect that rules will always be enforced. They probably exist, rather, to provide *some* limit to their violation. As has been noted, "full compliance with the rules at all times (is) probably dysfunctional for the organization . . . and complete and apathetic compliance may do everything but facilitate the achievement of organizational goals" (Mechanic, 1964, p. 148).

In providing guidance, the supervisor should do so as unobtrusively as possible if a worker feels that he does not *need* help. She will, in any case, want to mute any criticism of a staff member that might be inherent in her instruction so that he does not become defensive. One of the ways of dealing gracefully with a worker's "honest" mistake is to underplay the nature of the mistake, defining it as common for someone in the worker's position. Another is to share responsibility for it ("I should have anticipated . . . I probably should have told you that . . ."). A third is to soften the criticism by pointing out some of the positives in what the worker has done (if there are legitimate positives) before leading into the discussion of the worker's error.

Another means of providing "unwelcome" direction or diffusing criticism is to raise the matter in a general way in a group meeting rather than facing the worker individually. One supervisor, for example, decided to use the group when she anticipated a worker's strong negative reaction to an assignment she planned to make. Rather than threaten the worker directly with sanctions in the event that he resisted the supervisor's assignment, she raised the matter of these types of assignments at the weekly staff meeting. In the course of the discussion, she indicated the consequences of recalcitrance without directing her comments to anyone in particular. Ultimately, when she made the assignment, the worker clearly understood his choices without the supervisor's having to be explicit. It is important, however, that the group discussion relate to some common problem or issue and that it does not appear to be aimed at the attitude or behavior of any individual worker. A rough rule of thumb is that while praise may be public, criticism should be tendered in private.

There are times, however, when it is helpful—and may even be kind—to confront poor performance or worker resistance directly. It is particularly appropriate when the supervisor-supervisee relationship is sufficiently well developed or the worker regards the intercession as useful feedback for other reasons. If, however, the supervisor is so uncomfortable with confrontation that she experiences her comments as an attack on the worker, the latter is more likely to experience it in that way as well. Supervisory effectiveness requires that the supervisor be able to confront difficult situations without excessive tension, regardless of whether she decides on a confrontation approach in a specific circumstance. To the extent that her feedback is clear, specific, and concrete and the identified behavior is within the control of the worker to correct, it is more likely to be perceived as an attempt to encourage the supervisee's growth and to serve an educational function.

In each instance the supervisor must weigh the cost of using her authority against its benefits. Inexperienced and "brave" supervisors sometimes feel that every issue must be handled. If intervening is costly to the supervisor-supervisee relationship while the return in improved performance is minimal, avoidance may be the best course. When the worker is not totally adequate to the task, guidance or criticism may serve no supervisory purpose. Take, for example, the supervisor who has evidence that a worker does poorly with a particular type of client or problem area. In such an instance, supervisory responsibility may require that she protect a vulnerable client from the inadequacies of the worker. Or even if the client is relatively intact, she may nevertheless assess that the worker's deficits are too ingrained to respond to correction with certain clients, and trying to overcome the worker's deficits may accomplish little beyond the generation of tension between them. A more functional strategy would be to have her concentrate his assignments in areas of his greater strengths.

On the other hand, it is sometimes impossible to avoid the assertion of supervisory authority. This is particularly the case when it would be obvious that the supervisor was ignoring some issue, thus suggesting that she was afraid of or unable to deal with it.

Avoidance may also be impossible when there is contention between two or more workers and the supervisor has to adjudicate the differences between them. Obviously, it is better if the argument can be dealt with before it has become full blown or if a ready compromise is at hand. When these solutions are unavailable, the supervisor is almost inevitably put in the position of favoring one worker over the other. Here, as elsewhere, she must balance the importance to her of the matter at issue against the cost of deciding in one or another worker's favor. Thus if supporting one of the workers is critical to the long-range benefit of the unit, the supervisor may decide in that worker's favor even when she believes that the worker is not totally correct on the substance.

However much one is attuned to the unobtrusive or impersonal exercise of authority, and with whatever grace a supervisor is able to exert her authority, there are occasions when the supervisor must provide structure regardless of potential resentment, and even sometimes when she must provide it with a heavy hand. She must not, however, ever lose sight of the worker's humanity in the process.

Special Agency Circumstances

Before concluding this section on supervisory directiveness, brief mention should be made about the impact of special agency events on the modification of supervisory structure. We have made passing reference to the influence of agency context in our discussion of tasks and structure, and it is clear that the agency and its policies are major determinents of a supervisor's propensity to provide either structure or support. Here, we wish to note special agency circumstances: a crisis, out of the ordinary time demands, a distinctive project in the offing, and the like. In these situations the supervisor must provide additional structure to ensure the desired outcome. Ordinarily, staff members welcome the increase in direction and find it helpful. It has been found, for example, that correlations between high structure and improved performance are most likely to occur in instances when considerable time pressure is felt. (Dawson et al., 1972). For the staff to welcome the increase in structure during unusual events, or to reduce potential resentment at its abrupt increase, however, they and the supervisor must view the special circumstances similarly.

Although there is no fixed process that follows all organizational crises, one pattern may be relatively common. Participant reactions to serious crises such as a virulent public attack or a deep budgetary shortfall are likely to vary depending on the participants' positions in the organization. Those with most responsibility for solving the crisis will experience the most trauma and need to cope with the situation. This is often less true of those without responsibility whose positions in the organization are secure such as faculty with tenure in a university or staff with civil service longevity in a public agency. Indeed, the latter's frequent predisposition is to view the crisis as exaggerated or even nonexistent, or short of that, to act functionally as if it did not exist. This response is particularly likely if the event requires much extra effort or sacrifice on their part. Responsible participants, on the other hand, are prone to see the need for radical modification in programs or procedures to counteract the emergency situation. Nevertheless, there are also times when a relatively common definition of a crisis is shared throughout an agency. Then, the participants tend to coalesce around activities that abet the agency's well-being, and cohesiveness among the participants is strengthened. If the crisis is protracted, however, the consensus may well break down, and participants may start blaming one another for the organization's lack of success in handling its predicament. In a protracted crisis, the different stakes and perceptions of those in different positions then comes sharply to the fore. Thus, in crisis situations, the need for supervisory structure may vary, depending on the time in the sequence of the event.

The supervisor of a large social work unit in a voluntary hospital dealt with the stress of a protracted strike by support and maintenance staff by instituting a 30-minute unit meeting every morning during the strike. The stated purpose of the meetings was to problem solve around operational issues raised by the strike. Although the discussions addressed functional impediments caused by the strike, allowing the supervisor to direct staff activities in a much closer fashion than normally would have occurred, the staff also experienced the unit meetings as being very supportive. They managed well during the course of what was a stressful situation for everyone, attributing their ability to do so to the supervisory guidance and collective support that the meetings provided.

Finally, we call attention to a dynamic that has been inferred throughout our discussion of structure but which we should make explicit. Our focus throughout has been on the supervisor's provision of structure to influence subordinate behavior. But the influence is, in fact, mutual. How supervisees behave or appear to behave shapes the supervisor's response as well. For example, a worker with minimal commitment to his work calls forth increased oversight on the part of the supervisor and is likely to incur her resentment as well. He in effect induces the supervisory intervention. The worker, in the ensuing interaction, views the intervention as unfair, resents it, and acts accordingly. The two have thus started a cycle of behavior that is likely to engender persistent strain. The cycle may, of course, be necessary to get the job done. Nevertheless, it is an example of social exchange, albeit a negative example, in which the behavior of each is influenced by the other. Of course, a positive exchange could have served to illustrate the dynamic as well.

This point is important in supervisory practice. For one thing, it suggests that if interaction is mutually shaped, it is incumbent on the supervisor to examine her own role in how it has developed. She needs to determine whether her responses to the worker are instrumental or affective; that is, whether they are designed to encourage worker performance or whether her responses are because "she feels that way" or "he deserves it." However she comes out in the exploration, whether she deems herself not at all responsible, partially so, or totally so, her self-questioning is essential to ensure effective practice.

Further, the mutuality of interaction—each party influencing the other—calls attention to process in supervision. Too often a position is taken or a comment made as a result of the position or comment of the other without sufficient consideration of any further potential response and counterresponse. In other words, in acting in the immediacy of the moment, as she inevitably must, the supervisor should also factor in the longer-range consequences of her interventions.

Parenthetically, this dialectic is also exceedingly important in the exercise of power, although it tends often to be overlooked. An illustration may be useful, although it is drawn from a different context. The unit supervisor in a day treatment agency believed she had leverage with a particular unit supervisor in a referring agency because she knew that the referring supervisor needed her agency as a resource for many of her agency's clients. The day treatment supervisor wanted a procedural change in the unit of the other agency, and when the unit supervisor resisted, she threatened the withdrawal of her agency's services as a referral source, although the position taken by the day treatment supervisor was one that would be viewed generally as unprofessional. The day treatment supervisor had power over her colleague in the other agency, in that she controlled a resource that her colleague wanted and she decided to exercise that power with her threat. She overreached, however, because she neglected to consider either the response or potential for influence of her adversary. The referring supervisor raised the matter with her executive, who knew the executive of the day treatment agency and reported the matter to him. As a result, the day treatment supervisor was exposed as having behaved improperly, and her threat of the withdrawal of services to her colleague's clients was forgotten.

In short, if supervisors are to be effective in any context—whether with their supervisees, peers, or superiors—they must anticipate the components of interaction. Whatever the disparity of influence between supervisor and supervisee, their ongoing interactions reflect degrees of reciprocity in influencing the other's behavior, and decisions regarding structure, and affective interventions as well, must be predicated on this.

Providing Support

The affective dimension of supervision, we should note at the outset, is probably what social workers in supervisory roles do best. Thus a study by Kadushin (1976, pp. 269–270) asked workers to rate their supervisors on six dimensions culled from 39 statements: (1) the supervisor's interest in the worker, (2) her empathic understanding, (3) her acceptance, (4) her willingness to grant autonomy, (5) her openness, and (6) her competence. Workers in the study rated their supervisors more highly on the expressive-relationship aspects of supervisory practice as reflected in the statements than on the technical competence-instrumental ones. Similarly, Shulman (1982, p. 83), in replicating one of Kadushin's questions, found that workers felt that their supervisers created an emotional atmosphere that was supportive "a good part of the time".

In view of the emphasis in the human services on support and helping, these findings are not surprising. Indeed, it is worth noting that Kadushin's six dimensions were drawn from supervisors' conceptions of ideal supervisory practice, and five of the six dimensions are affective in nature. The structural-instrumental elements of supervision appear to receive short shrift in this list of the components of ideal practice, and political interventions are apparently ignored altogether. We shall thus only summarize some practice prescriptions associated with the affective dimensions of supervision, then conclude with some cautions and qualifications that should be considered in the practice.

The Dimensions of Supportive Practice

Kadushin's dimensions are a useful guide. The first five constitute a thumbnail description of what is generally considered to represent support in practice.

Interest. Interest in the worker, both in him as a person and in his practice, must be communicated by the supervisor. To some degree, this entails observing amenities: inquiring about personal events, reflecting his concerns, and engaging him in meaningful content, whether related to his practice or to more general matters. For example, one supervisor has reported to us that she makes it her business to discover some interesting personal and nonjob-related matter to engage her nonprofessional supervisees in friendly, if brief chats. With one secretary, the subject is the work she does as a volunteer tenant organizer in her building. With another, it is the progress of his son's college education, of which he is obviously proud. With a case manager, it is the progress of his own education, which occupies his evenings after work. This supervisor reports that these periodic informal engagements with her staff provides the context for indicating her interest and support for them as individuals and results in their increased morale and positive regard for her as their supervisor.

Obviously, interest that is genuine offers greater opportunity for effective practice. This suggests that the supervisor must seek something in the worker that is "connecting." At the least, however, the supervisor must *appear* interested. The risk in the latter instance is that her expression of interest will be mechanical and thus perceived as insincere, or the supervisor may compensate for minimal interest in a worker by excessive or overly positive reactions to him. Monitoring oneself to avoid overcompensation or mechanistic responses is the principle here.

Obviously, too, supervisory interest is communicated to a worker through her accessability. Although it is not directly related to communicating interest, Sayles (1979, p. 65) reports on an interesting research study by Richardson in which there were distinct differences in the accessibility of managers who were ranked as superior or inferior. Superior managers spent a considerable amount of their time (four to six hours each day) interacting with other people. Superior managers also tended to distribute their contacts with others widely, whereas ineffective managers favored some people and ignored others.

Workers experience their supervisors as accessible or not by whether their attention is relatively undivided during most conferences or if, conferences are marked by consistent and frequent interruptions. As Kadushin notes (1976, p. 223), the supervisor must not only be physically and administratively available, but psychologically available as well. He suggests that social distance factors are inevitable because of the hierarchical nature of the relationship and that they act as psychological barriers. The supervisor must thus actively attempt to mitigate social distance to encourage free communication with her workers. Expressions of interest in them and a relatively open door in part constitute such communication aids.

Empathy. To be empathatic—understanding how a worker perceives his world and feels about it—is critical to providing support. It entails taking the role of the other, being able to answer the question "How would I react in his place?" with some degree of accuracy. Acknowledging or articulating how the worker feels makes a connection with him that, more often than not, generates worker responsiveness in turn. To be able to get inside another's head (or heart) also provides a base for choosing when and whether to intervene and shapes what these interventions might be. The point holds, incidentally, in other contexts. An accurate reading of a superior's thoughts and feelings, for example, provides the foundation for effective influencing in political engagements as well.

When supervisors are aware of their own feelings, they are more likely to recognize the feelings of others. Those who can recall what it was like to fill particular roles (e.g., student or new worker) better understand the thoughts and feelings of workers who fill those roles. Similarly, if they can recapture how they felt during particular events—anxiety in performing a difficult task, for example, or being overloaded on the job— they are better prepared to attune themselves to workers in similar circumstances. Supervisors have an advantage in one respect. Located in the middle of the hierarchy, they experience what it is like to be both a superior and a subordinate. To the extent that they are attuned to their own feelings in each role, they are well positioned to empathize with both workers and executives. Some supervisors are intuitively empathatic, and remembering or connecting comes easily to them. Those who are less so, however, must consciously attempt to call back how they felt in prior roles and events or otherwise, cognitively and emotionally, put themselves in the other's place.

As implied, empathy is furthered by commonality. When the worker and the supervisor also share a similar ethnic or cultural background, the grounds for understanding the other's thoughts and feelings are more likely to be present than when their backgrounds are dissimilar. Ethnicity and culture significantly influence the meanings people ascribe to events, and the supervisor must understand and appreciate worker differences from herself as she interprets their behavior and responds to them.

To be effective, the supervisor's responses must be authentic. Otherwise, they will seem to be rote. Thus statements like "I know how hard this is for you" resemble a standard script more than a feeling response unless the supervisor actually *does* feel how hard it is for the other. And even so, however much a supervisor relates to a worker's feelings, she will be subject to the accusation of "social working" the staff unless she avoids the cliches of the field.

Acceptance. The statement Kadushin cites as representative of acceptance is, "The supervisor creates the kind of emotional atmosphere so that supervisees feel free to discuss their mistakes and failures as well as their successes." Creating a climate that permits free discussion is supported by a norm of the field that sharing feelings and admitting mistakes is professional and a requirement of learning. A practitioner ordinarily gets more credit for owning up to an error than he is blamed for making one. Students in graduate schools are socialized to accept this norm, so that the agency supervisor starts somewhat ahead of the game. Yet the dynamic is a complex one, and there are some thin lines she must tread.

When one encourages a worker to express feelings and he does so, the worker expects approval for his expression. Indeed, it is through such approval that the behavior is reinforced, and a free flow of discussion develops. Yet what the worker has shared may be so problematic with respect to his performance that the supervisor must confront its substance. The worker may then feel that he was trapped into admitting too much and criticized for his effort. Essentially, the supervisor has to balance encouraging worker openness, on the one hand, with sensitivity in engaging negative issues that surface as a result of his openness, on the other.

If the supervisor likes a worker or respects him, communicating acceptance is a relatively simple matter. By and large, it comes naturally. Curiously enough, supervisors generally tend to like their supervisees more than one might expect and certainly more than they would if the interaction were purely social. This may be so for a number of reasons. For one, the supervisor *wants* to like the supervisee; it makes her job more pleasant. For another, she invests something of herself in him, and to the extent that the investment pays off, however minimally, some part of her becomes part of him. Finally, the fact that they need each other or hold common goals is a further incentive for mutual attractiveness and acceptance.

This is not meant to suggest that supervisors universally care for their supervisees. Such is hardly the case. But when a supervisor does feel less than positive about her supervisee, she must discipline herself so as not to "leak" her actual feelings.

One of the ways in which supervisors demonstrate their acceptance is to react with equanimity to expressions of worker "badness" such as anger at a client or retaliating because of some colleague's offense. Workers are often troubled about feeling or acting in less-than-ideal ways, and they frequently exert considerable energy to keep their less-shining moments or emotions hidden—all to avoid being judged badly. Probably everyone has secrets of this sort. When the secrets are shared with the supervisor or the supervisor articulates them from cues she has gleaned, and her reaction is nonjudgmental, the worker is likely to feel supported.

Another means of communicating acceptance is to be reassuring, particularly with regard to workers who are uneasy about handling some problem or who generally lack a sense of self-esteem. There are, as a matter of fact, practitioners whose anxious behavior fairly demands the supervisor's reassurance, and with some workers, the anxiety may even be unconsciously.designed to elicit comforting responses. Too-ready reassurance, however, as with too-avid praise, may lack credibility if it has been proffered too frequently or too lavishly. Some workers with low self-esteem use various mechanisms to stave off any risk that reassurance will change this image of themselves. For example, a supervisor's praise in regard to the worker's handling of a case can call forth some variant of the following reactions: "It's clear I did a good job." "She doesn't mean what she's saying—she just wants to make me more self confident." "She doesn't have a real grasp of what happened—I'm good at fooling people into believing I'm able." For the worker with low self-esteem, the two latter accomodations may be more frequent. If the supervisor believes this to be the case, an appropriate response would be to confront the matter directly. If the supervisor reflects back that the worker seems not to believe her or that he has fooled her, she has opened a discussion of the worker's distrust of praise. Done empathetically, challenging the worker on his lack of trust will ultimately encourage him to give more credence to the praise. Praise, we should note, is a more valued currency when it comes from a supervisor who has been observed or is known to be confrontative when confrontation is appropriate.

Autonomy. The supervisor's actual confidence in a staff member can be measured more by what she does than by what she says. She will be viewed as supportive in direct relation to the latitude she permits him and the latitude he wants. The operative word here is *wants*, because as stated earlier, workers vary in their desire for close or loose supervision. Nevertheless, because generally speaking professionals are thought to be entitled to practice autonomously, most social workers are appreciative of supervisors who respect this symbol of their professional status. Supervisors are usually counseled to allow supervisees to make their own mistakes, and by and large, this is good advice.

But to propound autonomous professional practice is to oversimplify a complex matter. The case for autonomy by professionals can justly be qualified on value grounds: the predisposition of guildlike self-protectiveness on the part of professional groups and the rights of clients to representation of their interests. More immediately relevant, professional practice that is organizationally based demands, coordination which itself limits practice freedom and requires accountability to the organization's constituencies and various sources of support. The supervisor is the organizational actor responsible for both functions with line staff.

Further, in actuality organizations extend more or less freedom to the staff, depending on the particular activity in which the staff is engaged. Thus wide latitude is usually allowed for practice with individual clients (unless there is the potential risk of critical attention from the outside), less latitude is permitted for services that are highly visible, and the least latitude of all for acts that affect the agency's relations with other organizations or powerful constituents. Both the supervisor's responsibility for accountability and the agency constraints to which she is subject, therefore, circumscribe her ability to permit unfettered freedom of action.

With workers whom she can trust to perform with sensibility, the supervisor can afford to permit more autonomy than with less-skilled staff. Even when she may disagree with some of the positions taken by competent workers, the potential negative consequences of permitting them freedom of action are often less important than the positives that accrue from communicating her confidence in them. She must be considerably more circumspect with less-talented staff, however. She must weigh the advantage to the worker and to her relationship with him, on the one hand, with the level of his skill, the requirements of the specific task, its visibility, and the political and other consequences of less-than-perfect performance, on the other hand. The task is for her to find enough occasions to let the worker have his "head" while ensuring that the risk of a negative outcome is kept to a minimum.

Openness. The reference here is to the supervisor's openness, her willingness to own up to difficulty, inadequacy, or failure. Because she carries the aura of authority, her openness may well be perceived as modesty—at least to the degree that the staff respects her competence. Openness humanizes her and tends to mitigate the social distance inherent in their respective roles. Admissions of uncertainty or error also provide a model for nondefensiveness and make it more comfortable or at least easier for workers to share their own practice doubts.

Exploration and Elaboration. We noted in our discussion of empathy that a supervisor is at an advantage when she has the skill to view events from the perspective of the worker. The concept is a simple one, but it is exceedingly difficult to translate into actual practice. It requires hard work: listening (which is not merely attentive silence) and the ability and willingness to explore the meanings behind the worker's words. We discuss exploring and elaborating the comments, questions, and issues put forth by a staff member here, but they are important beyond providing support. Exploring and elaborating are also necessary in informing the supervisor regarding appropriate degrees of directiveness.

A common error of inexperienced supervisors is to neglect to probe sufficiently to get to the core of a problem. Rather, they ask a question and then settle for a more superficial response than is useful. A related, though somewhat different, error is for the supervisor to respond to a worker's request for advice by giving the advice too quickly. We do not believe this is so because workers find it is necessary to "invent" their own solutions to problems, although that is sometimes preferable. Rather, advice is often given too quickly because the supervisor has not yet *really* heard the problem. She may not know its meaning to the worker or have sufficient information regarding its background or history, other potential definitions of the problem, how various solutions would impinge on various participants, and the like. To insufficiently probe a worker's comments or questions risks skimming the surface of an interchange rather than actually dealing with the worker's thoughts and feelings or the substance of the issue.

Workers' responses to a supervisor's questions are sometimes general. An overly general response may be due to the worker's reluctance to share his views or due to his ambivalence about sharing them. Or it could be more innocent than that, representing the worker's style of thinking or his own lack of awareness of the nuances of what he is feeling. In those instances, the supervisor would be wise to probe these general statements until she is either clear about what he means or decides there is little profit in exploring them further.

When workers are ambivalent about what they wish to discuss, they may initiate a conversation that makes only indirect or obscure reference to the real issue. It becomes an agenda item in supervision only if the supervisor recognizes and raises the concern that the worker has expressed by indirection. One supervisor characterized the process as analogous to a worker picking up the corner of a sheet of paper on a desk, exposing only a partial view of what was under it while implicitly inviting the supervisor to peek. Only when the supervisor's responses demonstrated that she had caught on did the worker then reveal the rest of what had been hidden.

It is also true that workers often do not want to share their thoughts or feelings with the supervisor regarding certain matters. Supervisors should be sensitive to that possibility before they raise a potentially loaded issue. At the least, the supervisor should be listening for any cues in the worker's response indicating possible reluctance to discuss a topic. Whether she will let him off the hook without going after the unshared data will depend on two factors. One is how important his reactions to the particular topic are in promoting the effectiveness of his practice. The other relates to the costs or benefits to their relationship of her pursuing the matter further.

Two Cautions in Proferring Support

Supervisors whose style is to overuse affective interventions may well neglect what really may be most supportive for their workers in particular circumstances. For example, the worker who is overloaded will not feel most supported by a good relationship or the supervisor's approval but by an environmental change, the reduction in his caseload. (As one worker said to her supervisor, "Your compliments are all well and good, but are you going to try to get a raise for me?") Thus Kadushin (1976, p. 222) notes that in cases of worker stress, the supervisor can be supportive by temporarily shifting his caseload to less-difficult clients, arranging an increase in clerical help, providing a loss-noisy office or other environmental modifications. As already suggested, structure is often a highly significant source of support—the regularity of a supervisory conference, for example, or the reworking of a supervisory contract.

More important perhaps, perspective in the supportive aspects of supervision is sometimes skewed because there is some question about where support in supervision stops and "treatment" of the worker begins. Some clinicians ignore this distinction and hold that therapeutic interventions advance service interests. One, for example, speaks glowingly of a good manager as also being a good therapist and suggests that the concepts of therapy should be applied to management situations (Gibson, 1983). In the main, however, the social work literature on supervision advises against a supervisor assuming a treatment role with her staff. Nonetheless, the lines do get blurred, and even theorists like Kadushin who counsel the avoidance of treating the supervisee come dangerously close to the edge—or at the least, they appear disposed to psychologize the staff. Kadushin (1976, p. 208) suggests, for example, that "as is true for any highly cathected, meaningful interpersonal relationship, [supervision] becomes infused with transference elements, with ambivalence and resistance, with residuals of earlier developmental conflicts . . . . The supervisor-supervisee relationship evokes the parent-child relationship and, as such, may reactivate anxiety associated with this earlier relationship." A position such as this inevitably grants license for locating what occurs in supervision to transference elements and earlier developmental conflicts rather than focusing on what is occuring in the current interaction. And the position ignores the social context of the supervisory encounter altogether.

Supervisors must clearly resist a worker's invitation or their own temptation to move supervisory interactions into a clinical or treatment arena. However helpful either the supervisor or worker might believe the supervisor as therapist could be, she must be mindful that in service organizations where clients stand to gain or lose depending on the actions of the direct service staff, the role of the supervisor and the role of the therapist are fundamentally contradictory in character. The grounds for this argument are suggested in an earlier chapter. *Trust* in a clinical relationship presumes that the clinician holds the client's best interests to be paramount; it involves mutuality and shared decision making, confidentiality, and full disclosure. Implicit in the relationship between supervisor and supervisee, however, is the understanding that the supervisor, although respecting the needs and interests of supervisees, does not hold them paramount. To the extent that there are conflicts of interest, it is the needs of the clients and sometimes of the organization to which the supervisor holds primary allegiance. The potential for difference between worker needs or interests and the issues for which the supervisor is accountable generates a political tension that is inherent in the supervisory relationship. Its character leads to a much narrower definition of trust than is appropriate in clinical relationships. In the supervisory encounter, the worker should be able to trust that the supervisor will be open with regard to unit goals and directions and that she will be consistent in regard to what she says and does. But that is about as far as his trust may rightfully go. He must also expect that she will promote worker interests at one juncture and take positions that go counter to those interests at another.

This split allegiance renders the supervisor an inappropriate candidate as a "therapist" for a supervisee. A clear example of this is when, in a supervisor's engaging a service worker "therapeutically," personal difficulties are disclosed that compromise the quality of the service that the worker offers to his clients. A clinician in that circumstance would first have to "accept" the character and extent of the difficulty. How the problem was manifest in the varied aspects of the worker's life would probably be explored, and the therapist would place major responsibility on the person for dealing with the problem and the pace at which it was to be addressed. A supervisor's response, on the other hand, would necessarily entail a considerably more limited degree of "acceptance"—for otherwise she would be implicitly sanctioning a lesser quality of work from the supervisee. She cannot remain true to her function of assuring the quality of the service and engage staff in interactions that sanction its compromise.

From the supervisee's perspective, too, the supervisor's provision of treatment is highly questionable. It risks the worker's revealing "weakness" in one context—the personal—that could get used in another—the workplace. It has the potential for increasing the worker's dependence and the supervisor's control, both characteristics that usually have little need for enhancement. Finally, it places their relationship on a level of intimacy that may transcend the boundaries that the worker would choose or is appropriate for the particular organizational circumstances in which the two find themselves.

Supervisors who uncover personal difficulties that act as impediments to effective practice must, of course, raise them. There is, however, a question of timing, and the supervisor must weigh three factors: the quality of the supervisor-supervisee relationship, how seriously the problem impacts on the worker's practice, and how much evidence there is for the supervisor's interpretation of the difficulty. If the evidence is relatively scant, it is possible for the supervisor to identify the worker's problem tentatively, as perhaps only an impression, in order to speculate with him regarding its accuracy. If it is denied but is in fact correct, the supervisor can let the point go with the knowledge that additional evidence will emerge, as it does with any patterned behavior.

To say that the supervisor does not become the worker's therapist is not to say that she may not be of significant, even personal, assistance to staff members. There is a significant difference, of course, between helping a worker to examine his reaction to a particular client and exploring "why" it occurred (e.g., what in his family life explains the reaction). By highlighting or specifying the worker's current difficulties, she may assist him in mobilizing appropriate anxiety with respect to the problem without delving inappropriately into root causes. The heightened anxiety may then serve to induce the worker to struggle with the difficulty, either on his own or with the help of another. Second, the supervisor and worker may problem solve together, exploring how each of them experiences the problem and identifying available alternatives. If the supervisor views the difficulty as basic to the worker's personality and a serious barrier to his potential, she may in addition suggest his seeking professional help.

However empathic the supervisor may be with respect to the worker's problem and however helpful to him she might want to be, the supervisor may have to define limits with regard to the acceptability of the problem on the job. She may need to be explicit about the consequences of the worker's failure in dealing with his difficulties. For some workers, the problem will limit their potential but will not stand in the way of their performing well, if not outstandingly. For others, the difficulties may be of such a nature that the worker will be viewed as limited and therefore not as a prospect for advancement in the agency as new opportunities arise. Or the problem could even be as serious as to hold the potential for termination. The supervisor owes this information to the worker. It puts the worker in charge of the choices related to his destiny in the organization. Although it may not feel so to either party, the provision of this information for the worker by the supervisor is another means of helping him.

We note in conclusion that in addition to reaping such benefits for workers as increasing their motivation, relieving their anxiety, or promoting their self-esteem, supportive supervision has a serendipitous advantage for supervisors. When a supervisor is perceived as supportive, workers are likely to be more understanding of the pressures on her, to interpret her behavior more benignly, to have a greater sense of loyalty, and to respond to her blunders with more "forgiveness." Because supervision is a transactional process, understanding on the part of one actor triggers the understanding of the other.

Managing Sanctions
and Sharing Influence

A comprehensive survey of theory and research on leadership in organizations suggests that there are four major classes of leader behavior: initiating structure, consideration (or support), managing sanctions and inducing participation. (House and Baetz, 1979, p. 407). These classes of behavior are relevant to supervision as well. In the preceding chapter, we explored practice issues related to providing structure and support; here we consider the supervisor's management of sanctions and issues regarding participation and the sharing of influence with her staff.

Supervisors' power to dispense rewards and penalties constitutes a major resource in their ability to influence their subordinates' behavior. Indeed, the mere availability of the resource, without its having to be used, acts as an incentive to encourage worker compliance. And there is little question that, effectively managed, positive and negative sanctioning are important elements in successful supervision. A number of studies have demonstrated that when rewards are granted on the basis of an actor's performance, subsequent performance is improved (Sims, 1977). Indeed, one research study found that the correlation between a leader's applying rewards and desired worker performance was stronger than the correlation between desired worker performance and the leader's initiating structure or profering support (Sims and Szilagyi, 1975).

Managing Sanctions

Operant conditioning has been used to explain the impact of positive and negative sanctions on behavior. Put oversimply: behavior in significant measure is determined by the operation of reinforcements in the environment. Rewards are positive reinforcements; when rewards are linked with specified behaviors, the behaviors increase in frequency. Punishments are negative reinforcers, and when linked with specific behaviors, they are expected to reduce the frequency of these behaviors.

As formulated above, the point is too general for use in practice. For one thing, a sanction is in the beholder's eyes. What serves as a reinforcer varies from person to person and even for the same person at different times. Furthermore, the impact of a reinforcer depends on the history of its use. As noted in another context, social support—praise, a smile, a pat—probably does little to encourage desired behaviors when the approval is tendered too often.

Other factors relating to the frequency of using a sanction are also relevant to the effectiveness of sanctions as reinforcers. One-to-one reinforcement, when the reward is forthcoming every time the particular behavior occurs, may be distinguished from periodic reinforcement, in which the supervisor frequently but not always rewards the desired behavior. Under one-to-one reinforcement, desired behaviors fall away quickly once the rewards stop coming. Periodic reinforcement is recommended as a better method of ingraining a pattern of behavior because it endures even after the praise or negative sanction is no longer forthcoming (Dowling and Sayles, 1978, pp. 194–195). Although the recommendation may sound mechanistic, the basic principle of using reinforcements periodically rather than consistently is empirically sound.

The conscious use of rewards and penalties to reinforce or extinguish behaviors is regarded with apprehension by many social workers. They see behaviorist interventions generally as manipulative, a violation of norms of self-determination and thus inconsistent with social work values. Because it relates to supervisor-worker interaction, they argue that a carrot-and-stick approach demeans the professionalism of the staff. Providing quality service, adhering to professional norms, responding to coworkers in a colleguial fashion, and the like do not demand reinforcement, as these acts in themselves define the professionalism of staff. The use of sanctions for purposes of reinforcing good practice or discouraging bad practice is not only unnecessary but worse, dehumanizing.

It is one thing, however, to consciously use positive and negative sanctions as reinforcers as sole or primary techniques and another to use them as part of a broad variety of interventions. Further, the moral valuation of sanctions depends on *how* they are used, as well as how effective they are in achieving the supervisor's desired ends. To eschew the use of sanctions completely is to relinquish a potent lever for exercising influence.

One cannot avoid the use of sanctions in any case; they are common aspects of everyday life. To appreciate what someone does, for example, rewards that behavior; to disapprove and express displeasure penalizes the action. The issue, then, is whether one *consciously* takes into account their impact in shaping behavior. The consequence of not doing so may be to reward undesireable acts and penalize desired ones. Many supervisors do just that—and indeed, agency structure and policies also often result in rewards to workers who act in ways that go counter to agency aims. A common example is the supervisor or agency that espouses innovation but erects inordinate barriers to worker initiative or program change. Kerr (1975) cites numerous examples of such dysfunctional reward systems. Critical to organizational practice is identifying the ways in which worker behaviors are rewarded (or punished) to ensure that the fit is organizationally or professionally appropriate.

Nevertheless, the apprehension of some social workers with regard to the use of sanctions is well founded in certain circumstances, particularly when the reward is directly and explicitly linked to the desired behavior and/or when the reward is extrinsic to what the worker has done to "deserve" it rather than flowing naturally from his behavior. Repeated transactions of this kind—in which the supervisor offers "special payments" for service—tend to have the effect of giving the supervisory relationship an "economic" coloration. The reward is viewed as a payoff rather than an expression of the supervisor's appreciation. And as Yukl has suggested (1981, p. 55), "It is more satisfying for both [supervisor] and subordinate to view their relationship in terms of mutual friendship and loyalty than as an impersonal economic exchange." As is true in much social exchange, the trade, to be satisfying *and* effective, must not appear to be a trade at all.

The use of sanctions are not similarly available to all supervisory staff so that some supervisors are more advantaged in this regard than others. More powerful supervisors are given the authority to hire or fire, whereas others have considerably more modest sanctions to dispense. Obviously, a discussion of influencing staff through the use of incentives is irrelevant unless the supervisor has some incentives to dispense. Whether the supervisor seeks executive authority in advance regarding her license to use particular sanctions or chooses to negotiate around specific incidents, she must, of course, be certain about her perogatives before she employs rewards or penalties to attain desired behaviors.

Even a supervisor whose resources are relatively modest, however, can shape rewards that her staff find attractive or penalties for them to avoid. To a considerable degree, the supportive behavior described in Chapter 4 can be conceptualized as rewards designed to motivate staff to act in an organizationally proper manner. Recognition, for example, is one favor that almost every supervisor can offer. The recognition may be limited, as in a private communication, or it might entail public acknowledgment, as at a staff meeting or in a memo to the agency executive. Related is the recognition that comes from asking a worker to report on an area of his expertise, to present a case representing particularly able practice, or to conduct a staff seminar in an area that has emerged from the worker's special effort or high-quality performance. Public recognition or praise is a higher-intensity act than private acknowledgment and praise. It is worth more to the worker and tends to generate further commitment on his part. It entails some risk for the supervisor, however, but that is an issue to which we refer later.

Altering the characteristics of a worker's job is another reward (or penalty) that is available to most supervisors. The shaping and rearrangment of assignments are often meaningful to staff. For workers with an interest in increased responsibility or for those whose current tasks are repetitious or monotonous, the promise of job changes may constitute a significant incentive for "good" behavior. Attendance at conferences or special seminars and appointment to ad hoc committees or task forces in other components of the organization may be perceived by staff as rewarding, and can often be structured by the supervisor, either directly or through recommendation to higher-ups.

Other relatively modest rewards, albeit significant to many workers, are the supervisor's willingness to bend the rules or waive some agency requirements. To permit these "infractions," the supervisor must be sure of executive support, and she may need to keep the exceptions relatively invisible within the agency. Available to most supervisors too is the ability to share inside information with a worker.

It may be worth noting parenthetically that sharing information has other advantages. In giving information, the supervisor ordinarily gets information in return, and data about the thoughts, feelings, or experiences of other organizational actors provide a grounding for intelligent decision making. The supervisor who plays things overly close to the vest reinforces that behavior in others and tends to limit her sources of data. The question, of course, is what can be shared and with whom without committing major indiscretions.

Some of the rewards cited above are not only intrinsically gratifying, but they contribute to career mobility as well. For example, public recognition of quality performance and assignment of tasks of greater responsibility or projects of heightened visibility all have that potential. Other more direct and concrete career-oriented incentives such as salary increases and promotions also fall within the purview of some supervisors, either because their recommendations carry weight with their bosses or because they have been delegated major responsibility for decisions of this kind. In short, whatever formal or informal influence a supervisor has "earned" from her superiors, to a large degree the very position of supervisor allows the calibration of sufficient rewards and penalties to help motivate desired staff behavior.

Conditions Conducive to Sanctioning

There are three conditions that should obtain if the effectiveness of positive or negative sanctioning is to be assured. The first has to do with clarity between supervisor and supervisee—shared understandings with respect both to task goals and to the range of processes and procedures used to fulfill these goals.

We have already suggested the importance of clarity in a number of differing contexts and need not develop the point here. Suffice to say that priorities among goals and the means of achieving them require joint supervisor-staff attention. Agency purposes and processes may be clear and well understood. Often less apparent, however, is the fact that the pursuit of one goal or engaging in one activity entails *not* pursuing some other goal or engaging in some other activity. A simple example is when the agency requires extensive recording for third-party reimbursement and simultaneously demands an increase in the interview count of the staff—two mandates that on the face of it strain against one another. Unless the supervisor and supervisee share the same definitions of what takes precedence, the basis for the supervisor's rewarding or penalizing her staff may be—or appear to be—arbitrary to them.

A second condition necessary for the effective use of sanctions is the demonstration of follow through. Through experience, staff must come to believe that the supervisor is actually prepared to employ one or another sanction to implement her priorities. Workers should, in other words, have advance notice that the supervisor considers certain issues to be of sufficient importance that she will reward particular effort and penalize noncompliance. Sometimes, in cases such as these, the supervisor's communication may be implicit so that she does not appear to be "bribing" or "threatening" the workers. At other times, depending on the importance of the issue and the previous experience of the parties with issues of this kind, the communication can be quite direct, clearly a "bribe" or "threat." In either instance, however, if the supervisor promises some reward or warns against some penalty as an incentive to incur a particular response, she must be ready to act as she said she would and to do so consistently in similar circumstances. In the case of a negative sanction, failure to warn staff in advance is likely to sharpen the expected bitterness, and failure to follow through on promised rewards is likely to undercut her credibility and constrain her influence in subsequent encounters.

The third condition that should accompany the use of a sanction depends on its "fit" with agency norms and on the organic nature of the sanction.

Equity in using sanctions, or "fair treatment" generally, is an oft-cited organizational norm. (Austin, 1981; Strauss and Sayles, 1980). The advice of these authors is generally sound: treat people equally, avoiding either the tendency to favor the passive "good" supervisee or to pay most attention to the aggressive "squeaky wheel" type of staff member. Further, the norm is that the supervisor should be impartial in allocating rewards or leveling penalties. Personal relationships, the worker's support of the supervisor's positions, and the like should have no bearing on who gets rewarded, nor should disliking or dissenting determine who gets punished.

This norm is difficult to implement, however. What a person expects from another strongly shapes his or her reaction to an interaction with the other. *Perceptions* of fair treatment vary with the expectations of individual staff members regarding the supervisor. Thus it is likely that there will be a variety of definitions of fair, and the supervisor cannot possibly satisfy them all.

To some degree, organizational norms regarding fair treatment do shape workers' expectations for supervisory behavior. Nonetheless, individual expectations not only vary within the group's norms, but no supervisor could treat all workers in ways they would perceive as fair, even if she wished. For one thing, she must clearly reward or reinforce "good" organizational behavior and penalize "bad" organizational behavior. There is no way workers subject to the latter are likely to define the supervisor's acts as "fair"; their first lines of defense are often that her displeasure stems from bias, personal ire, or a personality conflict. Similarly, staff members who perceive that some workers are rewarded while they do not receive similar benefits often feel as if they had, in effect, been penalized. The grounds for charges of being unfair are rife.

Although equity is a strongly held norm, the uncertainty about the possibility of implementing it makes some workers monitor the norm closely. They do not trust that the supervisor can or will do other than play favorites. It is anomolous, but the very fact that the supervisor may be expected to be somewhat more responsive to favorite staff members provides her with a zone of discretion in exercising the norm. Within circumscribed parameters, she may maneuver some modest rewards for supporters or some limited penalties for opponents without seriously violating staff expectations. Because they expect her to do so in any case, they are more prone to accept some use of favoritism on her part, even if only unconsciously. That she may decide to do so is suggested by the fact that even if she does not, the accusation of partiality may be leveled in any case.

Nevertheless, it is important to guard the *appearance* of equity. Some rewards can be tendered in private or are generally invisible. There are occasions, for example, when supervisors grant the special requests of workers, but it is unnecessary to acknowledge that either the supervisor or the worker perceives her as acceding to the request as a reward for something the worker has done. The supervisor must also have a relatively acceptable explanation for any reward or penalty that is likely to become public. (The definition of acceptable here is that a neutral observer could grant a supervisor who has been less than totally equitable the benefit of a doubt).

The organic nature of the sanction—its appropriateness and fit within the organization—must also be considered. To reward or punish workers who are unable to accomplish or avoid some goal or task as a result of circumstances over which they have no control is to administer sanctions "unfairly." Some rewards or punishments are also out of proportion to the behavior that calls them forth, and others are seen as out of bounds within the agency. For example, whereas an especially responsible assignment would be an appropriate reward for meritorious work, rewarding the same performance with a work schedule that was better than the work schedules of other staff would seem untoward. This is so because the reward (i.e., the assignment) is intrinsic to meritorious performance, and when a reward is intrinsic, it seems more natural. Thus when the reward for competence is increased recognition, a more important role in the agency, or advancement, the reward is perceived to be organic to the processes of the unit. It conforms to the traditional organizational norm that dictates that it is the most capable who will advance.

Some organizational theorists have argued that rewards should be made sparingly and punishments even more sparingly (Caplow, 1976, p. 92). Although this position is probably overstated, it does contain more than a kernal of truth. As we have said, public rewards are often experienced as penalties by those who do not receive them. The idea, then, is that every reward to A holds the potential for generating resentment on the part of B—unless A is so obviously deserving that none of the many Bs in the agency can quarrel with A's good fortune. And even then it can generate ill-feeling. In other words, reserving rewards for those who demonstrate superior performance can engender an undercurrent of tension irrespective of how skillful the supervisor is in administering the sanction. Such tension is unavoidable, however, and a certain degree of tension may even be healthy.

Maintaining a balance between tensions that are inevitable and possibly useful and tensions that generate intense competitiveness among workers or strong resentment against the supervisor is a delicate task. The critical criteria for maintaining an appropriate balance has to do with staff behavior; feelings—either the supervisor's own feelings or the staff's—are secondary. For her part, the supervisor may feel uncomfortable in the face of even mild resentment. Such discomfort goes with the territory, however, and if the primary criterion of her decision making with regard to sanctions is her own feelings of comfort, she risks making inappropriate choices. Similarly, although supervisors must take staff sensibilities into account, exclusive attention to their feelings is unwise. Staff who are not working to capacity, regardless of the reason, *should* experience a degree of discomfort. Moderate levels of discomfort can serve to spur higher-quality performance, especially if workers have some assurance that the supervisor will be responsive to their efforts. If, on the other hand, the supervisor has set performance standards that overtax the capabilities of most staff members, they will perceive rewards to be beyond their reach and thus not be an incentive.

Disciplinary Action

The dictum that punishments should be made very sparingly is, in our view, wise. Frequent resort to the use of warnings and penalties has a chilling effect on staff, straining relations and generating distrust. Negative sanctions are justified only in isolated instances in which the failure to use them might result in an erosion of norms of staff conduct and in cases in which there is broad understanding, if not active approval, on the part of most staff members with regard to a given sanction's use.

Basically, negative sanctions should be reserved for two situations. One is when standards of conduct fall below an accepted minimum (flouting supervisory authority, irresponsibility in relation to clients, violation of time norms, and the like). The second is when the behavior is highly visible so that the supervisor's failure to check it is likely to compromise her authority and implicitly to suggest to others that what the worker has done can be tolerated.

In units in which standards of conduct have been established, the maintenance of those standards is usually accepted by subordinates, and failure to maintain them may well have negative consequences. When, for example, one staff member is unreliable in meeting commitments or consistently does inferior work, this frequently translates into an added burden for other staff personnel. In such instances, if the supervisor fails to enforce the rule or standard, workers may appropriately feel that the supervisor's avoidance of confrontation or coercion has been at their expense. Furthermore, some staff may feel sufficient resentment at someone's having gotten away with an infraction and conclude that they, too, should be able to get away with it.

As is the case in dispensing rewards, standards must be understood before the supervisor resorts to negative sanctions; her willingness to use sanctions must be clear, and their use must be equitable or have the appearance of equity. It is well, in addition, for negative sanctions to be administered promptly—in the hope that the problem can be handled before it gets out of control.

Actually, discipline often entails an incremental series of steps. Some situations may be remedied simply by a discussion in which the supervisor expresses her concern or feeling of being upset. After a few such conversations have taken place and the problem behavior persists, one or more verbal warnings is the next step. Ultimately, a written warning is necessary for disciplinary action that is formal such as an official reprimand or the recommendation of suspension, demotion, or dismissal.

Most often, a gradual escalation can alter the situation before radical steps have to be taken. Whether the infractions cease or not, however, the supervisor who anticipates that she may ultimately be forced to take formal action must be prepared early in the process to make an adequate case for her position. She should be precise with the worker regarding the activities that are required for him to avoid disciplinary action. Such specificity sharply defines the areas of difficulty and allows the worker to monitor his own compliance. It also lessens any implication that the supervisor is handling the matter in an arbitrary way.

Sometimes a documented case is required, because of contractual arrangements between worker and agency, to satisfy grievance procedures, or to construct a presentation to a regulatory body such as a civil service commission in the anticipation of an employee complaint. Even when documentation is not required, it is well for the supervisor to make the case so as to appear reasonable to other workers or third parties in the event that the issue draws public attention.

The Issue of Loyalty

Our focus up until now has been on the use of sanctions to influence unit practices and services. Another arena is worth noting in which the use of sanctions is important—namely, the relation of sanctions to staff's commitment to the supervisor herself.

A supervisor is often uncomfortable seeking the loyalty of her staff; she may worry that she may be after self-gratification or will appear to be. Some are uncertain about the extent to which their expectations of staff loyalty transcend the limits of professional responsibility. Others may also be concerned about appearing to favor only those workers who agree with them. The matter is further complicated by the difficulty of assessing who among the staff is actually supportive. Measures of staff support are usually informal, often times observed only implicitly, and frequently rely on secondhand information. Nonetheless, the supervisor who is interested in maximizing the influence of her role must be clear on the issue. Staff loyalty is a significant ingredient in the effectiveness of a unit's functioning and should be pursued. The issue is a matter of position, not person.

The converse is also true: staff disloyalty mars unit effectiveness. Typically, the challenge to supervisory authority is indirect, often masked as substantive difference. The fact that it passes as a substantive disagreement rather than as a challenge to authority is not to say that content differences do not also exist. But often the differences act as a cover for some hidden agenda.

On any given issue, it is reasonable to suppose that individuals will differ; some will favor a particular position, and others will not. But over time, positions that staff members express with respect to support for or resistance to supervisory guidelines become increasingly consistent. There are those who can be counted on to endorse supervisory positions, those whose responses vary, and those who may be expected to dissent. When positions become that predictable, one may presume that the first group are supporters regardless of the issue and the third are adversaries. Even so, often a supervisor is reluctant to confront the consistent dissenters—perhaps for fear of seeming to personalize an issue or because she is afraid it will appear that she cannot tolerate dissent. Instead, she facilitates the airing of the views of the dissidents, dealing with the manifest rather than the latent content—and, indeed, scrupulously adopting an impartial stance. She avoids any implication of unfavorable treatment in scheduling, making assignments, and the like, and she may even end up favoring the dissidents by bending over backward to be fair. Her impartiality can also extend to appointing dissenting staff to decision-making committees in the hope of coopting them or to gain the political advantage of having their views presented. In these ways, a message is implicitly sent to the rest of her staff that the positions of the consistent "nay-sayers" deserve credibility. In short, the supervisor has colluded with forces that undermine her leadership. Functionally, she may have put herself in the position of rewarding a subgroup for their disloyalty.

Because loyal or disloyal behavior feels and appears so personal, its management poses a delicate issue for a supervisor. Nevertheless, it is important that she communicate, through words or acts, the importance of the staff's supporting her leadership. Those who are supportive should be rewarded—privately if necessary, but publicly if the appropriate conditions are met. As for the others, it should be made clear that although the supervisor values differing views and may encourage staff debate, once a decision has been made, everyone must adhere to it. The supervisor should confront a consistent pattern of nonsupport privately through discussions and problem solving and then initiate a sequential strategy of informal sanctions and isolation from influence within the unit; and if necessary, ultimately the worker's actions may suggest that he should be transfered to another position or unit.

Throughout this process, the supervisor must herself have internalized that her concerns have to do with support for her *role*. When the relations with her staff are perceived as positional, the operative norms are different than when the issues between them are defined on personal terms. To accept a worker's assertion without correction that the supervisor is "biased because she doesn't like me" or "we have a personality conflict" is to place the arena of the conflict as one between peers and as such undercuts the supervisor's authority and prerogatives. Such a definition allows the dissident worker to call on the norms of interpersonal relations, in which the standards of openness, equality, or working things through apply. But if the issue is in fact one of authority, such standards obfuscate the real issue and diminish the supervisor's leverage in resolving the difficulty.

If the supervisor truly sees the matter as positional, she should, for her part, *not* personalize the differences between the worker and herself. If she indulges in feelings that the staff member is against *her*, she risks acting in anger or other ways that will reinforce those personalized feelings. Thus she will provide the worker with further grounds for shifting the definition of the problem. To the extent that the supervisor can engage her difficulties with a worker with personal distance and on the level of role and responsibility, she will remain more effectively positioned to manage them.

One final observation is in order. To incur loyalty, the supervisor must communicate that her staff members are influential in affecting the supervisor-supervisee relationship. Such communications are usually better transmitted implicitly than directly, but however it is done, the supervisor is responsible for making sure that the message has been received. There are a myriad of ways to transmit that their relationship is reciprocal and even that the supervisor is prepared to make the worker's commitment and support worthwhile. Gestures of support should be identified and rewarded in the same way that nonsupport should be confronted and addressed. The worker must understand that the supervisor stands ready to "play" and that the worker's actions will affect not only the nature of his relationship with his supervisor, but his fortunes in the unit as well. Similarly, workers must also understand that if there is no chance for the supervisor to "win," she will cease to "play." In other words, it is important for workers to understand that as long as their support can be influenced by the actions of their supervisor, she will find reasonable accomodations to win that support. On the other hand, once the supervisor concludes that this is not possible, the worker will, in essence, be written off and treated accordingly.

Influence Sharing and Participation

Sharing influence with the staff through their participation in agency decision making has been widely promoted in the human services during the past four decades. In addition to the presumed benefits of staff participation, enthusiasm for shared decision making has an ideological foundation. The fact that numbers of outcome studies show positive results is akin to icing on a cake. At its simplest, the value issue goes as follows: democracy is good; participation is democratic; therefore participation is good. Staff participation is congruent with the notion that those on lower levels of the hierarchy should be involved in the decisions that influence their lives and is also consonant with the social work values of self-determination and mutuality in client-worker interaction. The ideological issue is most directly put in Tannenbaum's statement that

"The question for many . . . is not whether participation works but rather how to *make* it work" (Locke and Schweiger, 1979, p. 267).

We believe that the context of the human service organization—the fact that its prime beneficiary is the client, not the worker—makes a difference in one's value judgment. Only insofar as it enhances client service do moral grounds exist for the supervisor's promotion of staff participation. It is quite possible for a supervisor who encourages staff participation to be passive and inept and for an authoritative supervisor to be supportive and competent. And regardless of one's value position, it is well to avoid confusing outcomes one would desire with outcomes that actually occur.

Research findings on the effects of participation are equivocal. By and large, the studies have focused on two outcomes: (1) job satisfaction or worker morale and (2) productivity, including the quality of the decision being made. In an extensive survey of the research, Locke and Schweiger (1979, p. 317) found that of forty-six studies that examined productivity, slightly more than half of them showed no difference between participative and authoritative decision making, and in the remaining studies superior productivity was divided equally between the two modes. The forty-three studies that explored job satisfaction evidenced more clearcut results; 60 percent of them showed that participation increased job satisfaction, 30 percent showed no difference, and in 9 percent of the studies, participation actually decreased satisfaction.

Participation Pros and Cons

In view of an equivocal empirical rationale for participation, what are the pros and cons that staff participation holds for the supervisor? It is commonly believed that staff members are more likely to support a decision they have been involved in making and that such involvement reduces resistance to change. It is assumed, therefore, that it is politic to gain their acceptance through participation. This is seen as particularly important when her staff have a significant role to play in implementing the decision. If a supervisor promotes participation to encourage the acceptance of a largely predetermined change, however, it should be recognized that there is an element of manipulativeness in encouraging it on this ground. In effect, one is ostensibly seeking staff input for the contribution staff can make or for its inherent value, when in fact there is a hidden agenda of seeking staff's endorsement for a change. Of course, it is possible to seek staff input to gain their endorsement *and* to improve the quality of the decision. But that is a different matter.

Whether their involvement actually encourages the workers' acceptance of a decision is probably situational—related to the particular worker, decision, or organization. For example, some workers might prefer *not* to take responsibility for contributing to some decisions. It is also unlikely that participation per se would increase workers' endorsements of decisions that went counter to their interests. Finally, organizational dynamics could play a role. Thus if there were grounds for suspicion that the organization was encouraging involvement to coopt the staff or to diffuse dissatisfaction, participation might serve to generate more rather than less resistance.

To take a reverse situation, suppose that the workers felt some anxiety about the turbulence in the agency or the profession and that the proposed change was less threatening to their welfare than at first it would appear. Suppose, too, that because of organizational norms, the staff expected to be involved in decision making. Under these circumstances, it is clear that the staff's participation would increase their acceptance of the resultant position. In other words, whether or not staff participation increases the staff's acceptance of a decision or increases their resistance to it is strongly influenced by contextual factors.

Under optimal conditions, staff participation influences the spread of knowledge and understanding within an agency. When staff members are engaged in problem solving about service issues that require on-the-line knowledge or understanding, the process entails the sharing of the workers' knowledge with the supervisor and/or other higher-level staff. In other instances, it is the workers who come away from the process with a greater understanding of facets of the service problem and thus are more ready to implement the decision as intended.

Because differing perspectives follow differing interests, one may suppose that when staff members with different turf interests are involved in a decision-making process, problems and issues may emerge that would otherwise have remained concealed, thereby improving the final product. It is possible that an open supervisor-supervisee decision-making process serves a related purpose. It provides the forum through which the supervisor and her workers can resolve some of their own differences through mutual concessions and exchanges of favors (Anthony, 1978). The issue of representation is put more generally by group theorists who hold that differences of opinion improve problem-solving outcomes, and empirical work has found that conflicting opinions did increase the quality of group decisions (Hoffman, Harburg, and Maier, 1962).

Nonetheless, it is well to remember the old saw about the camel's being an animal that was created by a committee. The risk of representation by differing turf interests in decision making is that their conflicting views will be resolved by solutions reflecting a least common denominator rather than solutions of high quality. There is evidence, too, that group decisions are inferior to individual decisions in large numbers of instances.

This is not to say that it may not be politically more important to ensure the representation of differing interests than to ensure the highest-quality outcome. Sometimes it is a matter of tradeoffs. Indeed, it may be argued that a major advantage of involving various staff members in decision making, albeit a negative argument, is the pyschic and political cost of *not* involving them. Yates (1985, p. 140) puts the point well: "An excluded party may well magnify the motivation lying behind the exclusion, is likely to run around trying to find out what happened [and] may launch a counterattack to get its interests heard."

If, organizationally, a decision is the supervisor's to make, it is also the supervisor's decision whether to include her staff in the decision-making process. Because there are both advantages and disadvantages in sharing influence through staff involvement in decision making, the criteria that guide her practice in this area need to be explicated.

Determinants of Participation

Three factors significantly determine the extent to which the supervisor might foster participation with respect to a particular issue: (1) the distribution of information and expertise among participants, (2) the importance of the issue to the staff, and (3) the locus of responsibility and accountability for the issue.

Information and Expertise. The quality of a decision, obviously enough, reflects the quality of the knowledge or understanding that the participants have contributed to the process of reaching it. The logic of this view is supported empirically; Lanzetta and Roby (1960) found in a laboratory experiment that when the most able group member exerted the most influence on the group's decision making, the groups performed more effectively than did those groups in which leadership and ability were less congruent. Interestingly, though not surprisingly, research also suggests that there is a decrease in equality of influence over time in participative structures when there are significant disparities in knowledge among the participants (Mulder and White, 1970).

In cases in which staff workers have relevant information to contribute or expertise that is not available to the supervisor, it would be foolhardy for her to exclude them from the decision-making process. When it is not politically costly, she may want to create subgroups of the staff who are most knowledgable in specific areas to help with relevant decision making, rather than involving the entire unit. On the other hand, it might be wasteful or worse for her to involve staff members on issues in which her own knowledge or expertise is clearly superior to theirs. It has been argued that "if a supervisor clearly knows the best solution, then she should properly assert her knowledge and make the decision" (Locke and Schweiger, 1979, p. 326).

The Significance to Staff of Participating. Two aspects of participation that are significant to the staff are the importance to them of having an impact on a particular issue and the importance they attach to participation as a process.

Issues vary greatly in their importance to staff. The most consequential are probably those that concern their professional or career interests or are job related (personnel matters, scheduling, and the like). The staff not only manifest greater interest in these areas, but their expectations for participation are likely to be greater when these areas are at issue. Conversely, even matters of considerable significance to an organization's well-being arouse lesser staff concern if the connection to their own activities or interests is relatively obscure. The supervisor's decision to seek staff participation need not correlate directly with the extent of the workers' interest in the issue, but their interest is an important piece of data in deciding which way to go.

It is also true that oftentimes staff are not interested in participating for any numbers of reasons—to eschew responsibility, to avoid meetings, because they are angry at the agency, or the like. Also, the pace of the unit's workload or the pressure it is experiencing generally may well influence a staff's desire to engage in decision making. Unless the decision making relates directly to reducing the pressure, participation may appear to them to be an additional burden to them.

Staff attitudes regarding participation depend in large measure on how much they *expect* to be involved in the decision-making process. Interestingly, there is considerable variance in people's judgment about the extent of their participation, even in the same organizational setting. Asking how much they participated in decision making, Mohr (1982, p. 151) found that a moderate amount of actual participation was recorded as very little by some workers and quite a lot by others. He interpreted the range of responses as anchored in the workers' expectations for participation. The higher the expectation, then, the more useful it is for the supervisor to accord workers the opportunity to contribute to decision making. If their participation is contraindicated, but expectations are high, it may be important for the supervisor to develop a strategy to reduce their expectations.

Responsibility and Accountability. The locus of responsibility for an issue and the nature of accountability for its outcome also constitute significant criteria for deciding who participates and to what degree. The criteria stem from the organizational principle that responsibility and authority should covary. Those who are held accountable for an outcome should have disproportional influence in deciding an issue. Responsibility in regard to a particular issue may rest with a single worker or staff subgroup, as when responsibility for a task or function has been delegated to them. In other instances, the supervisor alone or the entire unit may carry disproportionate responsibility for solving a specific problem. Whichever the case, the rule of thumb is that those who participate in making decisions and the degree of their influence should reflect who is accountable and the extent of the accountability.

We have already suggested that in addition to improving the quality of a decision, staff participation may be advisable for political reasons—to enhance staff's commitment to a particular outcome or to provide legitimacy for a specific decision. In regard to the latter, it is sometimes the case that a decision is viewed as improper if the input of some staff has been excluded. We believe, however, that when the criteria cited above collectively inform the assessment and ultimate choice that the supervisor makes concerning the degree of influence she will entertain, she will have to some degree depoliticized the matter of participation. This is so because the criteria are rooted in principles of organizational structure and process and provide uniform guidelines in assessing the appropriate degree of staff influence. When they are applied consistently, the criteria become familiar, and over time the staff may even come to expect that the supervisor will make the determination in prescribed circumstances.

Two other factors affect the supervisor's decision regarding staff involvement, although these are of lesser importance. One has to do with the time demands inherent in the issue. Clearly, the more immediate the need for a decision or the greater the sense of urgency in the agency, the less time there is available for staff deliberation. Participation may simply not be feasible or may seem inappropriate when time pressures are critical in problem solving. Whether a problem is a recurring one or is in some measure unusual also affects the supervisor's choice. Staff participation in solving recurring issues may be called for so that experience in grappling with the problem may be gained or the capability of dealing with it may be developed. Participation regarding issues that are less likely to recur cannot similarly be rationalized on these grounds.

The Decision-Making Continuum

Staff involvement in decision making ranges from complete nonparticipation, with the supervisor making decisions without staff input, on one end of a scale to the other end, in which the task is totally delegated to the staff. The choice among the various modes of decision making along this continuum flow in good measure from the criteria suggested earlier. Each mode has advantages and disadvantages and is appropriate or not depending on specific circumstances. Some considerations relevant to the supervisor's choice are discussed below.

Supervisory Determination. Here, the supervisor decides and informs the staff of her decision. Lest we still too quickly assume that her staff will resist supervisory determination, a number of empirical studies indicate that such is not necessarily the case. For example, Ivancevich (1976, 1977) found that of three possibilities in the pursuit of organizational goals—staff determination of the goals, supervisory determination, or open-ended in regard to the goals—the two former conditions fared similarly with regard to productivity and satisfaction; it was only when the goals were unspecified that the outcome was more negative.

Supervisory determination is most appropriate for issues that are either trivial or critical. Obviously, issues that the staff define as insignificant or not directly relevant to their day-to-day functioning are logical candidates for this decision-making mode. So, too, are nonrecurring decisions, because they do not require the development of staff capability to address in the future. Examples of these types of decisions include selection of reporting procedures that involve the staff only marginally, the scheduling of advance events that are sufficiently far in the future to preclude conflict, or the selection of a consultant for a special project.

Conversely, there are issues that are central to the supervisor's accountability to upper-level personnel or issues in which circumstances dictate little or no freedom to modify the decision. If the supervisor deems that *any* input from her staff might engender an expectation of influence when, in fact, none is possible, she does well to make the determination alone. Examples include a decision concerning disciplinary action, critical directives from the executive that may be onerous to staff but about which the supervisor has no leeway, or the adoption of a policy so important as to be nonnegotiable.

The advantages of the supervisor's making a decision without staff input is its efficiency in terms of time and the fact that it does not encumber staff personnel with matters of little moment to them. In cases of significant issues, supervisory determination has the advantage of minimizing the risk that the supervisor will appear to seek staff opinion but may then have to overrule it. Nevertheless, in view of the informational and political benefits for the supervisor of soliciting some degree of staff involvement, the burden of proof in selecting the appropriate mode should rest with the question: Why *not* solicit staff opinion? When the answer to this question does not argue compellingly for staff exclusion, the supervisor is advised to select a more participatory mode.

Supervisory Determination with Influence. This mode, a variant of the one described above, allows the supervisor to retain full decision-making power, but it also offers the benefit of soliciting staff knowledge and judgment. In addition, it provides the staff with the opportunity to persuade the supervisor of the wisdom of one or another course of action. In this case it is understood that the supervisor will make the final determination, but that she will not do so without taking her staff's views into account.

Soliciting staff opinion is appropriate in situations similar to those in which the supervisor decides that the decision is hers alone but that information or ideas are required from staff prior to making the decision. She may also solicit their views to assess their reactions to an option so that she can factor staff feelings into her decision. Consulting her staff is also appropriate when the staff *expect* to be consulted and the issue permits her to take advantage of the political benefits that accrue from their involvement. Issues in which this mode of decision making is indicated include those relating to program modifications, planning for the implementation of externally mandated procedures, responding to executive requests for recommendations, and most forms of meeting and special events planning.

The major advantages of soliciting staff opinion before the supervisor makes a determination is that she reaps the informational and political benefits without relinquishing essential control over the ultimate decision. Its disadvantages are twofold. Her staff may react negatively if they perceive their part in the process as less significant than they deem appropriate. And when the supervisor makes a decision contrary to their opinion, individual staff members may view her as having a pejorative judgment about them, rather than about their ideas. It has the potential as well of structuring a degree of staff frustration into discussions with the supervisor, particularly on the part of staff with a strong need to influence, because the visibility of their limited power may well be heightened by the process.

In using this mode the supervisor must not be ambiguous about distinguishing between input, on the one hand, and influence, on the other. The staff should understand that although they may discuss an issue and perhaps attempt to persuade the supervisor to select some preferred course of action, the ultimate decision-making perogative remains with her. Otherwise, when the decision goes counter to their position, they will feel deceived.

Collective Decision Making. Supervisory determination alone or with worker input can take place on either an individual or group basis, in contrast to decision making that requires the participation of staff as a collectivity. At some point an issue crosses an imaginary line at which the advantages of the supervisor's controlling the outcome or of acting with speed is outweighed by other factors. Usually, these are issues that are of moderate to significant importance to staff, but in which the supervisor has less investment in preferred alternatives than in resolving matters in a way that is acceptable to her staff. When a problem to be solved falls into these categories and is more relevant to the unit or a subgroup than to an individual member, it becomes the appropriate subject for a group decision. There are three patterns by which a group may reach a decision—through majority vote, with a minority veto, or by consensus.

Voting, with the majority determining a decision, has the advantage of being both efficient and effective as a participatory process. It is efficient because it is less time consuming than other group patterns—following the designated period for discussion, a vote is taken and the matter resolved. Its effectiveness stems in part from its symbolic significance in Western culture and in part from its intrinsic structure. It allows for a wide airing of views and the opportunity for people to persuade one another, and it culminates in a fair and democratic resolution in which the views of the many prevail. There is an associated normative obligation for those who participated in the process to go along with the outcome. One may suspect that people who disagree with a group's decision may be only marginally more committed to the outcome as a result of having participated in reaching it, but the norm places them on the defensive in any subsequent challenge to the outcome that they might want to make.

Minority determination or veto are two variants to the principle of assigning disproportionate influence to some subset of the staff unit in making a decision. Permitting a minority of the staff to unduly influence a decision or permitting them to veto it may be appropriate when an issue affects the interests, responsibilities, or areas of expertise of these workers more than it affects other workers in the unit. This is accomplished either by specifying the few who will make the decision (minority determination) or by indicating that disproportionate weight will be given to the preferences of a designated few (minority veto), rather than what the majority decides. In the latter instance, the supervisor initiates the discussion by seeking recommendations from the relevant minority or by identifying the format to be used to give their input the desired weight. She might instead meet with the subgroup alone, so that only she and they decide on a matter of particular relevance to the subgroup. The supervisor could use either of these decision-making formulas when a unit is considering the adoption of a policy that affects a particular category of client (e.g., ex-offender or substance abuser) and some subgroup of the staff has primary responsibility for serving that client group or possesses special expertise in regard to the problems or characteristics of the group. Similarly, when a decision disproportionately affects staff members with a particular function (e.g., outreach versus treatment), decisions that have a greater impact on the outreach staff may justify their having more to say about it, just as decisions that disproportionately affect the treatment staff may justify that group's having more influence in deciding. One caveat is in order, however. Should the supervisor believe that this staff subset has an inappropriate monopoly on the problem or that its position would be guided by protectiveness of its monopoly, her stance might be exactly the opposite—to open the issue to the entire unit.

Consensus, or unanimous consent, requires that the participants discuss a subject until all relevant observations, information, and opinions have been shared; closure is reached only when the group agrees by common consent to abide by a resultant position. Because the deliberations are open-ended and the group's position must emerge and be accepted by the entire body, it can consume an enormous amount of time and energy. Consensus is most often used in federated organizations in which the members represent various constituencies, all of whom must accept the decision. Sometimes it is the norm in smaller groups in which each participant finds it in his or her interest to reach unanimous agreement, perhaps, for example, to protect the turf of others so that their own turf will be respected in turn. As such, it constitutes a form of group decision making that supervisors might find troublesome and one that, because of its costliness in time, a supervisor would use only under extraordinary circumstances. One such case would be when even a single ruffled feather might be too high a price to pay for a particular outcome. Sometimes too, the supervisor's choice of the decision-making mode may be circumscribed, for example, when a consensual pattern is embedded in the culture of the organization. The task, then, would be to try to wean the staff away from consensual norms slowly.

In placing an issue on a group agenda for a collective decision, whether by vote, minority determination or consensus, the supervisor, in effect, calls on staff to resolve a problem, or at least she *appears* to do so.

Sometimes she is unaware that she is dealing only in appearances—for example, when her own position as leader inordinately influences the positions taken by her subordinates. Sometimes, too, she manipulates her staff into believing that they are making a decision when in fact their choice is circumscribed by the withholding of information or through controlling the alternatives available to them (Pfeffer, 1978). Although this may be done to appear to accomodate to staff demands for greater influence, its risks are apparent. The staff may fail to settle on her desired outcome, or the ploy may be revealed. It has been called a dangerous and shoddy game (Dowling and Saxles, 1978, p. 139) but it is a game that is frequently played, at times with some justification.

Delegation. At the most participative end of the decision-making continuum is delegation. In this mode the supervisor grants a single member or group of her staff the authority and responsibility for making decisions with regard to previously specified goals, tasks, issues, or functions. Constraints may be placed on staff's freedom to act without clearing particular decisions with the supervisor, but often the final authority to act rests with staff.

Delegation is appropriate when the resolution of an issue is insufficiently important to the supervisor to require her attention or because she deems one resolution as good as any other. It is also appropriate to delegate matters that must be decided on the line, particularly those requiring a quick response. When line staff have the responsibility for managing a particular set of tasks or achieving specified goals, delegating decision-making authority to them follows our-earlier cited organizational principle that responsibility and authority should covary. Further, issues in which a staff member's expertise is so overriding—for example, in areas in which the supervisor has limited knowledge or experience—are appropriately delegated to the staff. So, too, are those issues about which the supervisor feels sure that her staff can make a right decision.

The advantages of delegation are that it removes matters that are readily left to others from a too-busy supervisor's workload. With more-significant issues, delegation provides a signal to the staff that the supervisor has sufficient confidence in their ability to trust them to decide. There are two major disadvantages to delegating. Clearly, the supervisor's control is reduced with delegation. This can have negative ramifications apart from the potentially lesser quality of the decision. An example is when the worker's decision has an impact on other staff members and he has either not taken that into account or has consciously ignored its impact on others. Thus the supervisor, who must coordinate their efforts, may then have tensions between workers to resolve. A less-apparent disadvantage of delegation is that the staff sometimes define it in terms of supervisory detachment or lack of caring, rather than, as the supervisor might assume, a sign of trust.

Whatever the degree of staff input selected, the prerogative of selection must remain the supervisor's to make. Using different modes of decision making has a potential for generating heightened staff resentment unless staff is clear *in advance* which mode of decision making is to be used. Negative feeling is near-certain when the staff has been excluded from exerting influence on an important matter after they have been led to *expect* a role in deciding the issue. Supervisors sometimes make the unfortunate choice of setting a process of staff discussion or evaluation in motion without ascertaining that the staff is clear about who is to decide. Sometimes this is motivated by a commitment to process without considering the potential consequences of such a process. However good their intentions, supervisors must be sure that there is clarity regarding where a decision ultimately rests.

Skills in Influence Sharing

Although research on the effects of participation is extensive, there has been little empirical work on what constitutes skill in promoting staff decision making. We do not know, for example, whether productivity increases with participation in study A but shows no change in study B because of how the supervisors in the respective studies managed the participatory process. Until the research is sufficiently refined to distinguish between levels of skill, the results must be viewed as equivocal. Practitioners cannot, in any case, wait for empirical findings before acting, and in this concluding section of the chapter, we summarize some aspects of supervisory skill to induce staff participation.

As with all aspects of practice, a necessary if insufficient condition of effectiveness is goal clarity. Before she embarks on a participatory process, either with individual staff or in groups, the supervisor must have some notion of what she hopes to achieve. As we implied earlier, she may wish to involve her staff on substantive grounds (e.g., because their expertise will improve the quality of the decision). Or the goal of the process may be relational, to maintain or enhance a positive connection (e.g., when she consults with them because it is a unit norm or to gain staff's approval). Or her aim may be political, such as legitimating a decision or encouraging its favorable implementation. Although these ends are not mutually exclusive and there is often a mix of substantive, relational or political goals, her interventions will—or should—be influenced by what she wants to accomplish.

Consider, for example, a supervisor's choice to consult with individuals or a staff group on a particular occasion. Obviously, if her goal is to improve the quality of a decision, the choice of whom to include will be based on who has the greater knowledge or interest to contribute to the issue. She will also take into account the extent to which the decision entails interdependence.

Suppose, on the other hand, that her aim is relational. In that case the choice will depend on whose support or approval she is seeking. She may use some staff as confidants. Confidants give her advice and feedback in return for being on the "in" or for other favors. She would then want the consultation to be private and invisible.

Let us assume that her goal is political and that she wishes to legitimate some decision about which she has largely made up her mind. Here, the participation must be public and visible. Although group involvement assures visibility, she runs the risk of an undesirable outcome by employing group process. A number of options are available. She may explore the issue individually to be able to say that she has consulted the interested parties. In keeping them separate, she has strengthened her control of the process. She may have also diffused responsibility for the outcome to some degree. Or she may choose to partialize the issue as she engages in group discussion. She will deal with only some aspects of the problem and attempt to avoid its more-loaded elements. Or she may structure the group meeting to advance her desired outcome by discussing the matter with individuals prior to the meeting, so as to garner their support or to ensure that supporters will be primed to move the process in her direction. As noted earlier, spurious rather than real influence sharing raises value questions and also poses the significant risk of being found out. The point, however, is that the supervisor's clarity regarding her purposes in pursuing a participatory mode underpins her skill in promoting it.

Group Skills. For many reasons, inducing effective group participation is a more complex undertaking than consulting with individual staff. In both instances, skills in listening, communicating, confronting, and persuading are necessary, but the range of interconnections and interactions in a group compounds the supervisory task. Many supervisors find conducting unit meetings demanding, not only because of their inherent complexity, but also because their experience has largely been in work with individuals or treatment-oriented groups. Their tendency then may be to underemphasize the direction-setting function of a task group leader or in the course of the discussion to react as a participant rather than as the manager of the group's interaction. Skill in conducting staff meetings is a broader subject than our immediate concern with participation, but some aspects of skill in task group leadership are worth noting here.

Task group effectiveness depends on many factors, but three merit particular attention: clear, focused direction; a group composition that fosters competent work; and expert process assistance. It is the function of the leader—in our case, supervisor—to ensure the maintenance or enhancement of these favorable performance ingredients.

The need for a clear sense of direction and the group's engagement in the task suggest guidelines for practice. The purpose of discussing a topic at a meeting should be made explicit if it is not apparent, and the charge to ad hoc committees should be sufficiently well developed to permit focused deliberation. The importance of an issue should be underscored, particularly as it relates to the well-being and self-interest of the participants or to achieving collectively shared ends. The authority of the group to make the decision and the mode of decision making should be understood, and agenda items that do not entail decision making should, unless already clear, be labeled appropriately—for information, preliminary exploration, consultation, or the like.

Agenda items should be developed and distributed in advance of a meeting. If background material pertaining to subjects to be considered can also be distributed, participants will be more able to respond thoughtfully at the meeting. If data will be useful to solve a problem, its availability for presentation must be arranged. When an issue is controversial, the advance distribution of well-prepared material may serve two—albeit contradictory—ends. On one hand, the prepared material may sufficiently impress participants to predispose their support for an expressed position. Conversely, its distribution could also aid adversaries in marshalling their arguments or forces in advance of the meeting. In some measure, the supervisor's choice will be influenced by the agency's norms regarding advance preparation, along with the potential political consequences of flagging the material prior to the meeting.

Providing a clear sense of direction requires that the supervisor take charge of the discussion at the meeting. She does not let it wander off into irrelevancy, but rather redirects it to the problem at hand. Some wandering may be necessary for socializing and at times to reduce tension, but a too-unfocused discussion is a source of dissatisfaction and often generates a feeling that little has been accomplished. Studies of task-oriented groups indicate that participants are more likely to reach agreement or express satisfaction when (1) discussions are orderly without backward reference to previously discussed subjects; (2) matters are discussed one at a time; (3) give and take is allowed among the participants; and (4) topics are finished with dispatch (Collins and Guetzkow, 1964). The supervisor's responsibility as chairperson to achieve these results through focused leadership is apparent. At appropriate times she will need to summarize what has been said to move the discussion along, and when there is ambiguity she should rephrase a point to assure that there is shared understanding or agreement. It perhaps goes without saying that she must recognize all those who wish to speak—without favor to any point of view. This is a particularly important prescription in any instance in which she is suspected of supporting a particular position or harboring a hidden agenda.

A second ingredient in promoting the supervisor's goal for participation has to do with the group's composition. Here, the skill is in selecting who participates. One issue in this regard is size. Seven has been suggested as the optimum size for problem solving; that number permits each member to talk to every other member, whereas with more than seven, there is the tendency to direct communication centrally to the group leader. Nevertheless, the need to include a number of diverse interests may require more than seven members. In that case, the supervisor will have to decide which of these two competing conditions is most important in a particular circumstance.

We have already suggested that when some subset of unit staff are to be involved, careful assessment of the subset's composition is required. The criteria regarding staff participation are also operative regarding who among the subset of staff to include or exclude. For example, staff who by virtue of their longevity, knowledge, special capabilities, or leadership within the staff group could make a contribution to the quality of the effort would be likely candidates for inclusion.

We wish to add one other factor relating to group composition that has political overtones—the issue of whether the committee's membership is perceived as representative. Representation typically has shifting meanings among organizational members, depending on the issue in question and the range of interests within the collectivity. If the issue is benign, representation can be accomplished with minimal difficulty. When an issue is highly salient, however, or if there are disagreements within the staff concerning the issue, there is the expectation that *each* of the various interests or factions will be included or represented. Sometimes, too, interest divisions that superficially do not appear to be germane to the issue become important representational criteria for the staff. For example, if there is a controversy brewing related to a policy change, interests

such as various ethnic groups or those responsible for a particular professional function may seek representation, even though the issue does not
appear to affect the interests of that group disproportionately.

Ignoring a salient interest or one of the unit's factions might reduce the
quality of a decision. More significantly from a political perspective, it
could be damaging to the acceptance or legitimacy of the outcome.
When the supervisor has a special stake in a particular decision, she may
opt for *apparent* representation. Within any interest group or faction,
there are members with varying degrees of commitment or intensity. She
might then choose a member of a faction who is less committed to a
position that is different from hers to represent that faction. Or she may
decide to appoint a strong dissident but to add a sufficient number of
strong others so as to surround or isolate him.

The general principle is that the supervisor must assure that critical
interest groups are represented but that the total mix of players can be
expected to reach a reasonably satisfactory decision. Although this may
seem like rigging the process, it is natural for the supervisor to share
influence disproportionately with those who hold similar views. Furthermore, to constitute a decision-making group without assessing the relative
positions of the participants or anticipating the relationship between the
mix of players and the possible outcome is foolhardy from the perspective
of maximizing the supervisor's authority and influence.

A third condition of task-group effectiveness relates to the group's
process and whether it maximizes the members' potential for contributing
to problem solving. Bales (1969) makes a series of process recommendations for group leaders based on his work in analyzing group interaction.
He suggested that if possible, the leader should start the discussion of an
issue with factual material. Even if the facts are thought to be well known
to all the members, he counseled that a short review is seldom a waste of
time. The leader is advised to move next to values and opinions, or how
people feel about the facts and thus to allow sufficient time to lay the
groundwork for the final stage of soliciting specific suggestions for action.
One might add that participants should be encouraged to generate alternative solutions and to delay their evaluation until most or all of the
potential solutions are on the table. The supervisor must also prevent
deviant opinions from being too summarily dismissed without having
received thoughtful consideration.

Another function of the supervisor in guiding the process is to facilitate
the broad participation of committee or unit staff members. This entails
preventing some from dominating the discussion and encouraging the
more-reticent workers to express themselves. Both acts require sensitivity,

and in the latter instance it is important *not* to call on workers who seem to prefer to remain silent. One study is interesting in this regard. No correlation was found between the extent to which an individual talked during a meeting and his satisfaction with the group's discussion. The extent to which members *felt free* to speak was apparently the critical determinent of their satisfaction with the process (Heyns, 1969, p. 361).

Bales (1969, p. 379) admonished the chair when conducting the meeting to listen when someone else is talking and to react actively, whether her reaction is positive or negative. To some degree, being reactive provides participants with recognition. We would caution again, however, that much depends on the supervisor's purposes in regard to the particular agenda item—and to react or not depends on the issue and the extent to which it may be a loaded one. She ought to feel some responsibility, too, for directing the interaction so as to encourage her staff to communicate with one another, as well as directing their arguments primarily to her as chair. Bales also advised that good leaders make sure that their eyes are on the group as a whole when speaking, rather than on supporters or those they may be hoping to persuade. He noted, finally, that leaders should search constantly for reactions to what they are saying—and, we would add, to the reactions to other speakers as well. Much of what takes place during a participatory process occurs on a nonverbal level.

Obviously, there are no simple or inviolate rules for effectively encouraging group participation. We note, in concluding, the formulation by Hackman and Walton (1986). In the final analysis, it is the supervisor's function to monitor accurately the conditions necessary for the successful accomplishment of a task in any specific instance and then to shape her interventions accordingly.

Transitions:
Selecting, Promoting, and Terminating Staff

Personnel transitions such as the selection of new staff, promotions, and terminations pose both threats and opportunities to organizational participants. All hierarchical levels—line staff, supervisors, and top management—have a stake in shifts of personnel, and as in the case of other organizational events, the stakes vary, depending on one's location in the agency's structure.

Significant supervisory interests are involved when transitions occur or do not occur. Personnel changes represent an opportunity for the supervisor to influence the perspective or direction of her unit. They also hold potential for affecting staff morale, unit norms, and perceptions of the supervisor's competence, as well as judgments about her preferences, both within the unit and among other actors in the organization. Further, transitions may hold the potential for enhancing unit performance and engendering loyalty to the supervisor as unit leader.

Some of the common, yet sensitive, issues that transitions raise for supervisors are illustrated in the following four vignettes.

Joyce, a relatively new supervisor in a mental health clinic, has her first staff vacancy to fill. The clinic has been known for its traditional approach to practice, and many of its staff endorse pyschodynamic psychology as the singular theoretical underpinning of the clinic's work. Joyce wants to hire the most effective practitioner who can be found, and she believes that there might be some advantage in encouraging a cross-fertilization of ideas by hiring someone whose theoretical grounding differs from the clinic's current mold. Ultimately, she hires someone with a behaviorist orientation, and her action precipitates an underground of worker complaint. Although Joyce has often assured staff that she is appreciative of their skill and their approach to practice, her selection occasions speculation that her intention is to remake the clinic into a behaviorist enclave.

Joan, the administrative assistant to the supervisor of a large service unit, is an outgoing woman who enjoys warm relations with the service staff. She is often referred to as the mother hen of the unit, as she takes a personal interest in the staff. Her work, however, is shoddy; much of what she is assigned is done late, done poorly, or simply not done. Because her work concerns fiscal matters, maintenance of unit statistics, and other day-to-day details not related to the activities of the service staff, most of them are unaware of the extent of Joan's inadequate performance. The supervisor, after repeated efforts to bring Joan's work up to standard, makes the difficult decision to terminate her.

Betty directs a unit of eight practitioners assigned to a medical-surgery service in a large hospital. Following the resignation of the supervisor for a unit similar to Betty's, the position is open to applications from the social service staff. Several apply, including three of Betty's staff. Two of these applicants are considered by their peers to be well qualified for the position. The third is clearly a much less effective worker, but one who has managed nevertheless to impress those in authority in the hospital. Betty is consulted in the selection process and recommends either of the two more competent workers. When the controversial worker is chosen, Betty's staff react bitterly, cite agency politics, and question her possible role in the decision.

Trudy, the supervisor of a service unit in a large public welfare agency, is a well-respected old-timer in the agency. One member of her staff of seven is significantly less effective than the others. The worker handles cases involving acute emotional issues poorly; he is also unreliable in his work patterns and frequently absent. After attempting to improve his performance through close supervision and essentially failing at the effort, Trudy then seeks a consultation with her superior regarding the possibility of termination. The superior indicates that he will back Trudy if she is committed to firing the worker, but he reminds her how difficult such actions are in light of the agency's union contract. Furthermore, since the worker is a minority group member who has intimated that he has been subject to discriminatory treatment, there is the possibility that the agency will face the strain of a civil rights appeal. Following that consultation, the supervisor tends to ignore the worker's shortcomings, reassigning difficult cases to other staff. Although they like the ineffective worker personally, the staff has come to feel increasingly resentful that their supervisor appears to favor him and that more work is required of them as a result.

Each of the vignettes illustrates a different event, yet each of them holds important meanings for the participants, coloring the character of working relations within the agencies. For example, the staff perceived the hiring of the behaviorist as auguring a new direction, a threat to their traditional mode of practice. Firing the popular administrative assistant generated a concern that the supervisor was too hard-nosed, unmoved by that worker's warmth and caring, and therefore that she might be unconcerned if any of them were similarly in trouble. On the other hand, not firing the inadequate worker in the public welfare agency negatively influenced group performance norms, because in lightening the worker's load, the supervisor had rewarded lesser competence.

In each of these cases, the supervisor might have made an alternative choice. But the alternative choices would have had as important consequences for staff morale and staff evaluation of the supervisor and the unit's functioning as the ones that were made. Because of their complexity and importance, transition decisions require special sensitivity and thoughtfulness.

Key Factors in Transitions

The Symbolic Significance of Transitions

Truth is more likely to be found in deed than in word. How people behave, more than what they say, best reflects what they think and feel. Although inferences and interpretations may be drawn from words alone, inferences that stem from behavior are ordinarily deemed more reliable.

Nowhere is this more the case than in organizational life. Because organizations are composed of people with varying interests, they serve as arenas for attempts to influence perceptions that support one or another of these interests. And to the extent that there is distance between the participants, as is usually the case with hierarchically differentiated participants, trust between them is frequently attenuated. Thus even in organizations in which relations between staff and administration are positive, there is often skepticism on the part of the staff regarding an executive's statements. They may believe that he has taken a position to encourage worker response rather than as a simple assertion of what he believes. These assertions notwithstanding, the staff tend to assess executive commitments more by their observations of executive behavior and organizational events than by pronouncements.

With respect to personnel policy, therefore, the handling of hirings, promotions, terminations, transfers, and the like tends to constitute the "truth" of administrative intent. This phenomenon is so reliable that even when there has been consistent evidence of a favorable personnel policy, a single personnel action that can be interpreted as inconsistent with that policy is frequently read by the staff as indicating an unfavorable straw in the wind. For example, in an organization in which there has been a clear tradition of seeking qualified candidates for openings from within the agency, when a supervisory opening is filled with an outsider, the staff may well react with concern, experiencing the event as one in which promotional opportunities for which they would once have been considered will be closed to them in the future.

A similar issue is evident in one of our vignettes. Even though the entire staff of the mental health clinic held similar practice views, hiring one "deviant" professional was defined as reflecting the supervisor's intention to create a behaviorist enclave in the agency. The fact that Joyce had frequently articulated her satisfaction with the staff's work—and had no quarrel with their traditional orientation—was ignored in that single hiring decision.

In short, personnel transitions have important symbolic meanings for staff members. It is thus important to assess the range of possible messages the staff may hear as they witness personnel transitions that occur or do not occur about them. The primary message that is connoted by personnel actions concerns the system by which rewards and sanctions are distributed. Promotions, naturally, are considered to be a form of reward. When promotions go to those who are especially competent, the message suggests that competence will be rewarded—at least by those who perceive the promoted worker's competence. When promotions go to those about whom there is a more controversial view, the message with respect to the distributive system may be mixed, and the impact on staff morale is more problematic. Thus in the case of Betty's agency, the message suggested to her staff the precedence of agency politics in promotions.

The same dynamic occurs with respect to terminations. Terminations always provoke mixed reactions on the part of a staff. However justified the staff may believe a termination is, there may be some edge of discomfort stemming from their identification with the *role* of staff member. Because of this identification, they are likely to feel the terminated worker's pain more intensely than less-identified participants. Nevertheless, when clearly incompetent or inadequate staff members are dismissed, the predisposition of the staff is to assess the dismissal as fair, and they experience it as less threatening to their own welfare. The message that ineffectiveness cannot be tolerated will have been sent and received.

Just as transitions that *do* occur send messages, those that *do not* occur constitute a statement. This is suggested in the example of the worker who was unable to carry his share of the work in the unit and caused resentment among staff who had to take on extra work to compensate for his limitations. The fact that he was kept in the position was subject to a number of interpretations—that incompetence or irresponsibility was acceptible, that someone who was likeable or a minority group member could cut corners, or that friends of the supervisor manage to get a free ride. Obviously, none is a message that one would want to transmit. How the supervisor can influence the message so that a transition is defined by staff as closely as possible to the definition the supervisor prefers is the practice task.

The Political Ramifications of Transitions

Thompson (1967) and others have suggested that a primary dynamic of organizational life is the effort to reduce unpredictability. These authors note that beyond a point, uncertainty for organizational participants creates discomfort or stress. Transitions, of course, heighten uncertainty; when a colleague leaves a unit, what the effect will be on his fellow workers or on the conduct of their own daily activities is unknown, as is the impact on them of his replacement. For this and other reasons, staff transitions signal a degree of uncertainty that can be disquieting and may, depending on the circumstances, considerably heighten staff anxiety.

The degree to which transitions are unsettling is affected by their political implications for key actors. For line staff, the departure of one worker and the potential arrival of another can be important with respect to alliances and subgroup membership. This is of more or less significance, depending on the extent to which the unit has formed identifiable alliances or informal cliques. In the extreme case it can cause a major struggle over the attempt to influence the stripe of the new people who are selected and, once they join the organization, their recruitment into respective subgroups. But even in less-extreme instances, worker departures and arrivals have implications for patterns of cooperation, conflict, affiliation, and informal association among staff—and may have the further consequence of increasing or decreasing the power of one subgroup over another to shape organizational events.

Transitions also have political ramifications for hierarchichal relationships. This issue is perhaps most aptly embodied in the frequently expressed supervisory preference for hiring her own staff over inheriting staff from her predecessor. A newly hired worker is selected *by the supervisor* for the position, and as a result the worker may be expected to feel some indebtedness to her. In contrast to the inherited worker, the newcomer is dependent on the supervisor, at least initially, for the direction, information, and approval associated with being defined as successful on the job. Anxious to begin the position effectively and to impress the supervisor positively, the new worker tries to establish a relationship with the supervisor that demonstrates capability and respect. Put in social exchange terms, the indebtedness and dependency that characterize the initial relationship can be expected to forge a degree of commitment and loyalty to the supervisor that under other circumstances evolves only with considerable time and effort.

This dynamic may also have implications for the subgroup politics that were noted earlier. To the extent that relations with the supervisor or the desire for her support is an issue between subgroups, transitions in which the supervisor selects personnel to replace members of various subgroups can be expected to rearrange alliances over time in the favor of the supervisor. More significantly, under circumstances in which subgroup concerns relate to substantive policies or practices in which the supervisor has personal or professional stakes, line staff turnover can build consensus in the direction of the views held by the supervisor.

Faced with uncertainty, people act in ways to try to reduce it. When the uncertainty carries political overtones, the attempt to reduce it acquires particular urgency. One of the predictable responses to transitions in organizations is an increase in the likelihood of political behavior, that is, the effort to reduce uncertainty by maneuvering to control or influence possible outcomes. Staff members, either directly or covertly, act to prevent the change in personnel or to influence the choice of the replacement.

As suggested in Chapter 1, the organization's structure influences the extent to which political activity becomes rife. The more open the organization's system and the more decentralized its decision-making pattern, the more intense the political behavior is likely to be. But the proposition that transitions can be expected to trigger acts designed to increase influence or to win arguments, no matter what the character of the setting, is next to incontestable. When actors do not perceive their interests to be uniform, the transitional event will alert them to the possibility of pending threats and opportunities, and they will act in ways that they perceive to be in their interest.

The Process of Organizational Renewal

A final factor underscoring the significance of transitions has to do with personnel shifts as a primary means of change and renewal within a formal organization. Retirements, hirings, and promotions represent opportunities for organizational caretakers to "bring in new blood"—to reshape the organization in directions they consider to be desirable. Once we appreciate the significance of this process for an organization's vitality, it becomes clear why transitions are considered so important—or, at least, *should* be considered so important—by the organizational participants.

This renewal process is frequently not one that administrators or supervisors can influence at will. Within most human services organizations a set of constraints prevent managers from altering the mix of staff as they might ideally wish. Union contracts, personnel systems such as civil service, the tenure system, and protective legislation such as those precluding mandatory retirement before a specified age are all illustrations of such barriers. The extent to which such impediments to the renewal process are operative at any given time enhances the potential significance for an administrator of a particular transition opportunity when it does occur.

Supervisory Practice with Limited Control

Although a supervisor's stake in a transition decision is considerable, supervisors often have less than full control over the decision. In many organizations, the responsibility for the staffing of the unit is not delegated to the supervisor—because an executive chooses to maintain control, or the supervisor's level in the hierarchy is deemed too low to permit her such freedom of action, or she is new to the organization and not sufficiently trusted, or some similar reason. Under these circumstances, the supervisor is usually asked to make a recommendation, and the superior makes the final decision. In other instances the decision is defined as a shared one, to be made jointly by the supervisor and her superior, with the latter exerting varying degress of influence in the actual choice. But even when formal authority is delegated to the supervisor, there may be conditions that preclude full control. One example is when the supervisor has ultimate responsibility but the executive has a clear preference for a particular candidate or for a specific course of action. This was the case with the superior in the fourth vignette, who agreed to support Trudy's termination of an inadequate employee but who, in pointing out numerous problems the termination would entail, was in fact suggesting against the action.

When a supervisor has limited influence but significant interests are at issue, she may find herself in a bind. In transitions, as in other organizational events, she must face in two directions, assessing her interventions as they relate to both higher- and lower-ranking participants. Two major practice tasks are involved under conditions of limited leverage. With superiors, she must explore the means to increase her influence to affect the decision. With staff, her only recourse may be damage control.

Influence Enhancement

Increasing one's influence to affect a transition decision is an obvious option, but it is frequently overlooked nonetheless. Because the circumstances that limit a supervisor's control of the decision are typically associated with the perceived preferences of the boss, supervisors sometimes feel apprehension about offending him. The supervisor also may not attempt to extend her influence because of her assumption, stemming from past experience or observation of the failed efforts of others, that her chances of success are low.

Indeed, costs *are* sometimes associated with failed attempts to extend one's role in an organizational transaction that is seen as the prerogative of others. Executives may feel that the supervisor is exceeding her authority. Others may perceive her as making an incursion on their turf. Usually, however, skillful assessment of the prospect for an extended role and artful exploration with critical actors of the issues related to the transaction not only result in the supervisor's being better informed about the issues, but can be accomplished without too great an expense. If initial exploration suggests that it may be possible to influence the transaction, then appropriate action may be taken. If the exploration suggests that this option is unavailable, then useful information has been obtained at a modest cost. In either case, the exploration has been worth the effort. This is so not only because the supervisor may be successful in the current instance, but, as we have said, influence is developmental and the effectiveness of any influence attempts in the future is at least partially determined by what has occurred in the past. If, for example, the supervisor has not previously been involved in staffing the unit or some similar decision and is now included, it becomes more likely that she will be involved in such decisions in the future. Even the mere registering of interest to an executive may predispose him to consider including her the next time a similar decision is made.

Practice activities effective in extending one's influence with superiors (and peers) are detailed in the following three chapters. It may be well, however, to mention one of the principles that guides the practice here. Its premise is that although actors tend to operate out of many motives, high among them is organizational self-interest. For the supervisor to persuade the decision maker to agree with her recommendation requires that she frame her position so that it conforms to his interests. These interests may be instrumental (e.g., to move the organization in a particular direction) or they may be affective (to garner the approval of other participants).

Unless the supervisor is already aware of a decision maker's interests, framing her arguments in that context requires initial exploration of what her superior perceives his interests to be. Complicating her intervention is the fact that professional and social agency norms dictate that decisions should not be made on the basis of actor self-interest but on the basis of organizational goals and client needs. Skill is entailed, then, in making her case responsive to what has been assessed as the actor's interests but not to define them as such. Rather, her arguments must be presented in terms of approved professional and agency norms.

In seeking to influence agency decision making, the supervisor must maintain perspective. For one thing, she must not press harder than a specific issue calls for. Intense reactions to relatively unimportant matters are suspect, and she will risk being seen as controlling, someone for whom power is its own reward, rather than as the means to a desired end. She must also consider how frequently to engage in influence attempts, because being indiscriminate in attempting to "fix" every political situation will reduce her effectiveness in specific, and sometimes more important, instances. Her decision to intervene and how strongly to do so must depend, in short, on the importance of the particular transition issue.

However skillfully the supervisor may proceed, she may be unable to achieve the desired outcome—at the beginning of the chapter an unpopular internal candidate was selected for promotion after consultation with Betty, the supervisor. The import of the action for Betty transcends the fact that someone whom she did not deem capable was elevated to a position of responsibility in the agency. Her staff, aware that organizational protocol required that she be consulted, assumed that she might well have been supportive of the decision. Similar scenarios could be constructed for any of the range of transitions that might have bearing on a supervisor's sphere of activity. In each instance, the supervisor must then assess the consequences of her lack of success.

There are two potentially major consequences when a supervisor does not prevail. The first can be characterized as a lost opportunity, in which some desirable outcome would have followed or some undesirable one avoided if she had been successful. Losing the best candidate for a position or the inability to rearrange the staff mix in preferred ways are examples.

Apart from being alert to other opportunities as they arise, there is little that the supervisor can do in such an instance. Taking the loss in her stride and moving forward to other concerns is ordinarily the wisest course. If she feels resentment toward the decision maker for her failure to convince him, it is well that she does not let her resentment show. Lamenting her failure or preparing to engage in a round of the tempting, but self-defeating game of "I told you so" engender the irritation of upper-ranking personnel, reinforce impressions of powerlessness with subordinates, and raise questions about her professionalism.

The second problematic aspect of an outcome contrary to her preference is the supervisor's image or reputation with her staff and its consequent effect on unit morale. The supervisor who has "lost" on an issue of some moment to her staff is in a no-win situation. On the one hand, she may be perceived as lacking influence with her boss. As noted earlier, a supervisor who is perceived by her staff as influential with higher-ups is more able to gain the staff's compliance with her wishes. On the other hand, she may be viewed by her staff as complicit in an unpopular decision, even though she in fact took an opposing position.

Lest the situation appear overly bleak, however, it is worth noting that there is leeway in individual instances. It is only when the supervisor is overruled by upper-ranking personnel with some frequency or there are a series of unpopular positions for which she is thought to be responsible that there are negative long-range consequences for her reputation with her staff. Nevertheless, when significant staff interests are at stake and the supervisor is unable to affect the transition decision, she must consider repairing potential damage to morale or correcting the possible negative attributions that the staff may make regarding her role in the transaction.

Damage Control

There are three practice questions to consider in attempting to repair the potential damage caused by an unpopular transitional event: (1) whether to explain one's part in the transaction or to defend the decision, (2) whether to be direct or indirect in dealing with the matter, and (3) whether to engage the subject in public or in private. Although we discuss them here in the context of transitions, questions such as these are also applicable whenever upper-level administrators make an unpopular decision against a supervisor's advice.

The supervisor who explains herself to her staff may sound defensive—and in explaining, may also make the matter appear to be more important than it is. A supervisor who is self-aware relates to her staff's needs rather than her own need to explain; only when she has evidence of aroused feelings on their part are explanations in order. Even then, they entail a number of risks. One of the ways in which people who are uncertain about trusting another person come to a judgment about the person's trustworthiness is to observe how authentically he or she deals with others or refers to them in their absence. One risk, then, is that in violating the organizational norm that supervisors should support management decisions, she may be viewed by staff as disloyal to her boss—and therefore capable of being disloyal to them. A second risk of the "I fought against this decision but was overruled" argument is that it may underscore her lack of influence in the agency. Finally—and not the least of the risks—is the danger that her expression of disapproval to her staff regarding the executive's decision will be reported to him and result in some strain in their relations. The risk is somewhat mitigated if she has made her objections clear to him during the decision-making process, because she cannot then be criticized for double dealing. Better still, if the circumstances are right, she might find a way to suggest to her boss that it would be useful for her to share their respective positions with the staff.

Encouraging the staff's acceptance of the transition decision requires sensitivity as well. If the supervisor believes that the argument at her disposal is a weak one, she would do best to avoid the subject altogether. Nor should she simply assert that organizational life requires that managerial decisions be accepted and incorporated (although the assertion may be true), because she might thereby appear to be trivializing staff concerns or serving as management's mouthpiece. Perhaps the best that she can say is that, hopefully, the consequences of the decision will turn out to be less negative than now appears or that there is additional information which casts a somewhat different light on the action that was taken. The termination of Joan, the administrative assistant who was the staff's mother hen, is an example of the latter instance, for the supervisor informally made Joan's inadequate performance known to other staff members.

Generally speaking, the supervisor explains herself, defends the decision, or avoids the topic altogether because of two factors. One is the meaning superiors and staff members ascribe to the event, how strongly they feel about it, and her own assessment of its consequences. The second has to do with her relationship with the respective parties, including the extent to which she is perceived as responsible for the decision and the effect of that perception on her relationship with her staff.

How the supervisor engages the matter, whether directly or indirectly, is also a key practice issue. One advantage of direct reference to an unpopular transitional event is that the supervisor can be relatively sure that the message is delivered accurately and fully. Direct reference also encourages a staff member's feedback, thus furthering the give-and-take inherent in the expression of feeling and with it perhaps some diminution of tension. A major disadvantage of direct reference lies in its explicit nature. To the extent that the supervisor's statements might be unpopular with audiences outside the unit (e.g., her boss), a direct and quotable assertion of her views increases her external vulnerability.

The advantages and disadvantages reverse if one chooses an indirect reference instead. It is possible to imply a position regarding an issue without actually articulating it, but then the clear communication of the message is not assured, and her remarks are limited to a passing reference. For example, a supervisor who opposed an unpopular appointment might comment to a worker who referred to the action negatively, "Well, for better or worse, Bill (the executive) makes these decisions." Although not stating her opposition to the appointment, she uses ambiguity to imply her reaction and to distance herself from the decision. Indirectness allows one both to send a message without having directly done so and to move past the issue without actually engaging it.

An ambiguous comment permits the supervisor to justly deny her disloyalty. Even with the aid of ambiguity, however, the supervisor must ensure that if she is confronted by the boss regarding her statements to her staff, she can maintain her credibility. When ambiguity is used—and it should be used judiciously—it is well for her to take responsibility for having been unclear, rather than totally denying that she had revealed her disagreement or claiming simply that she was misunderstood. Let us assume, for example, that a supervisor opposed a transitional decision and in passing, implied as much to her staff. Further, assume that her boss heard about it and questioned her. Although it would be technically accurate for her to deny that she told her staff that she did not support his decision, it might be wiser to take a *degree* of accountability for the misunderstanding. Something like the following might increase her credibility: "No, I didn't tell staff how I felt about the matter. As a matter of fact, since I had such strong feelings about it, I made a conscious effort not to do so. In view of how I felt, however, it is possible that I communicated some of that sentiment. If so, I'm sorry." Using ambiguity in this way, the supervisor can, on occasion, successfully walk the tightrope of maintaining commitments to disaffected parties while, at the same time, not directly taking positions that would be offensive to either party.

The context or setting in which the supervisor discusses a transitional event with staff—either privately with one worker or publicly with some subgroup of workers or the entire staff—also influences the outcome. Public communications, by their nature, are more a matter of record than are discussions between individuals. If the supervisor wants her comments to be held in confidence, she will avoid the group setting, because in all but the most intimate and tightly structured groups, confidentiality cannot be assured. In part, this is because groups do not provide the same degree of relational intimacy that are possible in one-to-one encounters. In part, too, it is a function of the difficulty of determining accountability. When we share a confidence with another and discover that our secret is out, we know who is responsible for the breach and can act accordingly. But when a secret that was shared with a group of people becomes known, we have no way of fixing responsibility for the transgression. In instrumental terms, because there is no way to be certain who breaks a group confidence, the temptation to break the confidence—at least for those with cause—is significantly heightened. When confidentiality is important to the supervisor, therefore, she will avoid sharing her message in a public encounter, or she will shape the communication accordingly—either by omitting some elements of the message or by using ambiguity as a cover.

Employing private means for communicating information to the staff offers several advantages. There are occasions when norms proscribe a supervisor's sharing a matter with her staff, but she nevertheless wants to spread the word. It could be viewed as improper, for example, for a supervisor to discuss the inadequacies of a terminated worker, although the staff's knowledge of the worker's inadequacies may be important to their understanding of the situation. She might then choose to tell someone whom she expects will report the conversation to others.

She may choose a private communication to distance herself from the message for other reasons. If she is uncertain about the extent to which her staff is troubled about the transition decision, she may not want to appear overly concerned about it. Or she may wish, for other reasons, to make less of the matter than its confrontation in a public arena would entail. If, nevertheless, she wants her staff to know how she feels, a private session with a talkative staff member will probably do the trick.

Finally, if she perceives potential vulnerability for herself in expressing a position, she will need distance to avoid being held accountable for the message. In such a case, she might select someone to be the bearer of the message whom she can trust to honor her need for confidentiality. If her confidant has credibility with her staff, the message is strengthened by virtue of its association with a respected messenger.

Consider, for example, the situation cited at the beginning of this chapter. An unpopular staff member was promoted into a coveted position, and the remaining staff members were resentful that the supervisor seemed not to have tried to block the action. The supervisor believed that the executive would be perturbed if she were not publicly supportive of his action, and she decided to discuss the matter off the record with a member of the unit staff who had been helpful to her in the past. "Several of the staff are upset because they think you went along with the decision," the staff member confides. The supervisor indicates that, in point of fact, she fought actively against the unpopular selection, but she doesn't believe it would be wise for her to discuss it with staff. If her relations with the worker are close, she might ask him if he could find a way to inform staff. If she is uncertain whether he would be comfortable acting as a messenger, she might ask if he thinks the issue is important enough for her to try to leak the information to staff. In asking the question, the supervisor is implicitly requesting him to pass the word along. The worker can thus refuse without embarrassment to either of them. He may with good grace indicate that it is not critical to get the word out, or he may volunteer to let the staff know the supervisor's position. In the latter instance, both will then plan the most effective way to communicate the information without undue jeopardy to her relations with the executive.

Political communications of this sort are themselves risky. One must make accurate judgments regarding the loyalty and skill of the actors, as well as the fit between message, audience, and mode of delivery. It is also important to be prudent in using interventions such as these. If one develops the reputation for using or manipulating others, the effectiveness of future interactions are likely to be compromised. More importantly, if the supervisor's credibility in the organization suffers, any advantage gained by a successful political maneuver will be outweighed by that loss.

Selection, Promotion, and Termination

Because transitions hold meanings for organizational participants that transcend the specific transitional event, many similar practice issues arise in all such events. The steps in the process, the criteria for the decision, and the methods for sharing information with staff members must be considered, whether the event is a hiring, promotion, or firing. But there are also unique concerns that emerge with each. As we discuss the three categories of transition below, we emphasize the unique aspects of each. Those aspects common to all three types of transition are identified in context and thereafter are referred to only in passing, although in fact they may be relevant to all three.

Staff Selection

The supervisory effort required to ensure hiring an able worker at the outset is considerably less than the effort entailed in improving a marginal worker's performance through supervision and training. This fact alone underscores the importance of rigorous supervisory attention to the selection process.

Obviously enough, then, selection of staff personnel should receive prime attention. Nevertheless, at least two factors mitigate against the investment of sufficient time and care. One is the crisis nature of much hiring. The job must be filled quickly, because as long as it remains vacant, other staff members are burdened by additional work and some service or program may not be offered until the vacancy has been filled. A particularly dramatic example of this occurs when a time-limited project is approved or a grant is received shortly before the project is scheduled to begin, and a rush is on to fill a position. Whenever possible, vacancies must be anticipated, and even in the case of a new project, one can take all or many of the necessary steps, short of actual hiring, so that the program is ready to go when approval is received.

The second factor mitigating against careful hiring is psychological in nature. Often the supervisor so *wants* to find the right person that she overlooks or underplays the candidate's deficits and moves to closure prematurely. This happens particularly when the position is a difficult one to fill or when the supervisor finds the candidate's personal qualities or his ideological stance attractive. The latter is not to say that liking a potential worker is not relevant as a criterion for a supervisor's choice—indeed, in our subsequent discussion of promotions, we suggest that she has a right to like the people with whom she must work closely. The point, rather, is that the stake in filling a position effectively moves some supervisors to positive reactions with insufficient data. It is only as they recognize this that they can guard against it.

It might be noted parenthetically that another predisposition to watch for is overvaluing the candidate who appears to most resemble herself.

Studies of the accuracy of performance ratings, for example, indicate that the similarity of the rater and rated characteristics affects the favorability of the evaluation (Borman, 1974). Overvaluing—or even more so, undervaluing a candidate—is particularly problematic when the candidate is from a different race, ethnic group, or gender. It is incumbent on the supervisor in such a case to search her attitudes and when possible to seek the counsel of others to check her own reactions to the candidate.

Success or failure in selecting appropriate staff personnel takes place within the context of labor market conditions. If some particular expertise or some required combination of abilities is in short supply, compromises must be made. Assume, for example, that a position calls for both knowledge of the health care system and skill in training paraprofessionals and that these characteristics cannot be found in a single person. The supervisor and agency must decide which is more important, a decision that can have a considerable impact on the shape of the service. Much may depend on judgments regarding what knowledge and skill can or cannot be learned on the job or whether the lack of particular expertise can be compensated for by an applicant's other qualities. It is not unusual, nor should it be, for positions to be modified to reflect the skills of desired candidates.

Before embarking on a formal search, it may be useful for the supervisor to review unit goals and reflect on the fit between the expectations for unit achievements, on the one hand, and the current pattern of staff strength and weakness, on the other. A vacant position allows the supervisor to rearrange staff responsibilities and create a different job design for the vacant position that can extend the quality or breadth of staff capability, rather than simply duplicating it. Take, for example, a child welfare agency that offers protective and preventive services in which the caseload increasingly reflects a higher percentage of homeless families. In addition to its traditional services, its homeless clients require a staff with expertise in specific entitlement issues, housing resource development, special networking, and the like. In the past these cases were distributed evenly among all staff members, but with the advent of a vacant line, the supervisor has the opportunity of hiring a staff member with particular experience in work with homeless people. Such a change in the pattern of staff responsibility allows the supervisor to make the line more specialized and acquire a new area of service capability.

More formally, the supervisor is sometimes well advised to review or develop a job description that details the responsibilities and tasks of the position. Often, when a vacancy occurs an old description of the position is drawn from the files and dusted off for use. A formal obligation may thus have been met, but little else has been achieved. At the least, assuming the competence of the worker who is leaving, an exit conference should be held in which the supervisor reviews the current accuracy of the job description with him in order to update it.

There are at least three advantages to using an accurate and detailed job description and one disadvantage as well. In a hiring process, the chance of a desirable outcome is advanced when both parties to the transaction, supervisor and candidate, have a choice. Many applicants will not accept a position they believe they cannot fill successfully or will not find satisfaction in holding. Because the applicant is more aware than the supervisor of his strengths and weaknesses, likes and dislikes, the more he knows about a position he is offered, the more likely he will be to choose it on valid grounds.

A further advantage of a clear job description is that it is suggestive of the inventory of skills that qualified candidates should possess to merit serious consideration. In addition to carefully specifying for herself the practice competences that are desireable, it is well for the supervisor to have delineated the values, attitudes, service perspectives, and elements of personality that she feels are important for the maximum performance of the position. If these have been specified, her search is likely to be more sharply focused.

Finally, the job description may serve a serendipitous benefit—it forces the supervisor to devote attention to the details of the job. With the occurrence of a vacancy, there is an opportunity to take stock—to review which aspects of the position have been emphasized and which perhaps neglected, so that the mix can be modified or gaps in service revealed. A job description—as well as other facets of the hiring process—is significant for socializing whoever is employed to the agency, and can be used to encourage a fresh start.

The disadvantage of a detailed job description lies in the boundaries it places on the position. As conditions change, it may become less applicable to current circumstances, and bureaucratically oriented staff may use it to limit their efforts, eschew flexibility, or as a flashpoint for complaint. To some degree, if the description includes general and open-ended phrases, this danger is reduced.

A sufficient pool of applicants is a necessary, if insufficient, condition for finding the most appropriate candidate. A key to effective recruitment is the use of multiple sources. Word of mouth, particularly requests for referrals from agency staff and other colleagues, is only one—though perhaps the most usual—means. Others include letters to professional associations, organizations that might be in touch with qualified workers, ethnic and community groups, schools of social work, and specialized training programs. Advertisements in newspapers and professional publications are often required if the agency has affirmative action procedures in place, but even when not required, advertising is often useful. Depending on labor market conditions, it may produce a glut of applications and curiously enough, is sometimes avoided for just that reason. The inundation of resumes generates uncertainty, for the supervisor must decide on whom to follow up and whom to reject, often on slim grounds. Even then, she is often left with large numbers of people to see, and she may wish to avoid the time and tedium of extensive interviewing.

Nevertheless, it is a mistake not to cast the widest net possible to capture a diverse pool of candidates. The supervisor's willingness to do so has the added and not insignificant political advantage of lending an aura of openness to the recruitment effort. It will enhance the perception that her final choice—whether an insider, someone in a network that is closely identified with the agency, or someone from afar—was selected only after an exhaustive search.

Careful perusal of candidates' resumes serves as a device for screening a potential abundance of candidates, but it is also used as preparation for an interview—to develop questions and areas to probe in advance of the supervisor's meeting with the candidate. Her need to review key elements related to the job such as the relevance of his experience and the adequacy of his training is obvious enough. But a close reading of the resume may reveal more about a candidate than was intended, sometimes as much by what is omitted as by what is included. In part, a person's interests, values, and attitudes may be gleaned from what he has included or omitted regarding his activities or the organizations to which he belongs. Once that is said, a caution should be added. Social workers, trained to make inferences about people's behavior, need to curb any tendency to overinterpret what they find in a resume—at least until an interview has provided supporting data.

The interview is central to the selection process—although it must be added that there is question about whether enough is learned in an interview to ensure an effective choice. Some applicants are "interviewgenic," able to put their best foot forward, whereas others, because of anxiety or other reasons, are less effective in selling themselves. It helps to have more than one interviewer present. When two or three people meet with a candidate, more in-depth exploration is likely to take place, because the comments or questions of one interviewer can build on those of the other. There are advantages, as a matter of fact, in involving the staff in the selection process, as long as it is clear that the decision ultimately rests with the supervisor. Staff members are often effective in identifying requisite skills, as well as in designing activities to measure them. Intimately familiar with the day-to-day service issues that face the unit, they may frequently be quite sharp in assessing the relative strengths of various candidates. There is, in addition, a secondary gain in involving the staff. Staff collaboration in selecting the worker may help strengthen cooperative linkages within the staff unit, as well as significantly ease the process of entry for the newcomer.

The prime function of the interview is to *measure* the applicant's knowledge and skill and only secondarily to gain a sense of his persona. Although the interview itself cannot measure his competencies with assurance, considerable relevant data can be gleaned from a well-thought-out discussion. If the supervisor counts solely on her "people assessment" skills during the interview, as considerable as these skills may be, she is likely to have a less productive interchange than might otherwise be the case. The more specifically the tasks of the position have been delineated and the less ambiguity about its demands, the greater the likely relevance of the information the interviewer will receive and the more likely that her judgments about the candidate will be accurate as well. In addition to the value of specifying job definitions in hiring, the research clearly shows that the accuracy of performance appraisals is enhanced by job specificity (Kane and Lawler, 1979).

A combination of direct and open-ended questions in interviewing is helpful—direct questions to focus on areas of particular interest to the supervisor and open-ended questions to give the candidate an opportunity to expand on his attributes, such as the following: What parts of your previous job did you do best and least well? What parts did you like best? Least? What parts did you find challenging? Boring? What in this position do you find most, least interesting? From what you may have heard about the agency, what would you most look forward to, most wish to avoid? (Dowling and Sayles, 1978; Radde, 1981)

Probes that more directly disclose the candidate's practice competence are very important. One means is to select cases reflecting a relevant practice problem and inquire how the candidate would approach the case. Another is to ask the candidate to talk about cases from his past work—perhaps his shining moments and/or work about which he is less than proud. A simulation or role play with respect to a practice issue is a further tool for assessing skill. Written material (articles, case records) and tapes may sometimes be requested and reviewed, and even observation of the candidate in action can be arranged. The appropriateness of such direct mechanisms for assessing competence vary with the social context of the selection process such as the norms of the agency. But it should be noted that rigorous assessment procedures may well screen out less-able or motivated applicants who are unwilling to engage in a demanding selection process. Interestingly, those who do participate and are successful frequently express enthusiasm about the process and a positive predisposition toward the agency. Perhaps it is not unlike recruitment rituals in a fraternity; the candidate feels ebullient about his accomplishment in having passed the organization's demanding entry requirements.

A final step prior to the hiring decision is to check the candidate's references. A supervisor must respect an applicant's request that she not contact his current employer, but at a point of serious interest, he must of course free her to do so. She will, furthermore, often use not only the names submitted by the applicant, but potential references that she or other agency staff know, though except in rare cases, she should again request his permission. Named references often write puff pieces that are of limited value. But if one reads between the lines, references sometimes contain indirect or subtle criticism of the candidate that might be important to know. One technique that is used to refer to negative without calling attention to it is to frame the negative in developmental terms; that is, to indicate that problems in performance have improved or that the candidate has continued to learn. Telephone inquiries—in which respondents need not commit their evaluations to writing—are ordinarily more reliable than written references. As one author has suggested, "A skilled telephone interviewer who knows how to use silence or "uh-huh" replies [can] lure a person into being candid" (Carney, 1984, p. 66).

It should go without saying that in a field in which sensitivity to others is highly valued, supervisors should respond empathetically to the tensions that applicants bring to a hiring process. One manifestation of that sensitivity is to let the candidate know where he stands in the process, to inform him if there are to be delays in making a decision, and to notify him promptly if he has been rejected. Perhaps it is unnecessary to point out what is essentially a courtesy. But as many who have applied for jobs can attest, such courtesy is less universally practiced than one might wish.

Promotion

Substantive and political factors interact in all transition decisions, but in none do they interact with more consistency than in the case of promotions. Some combination of rationality and political behavior occurs whether a promotion takes place within a unit or entails a unit member from some other department of the organization. Both substantive and political issues must be considered in the way in which the opening for a promotion is announced within the agency, how the final decision is interpreted to unit staff, and the means by which the supervisor deals with exceptions to pursuing a rational process. We deal with each of these aspects of promotion in turn.

Promotion Outside the Unit. Promotions to positions outside the supervisor's unit raise more complex concerns for the supervisor than those that occur within the unit. Assuming the criterion for promotion is superior competence, the promotion constitutes a loss for the unit and the supervisor. Although it is unlikely that such a promotional decision is the supervisor's to make, she will undoubtedly be consulted and her observations regarding the candidate given weight in the determination. Is it essentially the case, then, that an external promotion is inevitably a net loss, depleting the unit of one of its most able staff? Not necessarily.

The negative effect of the void may, in part at least, be balanced by some positive consequences. For one thing, flexibility can be increased with the departure. Competent staff, especially those with seniority or a highly developed specialization, are often in a position to select choice assignments or to dominate specialized tasks, inadvertently blocking other staff members from developing their own capabilities. The departure permits the supervisor to redistribute assignments, thus rewarding other members of the unit. Two other benefits may also ensue, depending on the situation and the supervisor's political skill. One has to do with her relations with the promoted worker, the other with her relations with superiors or important other colleagues.

More than likely, the promoted worker's relationship with the supervisor will have been positive. As the worker leaves the unit, he therefore constitutes a potential resource for the supervisor in extending her network of colleagues who are predisposed to cooperate with her future influence attempts. It is only necessary that the transition be managed in such a way as to ensure the continuance of close personal ties or to maximize the potential for obligation.

The conflicting feelings associated with endings apply to both the departing worker and the supervisor. However irrational, the promoted staff member may feel guilty about leaving and perhaps experience some resentment toward the supervisor stemming from his guilt. On the supervisor's part, however much she may have been responsible for the promotion or pleased that it has taken place, she may feel deserted, upset with the worker for leaving the unit. Both may also experience some anxiety that, because their need for one another is no longer immediate, the relationship will diminish. And if the promoted worker is to become a peer supervisor in another unit, an edge of competitiveness may arise as well. At the least, it should be expected that some initial ambivalence will exist for both of them.

Our speculations may not apply in a particular circumstance, but it is important for the supervisor to be aware of mixed feelings if she has them—for the sake of her ongoing relationship with the worker, if not for the instrumental purpose of extending her influence within the organization. In regard to the latter, she should ensure that the worker knows the role she played to help in his advancement. If it is appropriate to their relationship and agency circumstances, she may—before the promotion decision is made—keep him informed privately of what she knows, how it is going, and, perhaps, that she has discussed the promotion with the decision maker. (She ordinarily need not specify the latter conversation, unless directly asked. Because the worker *was* promoted, it is a fair assumption that she expressed positive judgments). It is important, however, that the worker does not feel that the supervisor is consciously emphasizing or embellishing her role in the selection process. For favors to be obligating, obligations must not be underlined. If they are, the worker's feelings of indebtedness may well diminish, or worse, he may resent what could appear to him to be self-promotion.

The supervisor can also incur an obligation from an executive or from a colleague in the unit or department to which the worker transferred. If the promotion causes a serious gap in the supervisor's unit, the executive may even be asked or himself offer to make it up by meeting some other unit need. But even when the loss is less serious, the supervisor can imply her sacrifice for the agency's greater good by stressing the value of the worker to her unit. As in the case of exchange maneuvers with the worker, however, it must seem natural to be effective. By and large, this will not be difficult, for the worker's loss will indeed be felt, and the supervisor is simply expressing—perhaps emphasizing—a sentiment that she really feels. A tenet of these maneuvers is that they be deft and unobtrusive; to be effective, they *must not* show. To the extent that the supervisor errs in any direction, therefore, it should be in underplaying rather than overplaying another's indebtedness.

Internal Promotions. Promotions that take place within the supervisor's unit occur when the unit is large enough for some degree of hierarchy to exist. The distinctions can be within function, as is implied in the titles *caseworker* and *senior caseworker*, between functions, such as *intake worker* and *caseworker*, or when the unit is of sufficient size to involve multiple ranks such as *caseworker* and *case supervisor*.

Although promotions within the supervisor's unit occur with less frequency than those outside of it, the supervisor is more likely to be the primary decision maker in this case. For this reason, they raise a less complex set of political considerations, offering similar opportunities but lesser disadvantages than external promotions. For this reason we discuss here rather than in the prior section two decisions that must be made before an opening for a promotion is announced, although the decisions are relevant to both internal and external promotions. The first relates to the various criteria for the position, the second, to whether to look for an inside candidate or someone from the outside.

The primary criterion for promotions is, of course, competence or the potential for competence. Although this observation is obvious enough, it is sometimes more difficult to apply than one might assume. Often, in assessing a worker's ability to fill a particular position, the judgment is based on his competence in his current position, and this could constitute an error in predicting success in a new role. As noted in Chapter 2, the promotion to a supervisory position on the basis of clinical skills overlooks such aspects of the position as managing authority relations and effectiveness in working a system. A thoughtful assessment of the specific skills that constitute the task requirements of the new position and measuring potential candidates against these requirements are necessary.

A second important criterion is the candidate's loyalty to the supervisor, his willingness to accept her leadership. It is not untoward for a supervisor to promote someone she likes or with whom there is the potential for a close relationship. Mutual regard, we would argue, promotes more effective work. We hasten to add, however, that loyalty and mutual regard do not—or should not—demand unquestioned acceptance of the supervisor's positions. Supervisors are often greatly helped by staff members who express disagreement. Able supervisors are aware that they are bound to distort, overreact, or misperceive on occasion and welcome—or should welcome—staff who privately point those occasions out to her. The test, of course, is whether the worker is prepared to close ranks behind the supervisor once she has publicly declared her intentions.

Other relevant criteria for promotion emerge from the context of specific situations. The politics of ethnicity and gender, the acceptability of the candidate to important ascendent factions in the organization or the community, relevance of the candidate's experience in regard to current controversies or issues, and access to important constituencies or other resources are all examples of potential criteria. One caution with respect to these criteria should be noted, however. Although usually important and occasionally critical, they are often transitory and must therefore be kept in perspective. They are secondary to competence and loyalty.

The advantages of promoting from within versus seeking an outside candidate are relatively straightforward. An internal candidate is a known quantity, and his strengths and weaknesses can be more accurately assessed than those of an outsider. We note parenthetically that this is not necessarily a gain for the inside candidate, because his vulnerabilities, as well as his talents, are more exposed. Outsiders sometimes look good because it takes more intimate knowledge than is available in a new hiring for deficiencies to become apparent. A further advantage of promotion from within is that it permits the supervisor to reward good behavior. This has the salutory effect of indicating to the staff that there are payoffs in the supervisor's perception of them as competent and loyal, and if the promoted worker is generally popular with his peers, staff morale is enhanced. Of course, there can also be negative reactions to the supervisor's choice, whomever the promoted candidate may be, but that is a subject we discuss below.

There are two major advantages to outside candidates. For one thing, they bring a fresh perspective to the unit; because they do not have a stake in the status quo, they are freer to offer innovative solutions to unit problems. For another, outsiders selected by the supervisor do not have prior connections to current staff, and as suggested earlier, they are thus more dependent on her than current staff. All other things being equal, they are more likely to embrace her leadership.

How a supervisor comes out on the issue of promoting an insider versus an outsider depends on a number of factors. Apart from the availability of an appropriate internal candidate or the supervisor's propensity for risking the hiring of an unknown, a major factor has to do with the length of time the supervisor has been at the agency. If the supervisor has had an extended tenure and relations within the unit are stable, her tendency will be to choose an internal candidate. A new supervisor, on the other hand, usually wants to make her own mark on the unit's functioning, and one way to do that is to hire her own staff.

Dealing with Staff Reaction to Promotions. Because promotional decisions hold such symbolic meaning for staff, to the extent possible the supervisor should follow a process that appears to be open and objective. Such a process begins with an announcement of the opening, an articulation of the criteria to be used in the decision, an indication of anyone in addition to the supervisor who may share in the choice and, finally, an estimated timetable. The process should be managed in a fashion that in addition to striving to obtain the best possible candidate, the supervisor is also perceived as being equitable in her conduct of the search.

In addition to the openness of the search process, the climate and culture of the unit prior to the promotion decision significantly influences staff reaction to it. A precondition of the staff's acceptance of the ultimate selection is their prior clarity and acceptance of the performance standards that the supervisor holds, her definitions of excellence, and her determination to reward those who meet her standards. Much, then, depends on earlier feedback—how successfully she has communicated the linkages between supervisory expectations, performance, and potential rewards.

Staff members who are passed over for a promotion rarely feel that the choice is justified. A disgruntled worker should be prevented from obtaining wide support from the staff at large. Here, a comparison of the worker who has been passed over with the worker who has been promoted must clearly favor the latter. If the distinction has face validity, the supervisor has little to do. If the distinction is less obvious, the supervisor must anticipate potential dissatisfaction—and prior to the announcement of the decision—try to structure the situation so as to mitigate any complaint. How she would go about it depends on specific circumstances, but one means is to enhance the visibility of the to-be-chosen worker's contribution to the unit. Another is to discuss the matter privately with key staff members or supporters so that they are in a position to counter any invidious judgments about the decision that might arise. To the extent that staff *expect* in advance that the supervisor will select or avoid a particular worker, the sharp edges of potential negative reactions are softened.

Workers who do not get promoted are also less disappointed if they do not have inordinate expectations. This suggests the importance of workers knowing how their supervisor views their measuring up to performance standards—an integral part of the supervisory process in any case. Too often, the uncomfortable prospect of confronting staff members with negative judgments about their work leads supervisors to be overly lenient or nondiscriminatory in their evaluations. (Kane and Lawler, 1979). They do the worker no favor by such so-called kindness.

Sometimes, however, avoidance tactics may be unavoidable. It may serve no purpose, for example, to appraise negatively a worker who is committed to agency and unit goals, is conscientious, and performs at his maximum—if only adequate—capacity, but such a worker may expect to be advanced when a promotional vacancy occurs. On these and like occasions, the supervisor may tailor the criteria for the position so that the worker in question is ineligible. Even when he suspects that this may be purposeful, the uncertainty wreaks less havoc with his self-esteem than would outright knowledge. It also makes it easier for him to avoid the public embarrassment that a rejection based on performance criteria might engender.

Personal and Political Factors. We have suggested that personal or political factors may come in to play as the supervisor moves to fill a promotion. Although the supervisor's interests are often well served by following an open and objective process, she must expect that various constraints will frequently arise that make a rational process and choice undesirable. We conclude this section on promotions with three examples of such constraints.

Assume that the promotion requires a close working relationship with the supervisor. Of the potential candidates, one is somewhat more competent technically than the others. He is a committed and loyal worker as well. Unfortunately, the worker is humorless, and humor is an attribute that the supervisor values highly in those with whom she feels affinity. The supervisor does not look forward to extended interaction with this worker, and what is worse, his apparent need for a personal relationship with her is more off-putting still. Although of considerable importance to the supervisor, these are reactions of a personal nature and, as such, have no place in a rational process or among professional norms. And yet?

Another example involves a white department head whose department has four units, each headed by a supervisor who is also white. There are several minority group line workers, and the client population is predominately black or Hispanic. When one of the unit supervisor positions becomes vacant, the department head feels strongly that it should be filled by a minority candidate. Among the current applicants are two highly competent white women and two minority women, each of whom, although acceptable, is somewhat less able than the two white candidates. What to do?

Our final example, drawn from a large social service agency, involves a supervisor directing a service unit composed of twelve practitioners and two case supervisors. One of the case supervisors, an old-timer with many years of service and a secret drinking problem, is due for retirement. Because her retirement is imminent, the supervisor has covered for her during the preceding year by relying heavily on one of the promising workers in the unit. The supervisor has promised the worker that if he continues to provide informal support and leadership to the unit, the job will be his when she retires. The supervisor is thus faced with developing a selection process for a position that has already been privately promised.

Each of the three examples represent a typical kind of promotional situation. Our argument is that encumbrances to a rational or objective process are frequent and may be justifiable, and that it may be appropriate to eschew a "proper" process to achieve other important ends. We do not have a pejorative judgment about the supervisor in the first instance, because she decided that she could not appoint the worker who would cause her personal grief. And we agree with the second supervisor that she *had* to find a minority candidate. The third supervisor was also right, in our view, to promise the position in order to hold the unit together under trying circumstances.

Care must be taken, however, when personal or political factors intervene in a promotional process. To the extent possible, it must not be obvious that the openness of the search has been violated. If this cannot be done, the next best circumstance is to try to ensure that a public case cannot easily be made regarding the violation. Finally, when violations are clear or easy to infer, it is important that the supervisor's reasons for contravening the open process are understood and generally accepted. To achieve these objectives, the supervisor must try to structure the formal process as much as possible to accomodate whatever the specific constraints might be. She must also publicly defend the process as appropriate, if that is necessary, and informally attempt to build support or at least acceptance for her action.

Let us now consider how this played out in our examples. To avoid the candidate that she preferred not to hire, the first supervisor redesigned the requirements of the role so that the selection criteria included specialized competencies that the candidate did not possess. In the second instance, the supervisor weighed two options. One was to select one of the internal minority candidates; the second was to search outside the organization to find a minority candidate whose capability matched the top internal white staff members. Hiring an outsider in the face of several qualified internal candidates would not be a popular decision, but if she had chosen that option, she would have stressed the need to find the most qualified person for the position. In fact, after some further searching on an informal basis, she offered the job to one of the internal minority candidates. She knew that most staff members understood and accepted her commitment to hiring a minority group member, although how this preference affected her actual choice remained unstated, an organizational secret. In our final example, the supervisor included as one criterion for the case supervisor role, "the ability to work closely with and exercise leadership for unit staff," because this reflected a major strength of the worker she planned to select. It is, of course, not unusual to develop criteria for a position so that it gives a distinct edge to some preferred candidate. In this case, when the supervisor was asked whether the job was "wired," she responded that her intention was to consider all applicants, but that given the particular worker's performance over the past year, he had a great deal to recommend him for the position. To an active listener, her answer to the question was "yes" without her actually having had to say so.

Termination

Terminations are often painful and highly charged events. Employment is a primary need, and depriving a worker of his job, precipitating a loss of status, income, affiliation, and professional security, is fraught with stress. Nagging doubts are likely to arise as a supervisor contemplates such an ultimate rejection. Is it right to so hurt another person? Is it a consequence of her own failure to be sufficiently helpful to the worker? How will others perceive her if she takes the step? Will it cause trouble with superiors or others in the organization? Is it worth the time or energy or pain that the process entails? Little wonder, then, that supervisors are often prone to look the other way in the face of inadequate performance.

But supervisors must sometimes be hard-headed in the interests of their clients and the service. There are two ways in which terminations can be accomplished so that the process is somewhat less protracted or painful, although still difficult. One way is to find or invent the grounds for firing that ostensibly do not involve the worker's inadequacies. Some ostensible grounds are retrenchment, the need for different expertise than the worker's, or a staff reorganization. These rationales are sometimes used when contractual or other constraints on the organization do not readily permit a termination based on incompetence to take place.

Another means of easing the termination process is to encourage the worker to leave voluntarily. Depending on the specific circumstances, there may be ways to accomplish this with minimal trauma. But even when a resignation cannot easily be engineered, a termination should be the logical outcome of an ongoing process, rather than erupt as an isolated event. A consistent and coherent system of supervisory guidance and evaluation facilitates predictability. When supervision has been consistent, evaluations have specified difficulty, warnings have been issued (first verbally and then in writing), the final action, although still traumatic, nonetheless evolves as a natural part of the supervisory process. To the extent that this has occurred, it is more likely that the worker will abort the process somewhere along the way by leaving voluntarily.

Under the most ideal of circumstances, termination actions are difficult, requiring interpersonal and political sensitivity, persistance, clear priorities, and resolve. We now discuss four concerns that are important to consider. Although we discuss these tasks serially, in practice they tend to be interactive.

The Decision to Terminate. The criteria for a termination decision derive from a confluence of ethical and pragmatic considerations. Reasons why a worker does not fulfill job expectations obviously vary. Whatever the reasons, however, ethically the decision must grow out of a process in which the articulation of performance expectations, feedback on his performance, and the consequences of not meeting minimum criteria provide the worker with ample opportunity to take corrective steps. In other words, a termination decision cannot be the initial order of business. Ordinarily, as the process unfolds, there comes a point at which the supervisor decides that termination must move from the background as one of several options to the foreground as an increasingly likely alternative. A specific incident or the exposure of a serious deficit might trigger the process or act as its tipping point, but these are not sufficient criteria in themselves for termination except under the most unusual circumstances. The operative value is that the worker is given every opportunity to achieve an adequate level of performance.

How a supervisor feels about an inadequate worker undoubtedly influences the termination process and outcome. Conscientious and amiable workers, however incompetent they may be, are exceedingly difficult to fire. So, too, are workers whose inadequacies are the result of personal or emotional problems that appear beyond their control. In organizations with sufficient funding, or during times of expanding resources, it may be humane and appropriate to carry these workers. Positions may be found in which they make some contribution, however limited, or in which their opportunity to do harm is circumscribed. If they cause significant organizational damage, however, or absorb otherwise critical resources, they must be let go, and the natural predisposition to procrastinate must be overcome. In allowing a situation with such a staff member to build over time, the supervisor risks being charged with the admonition, "Why didn't you tell me sooner?" (Radde, 1981).

Privately, the supervisor may have interpersonal reasons for seeking to terminate a staff member. The worker may be so resistant to supervision or negative about the supervisor that she finds their day-to-day work together upsetting. Or the worker may try to organize a staff core of dissatisfaction that, if allowed to go unchallenged, would threaten the supervisor's leadership of the unit. In these instances, the supervisor may consider termination without undue pangs of conscience. In cases in which the challenge is severe or in which confronting the matter has not resulted in any change in the worker's behavior, it is our view that the supervisor is justified in taking drastic action. But the criteria for termination must focus on the worker's inability to perform the job adequately, particularly when there is any suspicion that personal feeling or interpersonal conflict is at the root of the issue. Interpersonal conflict is, after all, a matter of interpretation and ascriptions of fault very much a subjective affair. Whether, in fact, actual job performance is always the issue, it must always *appear* to be the case that performance and not interpersonal tension underlies the decision.

Pragmatically, the supervisor who is considering termination needs to ensure that there is adequate documentation of the worker's failure to meet minimum expectations before she moves to termination. If the agency has a formal system of performance appraisal, it should take place as a matter of course. In most instances, however, this is not the case, and there is ordinarily no reason for the supervisor routinely to document the difficulty or to communicate with the worker about the problem in writing. In the usual case, the supervisor will have engaged the worker informally, tried to raise issues in ways that have minimized potential defensiveness, re-raised the matter from time to time, and made little progress. If, on these grounds, she feels pessimistic about the worker's ability to make it, her next step is starting to document the difficulty and the process of dealing with it, usually by starting a file on her attempts to elicit acceptable worker performance and his responses. In most organizations, terminations are sanctioned only after a strong and documented case has been made. It is irrelevant that an appropriate process has already occurred through verbal interchange; until it is in writing, it may be ambiguous and is subject to misunderstanding and conflicting interpretations.

Organizational events take on added significance when committed to paper. Verbal exchanges between organizational actors that reflect difference or disagreement frequently occur and often pass without engendering resentment or excessive defensiveness. But the same content, when formalized by commitment to writing, takes on a more serious meaning in the culture of organizational life. One of the reasons written documentation is often lacking as a supervisor contemplates termination is precisely because, in the process of engaging the worker, the supervisor has felt that writing the criticism would seem too threatening. At the point when supervisors in this situation entertain the possibility that the worker may have to be let go, they also realize that there is no record of the worker's deficits or of their process in redirecting his performance.

Developing a written record in relation to a problematic employee holds two other potential benefits. First, the fact that the supervisor resorts to writing signals to the worker a level of seriousness that may have eluded him earlier. Perceiving the supervisor's resolve on the issue frequently has the effect of stimulating action on the worker's part. If he is serious about keeping the position and is capable of meeting expectations, the written exchange may induce him to take the necessary steps to improve, which other supervisory interventions have failed to achieve. If the worker cannot or will not improve, the written exchange frequently moves the worker to resign. Indeed, sometimes the mere *threat* of the supervisor's placing damaging material in his file may persuade the worker to leave, and supervisors sometimes offer not to put anything in writing in return for a worker's resignation.

A second benefit of the written exchange, no matter how late in the process it occurs, is that it gives the appearance of the supervisor's offering the worker another chance, further strengthening the supervisor's position as she seeks organizational sanction to move ahead on termination. Regardless of what has transpired between them earlier, the written communication provides de novo an opportunity for the worker to meet supervisory demands now.

Obtaining Organizational Sanction. A supervisor who seeks to terminate a worker is subject to the suspicion of superiors that the problem may be hers as well as the worker's. In cases of public conflict, often neither party to the conflict gains from the situation; both are ascribed some measure of fault for letting the situation get out of hand. Resorting to as extreme a measure as a firing may raise question about the supervisor's effectiveness or her professional perspective. She may be viewed as personalizing her difficulties with the worker and reacting vindictively. Administrators are sometimes loathe to fire employees on other grounds as well. It is the supervisor, after all, who is faced with the day-to-day difficulties associated with the worker's inadequate performance, but it is the administrator who may well have to deal with the trouble caused by the termination, such as a union grievance, discrimination suit, or an appeal procedure. Too, the normative predisposition of the human services field is to stress a humane and supportive approach to problems. Firing a worker, even one who evidences significant deficits, seems inconsistent with that value stance and may therefore be resisted.

Obtaining organizational sanction for a termination may thus be a difficult task. Although the criteria necessary to gain organizational sanction vary with the specific agency and situation, three factors are almost always present: compelling substantive grounds for the action, written documentation of the supervisory process aimed at assisting the worker to meet minimum performance criteria, and evidence that the worker has been warned about the possibility of termination and provided with the opportunity to improve. Showing that these criteria have been met in any particular case is, of course, a function of the quality of the documentation.

At a minimum, the supervisor's record of the difficulty should summarize the areas of worker deficit, the process of problem solving that has occurred, a detailing of those activities that were deemed to constitute satisfactory improvement, and any warnings that the supervisor has had the authority to impose. The documentation should be specific and include dates of relevant discussions, the content of those discussions, and descriptions of deficit behaviors, including dates of unexcused absences or other failures to meet job responsibilities.

During the process of documenting her case, the supervisor is usually well advised to consult with relevant superiors to assure that the circumstances and developing record conform with conditions that her superiors consider serious enough to require termination. Consultation is particularly important when the supervisor believes that the case may be a borderline one or one that her superior is ambivalent with respect to the termination. Consultation also has the effect of indirectly implicating the superior in the transaction with the worker. Once the executive participates in setting the conditions for the worker's continuation in the job, and the worker fails to meet those terms, the matter takes on a more personal meaning for the executive.

Communications with the Problematic Worker. Generalizations about maintaining communication with a worker who may be terminated are difficult to make. The supervisor's interventions are contingent on her assessment of the worker's reactions as the process unfolds and how she wants the process to take shape in response to his reactions. Ethically, she is responsible for keeping the worker informed of the potential consequences of his actions in light of the seriousness of the situation. This entails providing feedback about the worker's behavior and its meaning for next steps. If it is the supervisor's assessment that the worker is attempting to improve and shows promise of success, encouragement is obviously appropriate. If, on the other hand, she believes that the worker is misperceiving the situation, it is important that she make this clear to him.

A special caution regarding communication with a worker at risk of termination merits note. It relates to the understandable tendency for the supervisor to reduce interaction with the worker. Once judgments and intentions have been shared, their contacts are likely to be extremely difficult, frequently causing no less anguish for the supervisor than for the worker. In response to the stress and possible acrimony that occurs in such instances, the supervisor may find herself avoiding contact with the worker to limit the upset that each experiences in their dealings with the other.

The problem with a reduction in contact during the critical period of a pretermination procedure is self-evident. The supervisor's ability to monitor the worker's responses and the direction of the process are jeopardized. This is a period in which the worker's anxiety and possible negative feelings may distort his perceptions and precipitate extreme reactions. Because she must maintain clarity regarding the direction the process should take, success in resisting a predisposition to disengage is a necessary condition for making a fair and effective judgment. Once a decision to terminate is inevitable, however, it is well for the ending to made as quickly as possible, so as to prevent a potentially disgruntled staff member from behaving negatively with other staff or clients.

Handling Other Staff. When a worker is visibly not performing to standard, it can be expected to cause some resentment among other staff members. They will usually come to hold the supervisor responsible for altering the situation. But because they often identify with other staff personnel who occupy a similar place in the agency hierarchy, workers may feel threatened by the trauma of a colleague's separation anyway. Thus the fact that the staff members feel she should do something is often misinterpreted by the supervisor—and even by staff members themselves—for when she moves to terminate the worker, the action can occasion a flurry of appeals requesting that she reconsider. Or if there are no appeals, there is often an undercurrent of dissatisfaction among the staff, not publicly expressed but which privately censures the supervisor for her decision. Indeed, if the staff had previously complained about the worker, they may now also feel guilty and thus perhaps even more judgmental about the supervisor's "cruel" treatment of their colleague.

Supervisors preparing for a termination must recognize, therefore, that however the staff may judge the worker in question, they may be upset when a firing takes place, and that the staff may not be likely to be openly supportive of a termination for cause except in extreme circumstances. Her task, then, is to be sensitive to these potential responses during and following her engagement in the action.

Handling termination issues with the staff ordinarily generates tension. On the one hand, the supervisor must often ensure that the staff's understanding of what occurred is accurate. She must deal with any perceptions that the worker was unjustly treated. On the other hand, she must also be concerned about protecting the feelings and image of the terminated worker. Her protectiveness is important because, for one thing, it is the humane way to act. It is also expected that what occurs between a supervisor and worker is confidential, and she may be viewed negatively for violating a professional norm if she breaches that confidence.

Ordinarily, how the tension is resolved is determined by the specific circumstances of the termination. If the problem worker is actively attempting to gain staff support, widely spreading a distorted perception of the issue or promoting negative feelings against the supervisor, the supervisor is freer to put forth her own interpretation of events. Whatever the operative norms, their violation will be excused if it is done in self-defense. Even so, however, the supervisor does well to appear to be reluctant to put forward another side to the story, or if she puts it forward, to do so with a light touch. Whatever the provocation, the supervisor must appear to be moderate and reasonable.

Conversely, if the worker is interested in defining the termination as a resignation or is prepared to go quietly, the supervisor is in a position to behave with utmost consideration for his sensibilities. The one caution to note here is that she must feel assured that he will, in fact, go quietly. Otherwise, she risks being sandbagged into saying positive things about him or his performance that he could subsequently use as evidence to attack her criticism or the termination decision. She must, in other words, temper her inclination to be kind when there is a serious possibility that her kindness will result in damaging misperceptions among her staff or others.

A primary objective in handling terminations with the staff is to facilitate accurate perceptions regarding the implications of the termination for the *future* conduct of the unit. Addressing the specifics of the current case in the way we have suggested may often accomplish this end. But the supervisor should be aware as she discusses the case that she is communicating a message regarding the future use of sanctions as well.

One final point. Unless the termination has become a cause celebre and a unit meeting cannot be avoided, it is wise to avoid dealing with a termination issue in a group meeting. The nature of a group setting can cause dissatisfaction to crystallize and feelings to be intensified. The risk is that the participants' views will support and reinforce each other, thus making matters worse. Only in the most unusual of circumstances—when there has been a gross misunderstanding, for example—is the risk worth taking. When circumstances in a unit are highly charged, communications ordinarily travel very quickly, and informal means do spread the supervisor's point of view. Even if she must live with some unpleasantness as a result of her staff's reaction to the firing of even a popular colleague, organizational issues tend to fade over time if they are not reinforced. Ordinarily, then, she is best advised to wait it out.

In concluding this chapter on transitions, we also conclude our discussion of supervisory practice and leadership dealing primarily with direct interventions with supervisees. It should by now be clear that in our view direct work with the staff is only one element of supervision—albeit a most important one. The supervisor's organizational practice—how she interacts with and influences peers and superiors—is critical both to her direction of staff and to running an effective service. We thus turn in subsequent chapters to practice issues relating to her work with peers and the agency's upper management.

7

Working with Peers and Superiors:
A Mixed Game

Cooperation and Competition Among Colleagues

If two actors share similar goals, one would expect them to engage in collaborative interactions. In the nomenclature of game theory, the circumstance is a win-win game—for one party to win, the other party must win as well. Because the situation is perceived by both parties to involve commonality of purpose, each behaves collaboratively toward the other.

In the opposite instance, parties experience extreme disparity with regard to desired outcomes. Goals that seriously challenge another's influence or autonomy, affect their share of an organization's resources, or threaten their self-esteem—if they are engaged in this form—call forth intense dissensus. In that case, a participant can attain his goal if, and only if, the others with whom he is engaged cannot obtain their goals (Deutsch, 1973, p. 20). In other words, for one party to win, the other must lose (a zero-sum or win-lose game).

Cooperative relationships are characterized by friendliness and trust. Communications are open, and there is a shared recognition of the interests of each party. The actors demonstrate special sensitivity to commonalities and tend to overlook the significance of potential differences. Under these conditions, tasks are approached in ways that use the special talents of each. Task duplication is minimal, and the actors jointly search for ways to span whatever conflicting interests may exist.

By contrast, conflictual or competitive arrangements are characterized by a distortion of or a lack of communication. Such conditions encourage what Deutsch calls espionage, the covert attempt to obtain information about the other that he or she is unwilling to communicate. Perceptions of actors toward one another emphasize their differences and are characterized by hostility and suspicion. Pernicious interpretations tend to be made about the other's motivations. Activities are engaged in with the intent of imposing one's will over the other, and the predisposition to prevail at the expense of the other increases over time to encompass previously neutral or irrelevant issues.

Although these descriptions of "pure" cooperation and conflict can sometimes be observed in the day-to-day interactions among organizational peers, more frequently interprofessional relations fall somewhere between these two extremes. In this circumstance, each party accepts the validity of some of the other's interests and rejects others. Relations combine friendliness and distrust. Attitudes may be cautious—publicly accepting and privately uncertain—and interactions tend to be mixed as well. This type of situation might be called a mixed game, combining as it does elements of both cooperation and conflict or competition.

It is our premise that these mixed relationships are widespread among colleagues in human services organizations. Pure cooperative relationships do, of course, exist, as do pure competitive or conflictual ones. But the effects of the structure of human services bureacracies on middle-level personnel encourage a mixed game.

Jill is one of six unit supervisors in the Carswell Community Services, an agency serving mentally ill homeless people. Each unit is located in a shelter for the homeless in different sections of the city and provides a range of similar services, including outreach, case management, client advocacy and counseling. Each unit team consists of a supervisor, two professional social workers, and a number of paraprofessionals, plus students in nursing and social work. Jill has been there for eight years; at the agency's inception she trained as a student and was a line worker before her promotion three years ago.

Tom, the agency's director, was Jill's instructor during her student internship. They have contributed together to the agency's growth and reputation, and they have developed a close working relationship. Both believe that the services provided by the agency cannot be maximally beneficial for its clients unless housing for the chronically mentally ill is vastly expanded. Jill's unit has been significantly more effective in placing clients in permanent housing than the agency's other units, and Tom has proposed to Jill that she head a training effort designed to assist the other units in housing placement.

Jill has reacted to Tom's suggestion with some ambivalence. On the one hand, she agrees that the training would be useful for the other staff units; she is desirous of the experience, believing that it holds learning potential for her; she is also secretly pleased with the recognition that the activity will bring. She is ambivalent, however, because she is concerned that the visibility she will gain could cause tension in her relationships with the other supervisors. She is already concerned that they may perceive her as someone who too readily does the director's business. She has decided, nevertheless, to take on the task.

Jill and Tom have agreed that, prior to developing the training protocol, it would be useful for her to meet individually with the other supervisors, because the local conditions of each team, as well as the experience and capabilities of each unit staff, differ in the six locations. Following this informal assessment, Jill and Tom will meet again to decide on the specifics of the training program and curriculum. Tom has indicated that he will discuss the plan at the next scheduled meeting of unit supervisors.

Jill gets her first inkling that the task will be even more difficult than she had expected when Tom presents the idea to her colleagues. Although none of them opposes the notion, only Amy, a relatively new supervisor, expresses any enthusiasm for the plan. Sandra, one of Jill's good friends, does not participate in the discussion at all, even though Jill has spoken to her before the meeting in the expectation of garnering her support. One unit director asks Tom if he doesn't think that variations in housing placements have more to do with geography than with differences in worker skill, because, after all, some shelters are located in communities in which appropriate housing is less available than the shelters in other communities. Tom concurs that this certainly is the case. The training suggestion did not imply a criticism of the staff, he says, but was designed to hone their already considerable skills. Jeff, another of the supervisors, suggests somewhat incoherently that it is more important to help clients find their own residences than to "infantalize" them by doing everything for them. At the end of the discussion, however, they all agree to cooperate with Jill in planning the program.

Jill has held only four of the planning interviews. The fifth, with Jeff, was cancelled by him twice and he did not get back to her to reschedule it as promised. The unit director who had mentioned geography has argued that the agency would do better to invest in hiring a housing specialist than to spend precious staff time in training. Jill agreed that his idea was a good one but that it did not preclude training; nevertheless, she was unable to move the discussion to the specifics of his staff's needs. Bea, another of the supervisors, persisted in talking about Tom and his difficulty in understanding the pressures faced by the supervisors on the line. Although Jill was responsive to Bea's concerns, she was unable to redirect the interview to the training program except in the most general terms. Only Amy and her friend Sandra were helpful in identifying the specific needs of their staffs.

Jill now feels that she may be unable to get further cooperation without strong intercession from Tom, and she is uncertain about requesting it, because it might come at a considerable expense to her future relations with her colleagues. She wonders, too, to what extent Tom might privately think that she has not handled the situation with sufficient sensitivity. If she were to ask Tom to relieve her of the program, it would also cause some embarrassment with her staff, because she has told them about her special assignment—partly to explain her spending time away from the office and partly as a means of sharing with them the implicit credit that Tom had accorded the unit. In any case, what had seemed to her an opportunity has become something of a problem, and Jill feels stuck.

Jill is clearly experiencing mixed-game relations—relations that are simultaneously both cooperative and competitive. For Jill—and for supervisors generally—these relations pose difficulties of both an instrumental and affective nature. Often, a supervisor's success in launching a program, obtaining needed resources, or otherwise conducting her unit effectively requires the participation and help of her peers as well as of superordinates. Patti (1983) has noted that although program managers are held accountable for their unit's success, their formal power and resources are often insufficient for the task. To elicit cooperation, they must rely on persuasion, education, pressure, exchange, and negotiation with colleagues and/or executives. In other words, they rely on a range of interventions that are suggestive of both cooperative and competitive relations. "In the last analysis," Patti says, "the political skills necessary (to accomplish her goals) may be the most demanding aspect of the program manager's role" (p. 58).

On an affective level, too, there are strong incentives to maintain warm relations with one's colleagues. Obviously one's comfort in an agency and one's satisfaction with one's job is diminished when interpersonal tensions are present. Thus although Jill has felt frustrated by her inability to elicit the full cooperation of her peers, she has been nonetheless cautious in calling on her boss's help because it could be potentially damaging to collegial relations.

Mixed relations are more a consequence of the structure of relationships between colleagues at the middle levels of a human services bureaucracy than they are an outgrowth of the personalities of particular supervisors. We do not suggest that individual factors are unimportant; certainly the way in which people enact their roles and interact with others is shaped by their personalities and other nonorganizational influences. But we do argue that mixed relations are structurally inevitable, whatever the capability or goodwill of the persons who are actually involved, and that an understanding of these structural factors is a necessary grounding for effective practice.

The Strain to Compete: Structural Factors

Organization theorists have noted four bases for structuring departments or units (Gortner et al., 1987, p. 107). They may be organized by geography, as in the case of Carswell Community Services, Jill's agency, in which each unit is self-contained, offering similar services in varying locations. Another basis is client type, for example in a settlement house in which there are discrete units to serve members by age group (preschool, youth, adults, the aged). A third is by the category of service or process, in which units are organized around specialized skills. Hospitals, for example, are ordinarily structured by service categories, with doctors, nurses, social workers, and others with specialized expertise working in such services as the emergency room, medical-surgery, pediatrics, and the like. Closely related to the latter is a fourth form of organization, in which function is the organizing principle. In this instance, one unit may do intake; the next, day treatment; a third, job training; and another, job placement. Or one unit may be responsible for the program and others for management functions such as finances and building maintenance.

Agencies often combine these various structures. The important point for our consideration is that these unit structures entail either independent functioning by the supervisor and staff or interdependent work with colleagues, and that whichever is prevalent—independence or interdependence—competitiveness is fostered.

Functional Independence

Units organized by geography and client type are more independent from one another than other forms of unit organization. Exceptions can be found, of course, but in the main, the day-to-day conduct of the staff requires little coordination and interaction with the other sister units that comprise a larger department or agency. Primary accountability for goal accomplishment is circumscribed by the internal operations of the unit (and frequently by its interaction with outside entities such as other service providers in the community) and is not to any significant degree dependent on collaborative interactions with other agency units. Such is the case at Carswell; the success of Jill's unit and those of her peers do not require their coordination or cooperation.

Returning for a moment to the terms of game theory, for a supervisor to win, she is required simply to ensure her unit's effective functioning. Winning for an individual unit does not require that other units win or lose. To the extent that this structural arrangement obtains in any given case, then, unit supervisors can be thought of as being *structurally independent* of one another.

One might assume that structural independence would predispose cooperative relations. When parties neither need nor are dependent on one another, there is little to impede positive relationships from developing. In fact, however, structural independence interacts with another dynamic of organizational life that encourages competitive tensions in peer relations: the desire of most organizational members to look good—particularly in the eyes of superiors, but by peers and subordinates as well. The striving to be perceived as particularly able in one's professional duties stems in part from a sense of craft—and it is also an understandable response to the politics of organizational life.

As we have noted in Chapter 3, the perception of competence is an important determinent of influence in most professionally dominated bureaucracies. This perception is, naturally enough, associated with the delegation of increased responsibilities, the development of more effective exchange relations, an expanded role in decision making—in a word, increased power. Thompson (1967, p. 33) also points out that approbation and prestige are the cheapest ways of acquiring power, for if one finds it prestigious to exchange with another, the latter has gained a measure of influence without making any commitments in return. It is to be expected, then, that a committed supervisor should be concerned that she be viewed by others in the organization as competent.

Why this tendency to seek recognition interacts with structural independence to predispose competitiveness is an intriguing phenomenon. Neither condition alone—structural independence or the quest for recognition—is sufficient to lead to a win-lose situation. In the main, the supervisor does not require the cooperation of peers to be viewed as competent; nor is this perception of her dependent on others being viewed as less able. But if each unit supervisor is seen as highly effective, what is the significance of this for any given supervisor? We would hypothesize that because, relative to other supervisors, she will not be viewed as *more* special, she will not be accorded the added measure of power that typically accompanies the perception of competence. It is, at least in part, the desire for more influence than that of one's peers, that drives the competitive dimension of this phenomenon.

Recognition is not a scarce resource. As we have suggested, the currency of recognition may be somewhat debased when the resource is widely distributed. Nevertheless, all organizational participants can be seen as having areas of special competence and be recognized as particularly able. Power, on the other hand, is a considerably scarcer resource. In significant measure, its particular value for an individual depends on whether she possesses it to a greater degree than others. If this analysis is accurate, then the press for increased influence is inevitably a source of competition.

The competitive process is often a subtle one, for there are strong professional and organizational norms—to say nothing of the constraints associated with friendly and collegial relations—that mitigate against an open contest. Most often, practitioners do not publically denigrate the recognized accomplishments of their peers. Instead, competitive intent is more likely to be shown by an apparent lack of enthusiasm for the credit accorded a colleague. Informally, however, particularly among themselves, organizational peers may trivialize the accomplishments of colleagues—either on substantive grounds or by claiming that the boss is behaving subjectively or playing favorites.

This dynamic was in evidence in Jill's case when Tom assigned her to train staff, thus implicitly recognizing her skill in developing residential placements for homeless clients. The colleague who cited geography as the reason for a successful placement rate was, in fact, implying that it was not Jill's ability that was responsible for her unit's achievement. The silence and lack of enthusiasm of some of the other supervisors is also suggestive of their competitive reaction to Jill's recognition. Indeed, even her friend Sandra seemingly behaved somewhat competitively.

It should be noted that even in instances of structural independence, supervisors may have to work together from time to time on a common agency problem or issue. If in this work all have equal roles, cooperative efforts often follow. If, on the other hand, responsibilities are such that there is the potential for one supervisor to receive disproportionate credit following the cooperation of the others, passive or active resistance may well occur. A special assignment, as in Jill's case, often calls forth this response. Special assignments are ordinarily made to those whom the executive deems most qualified to do the work and serve as a signal to the supervisor and her peers that she is viewed in a particularly positive light. When such assignments require the active cooperation of these same peers, some of them may well perceive the situation as no-win unless they have a positive stake in the outcome on substantive grounds. If they cooperate fully, their colleague accrues the credit, and they are set back in the quest for relative status and influence; if they do not cooperate, their motives become suspect. The result, then, is a mixed response.

Functional Interdependence

Units that are structured by program or function usually require significant interaction among each department's staff for one or any of them to function effectively. Staffs providing different services need to coordinate them, because clients may require service from two or more units or because single units may be unable to do their work without the others. For example, a day treatment unit depends on an outreach or intake department if the agency is structured along these lines. Very often, the staff of interdependent units are composed of workers with varying specializations or professionals from different disciplines. Structures such as these may be said to be functionally interdependent—neither unit can achieve its objectives without input or output from the other.

If competition is encouraged by structural independence, when combined with the desire for recognition and influence, the case is even stronger in instances of functional interdependence. It is true that when two or more entities need each other, there is an incentive for them to develop a network of reciprocal relationships and thus to cooperate—at least on the surface. But it is also the case that to control their own program and thus to reduce uncertainty, units frequently develop vague or overlapping boundaries that are viewed by other units as incursions on their turf. Units frequently fail to coordinate or to disseminate consistent messages (Patti, 1983, p. 131). As one theorist notes, "A strong tendency toward bargaining . . . inevitably develops when the same participants are institutionally constrained to meet over and over again, with somewhat divergent goals, to make choices of importance to all." (Mohr, 1982, p. 170). And bargaining, we would add, is a tactic in mixed games.

There are a number of other reasons why the strain toward competition may be even greater than the need to cooperate in functionally interdependent circumstances. Although we have suggested that these units may have goals in common, they are likely to have divergent aims as well. For example, a day treatment program may want to accept only clients with particular characteristics, whereas an outreach unit may experience pressure to take other categories of clients. If the agency has a problem in maintaining its client census, blaming others or recrimination is a potential outcome. When two or more units jointly contribute to some outcome, the potential for claiming responsibility for its success or denying responsibility for its failure creates a ready condition for the generation of tension.

It is not only heterogeneous goals that cause conflict among colleagues, but differing values as well. Striving to achieve the ascendancy of one set of values or ideology over another is a common source of strain between agency subunits, more so in the case of functionally interdependent units than independent ones. Further, when supervisors subscribe to different technologies, the conditions for virulent disagreement are present. Nowhere is this more apparent than in cases in which the staff of these units is drawn from different professions. Competition between the leaders of such units is then often rife.

Units also vary in their degree of power. A power differential is experienced by the less powerful as a deprivation under the best of circumstances (i.e., even when the unit's effectiveness is not contingent on the acts of a more powerful party). But when the parties are functionally interdependent, the differential sharply reduces the ability of the less powerful unit to control its own destiny. Unless it is prepared to surrender, it will either "go underground" to gain its ends or will overtly press for increased influence. Whether overt or covert, the competition is likely to be intense. Social work departments in hospitals are a case in point. Their work requires interdependence with medical personnel who are more powerful than the social work staff. Whether through covert maneuvering, cooptation, direct confrontation, or other means, the attempts of social workers in hospital settings to resist and reshape medical influence is legendary.

The impact of differentials in unit power on the supervisors of these units is considerable. For one thing, most staff members develop identifications with their unit, but this is particularly the case for the leader who feels responsible for its functioning. Indeed, often a supervisor's identification with her unit is stronger than her identification with the agency as a whole. (If such an identification is obvious to her boss, however, she has probably been guilty of a significant practice error). More importantly, a good case can be made that a manager's power stems from the power of the subunit he or she directs. Empirical support for this proposition is suggested in one study with a large sample of organizations, where it was found that the managers from powerful subunits were significantly more able to get their way than the managers from less powerful units (Stagner, 1969).

Such may have been a dynamic in Jill's case at Carswell. Jill probably had more influence in the agency because she had greater access to the executive than the other supervisors, stemming both from her earlier role as his student intern and her longevity in the setting. But it is likely that Jill was also influential as a result of the work of her unit. When a unit contributes importantly to a central organizational goal—in this instance the ability to place homeless people in residences—the unit itself accrues influence. A unit's power may also arise because the technology or function of the unit is more critical to the accomplishment of an agency's central or priority goals. In any case, some of the restiveness in the response of Jill's colleagues to her assignment may have, consciously or unconsciously, derived from their awareness of these power dynamics.

We do not mean to imply in our discussion of dependence and interdependence that competition is the immutable outcome of these structural forms. We believe, rather, that they constitute a significant potential source of tension in peer relations. The tension may be heightened or mitigated by additional factors such as professional and organizational norms, common ideology, and other factors discussed now.

Access to Organizational Resources

Competition is also fostered by a scarcity of organizational resources. When the organization's resources are insufficient to meet the full requirements or desires of various units—a well-nigh inevitable occurrence—choices need to be made regarding how the resources that are available will be allocated. With scarcity, as one unit receives more, another obtains less (the zero-sum game). The greater the scarcity of the resource compared to the demand, the more effort supervisors will exert to gain it—an effort that comes at the expense of colleagues in other units (Pfeffer, 1981, p. 69).

Resources may be tangible or intangible. Funding and staff positions provide the clearest example of tangible resources that predispose competitive relations between departmental peers. Funds, of course, are a perennial scarcity in social agencies. If the potential exists to finance a new project or to add a position in one unit, it is less likely that similar funds will be available for all other units as well. Within certain overall agency constraints, it is a supervisor's *job* to represent the best interests of her unit—to advocate for new services and perhaps additional staff. Effective supervisors are sensitive to opportunities to gain access to such resources and, as such, are competitively linked with their peers in such dealings. Indeed, as one might expect, empirical studies suggest that when resources are scarce, power is more likely to come into play in decision making. Salancik and Pfeffer (1974) found in a study of four resources allocated at the University of Illinois, for example, that the use of power increased as the resources varied in their scarcity and importance. Thus as one supervisor is successful in obtaining these scarce resources, other supervisors are not only less successful in obtaining the tangible resource, but they face the visibility of their lesser power as well.

Contention, both overt and covert, also arises when the tangible resource is less significant than a unit's overall budget or the ability to expand staff lines. Whatever the nature of the resource, its very scarcity increases its value. Furthermore, when the distribution of a resource is clearly observable, more than the need or desire for the resource is at issue. Granting any scarce resource to one unit as opposed to another may carry major symbolic meanings. Thus if one unit receives something of as modest importance as a computer, but a second unit must wait for its allocation, the fact that tensions between them might arise would not be surprising. Even when other explanations such as relative need for the distribution are given, it can signify that the unit which received the computer—and therefore the unit's supervisor—is more important or more favored or more powerful with the agency's upper echelons than others—a factor that is hardly designed to endear the supervisor to her colleagues.

The scarcity of intangible resources is also a source of competitive relations between colleagues. We have already suggested that power is a scarce resource, by and large. Because it is in high demand—or should be in high demand if supervisors are ably representing their unit's needs and wants—it is probably the most critical resource of all in generating collegial tensions.

Over time, some supervisors are able to accrue a greater amount of formal or informal power relative to their peers. Initially, symmetry may exist in a department of several supervisors, each of whom share identical authority and are held accountable for similar responsibilities. As special needs arise, such as the case with Jill at Carswell Community Services, the superordinate will assign specialized tasks to one or another of the supervisors or units. With the assignment, the supervisor is accorded added authority—and increased informal influence as well—because it broadens the legitimate area of concern associated with the supervisor's formal role and enlarges her sphere of influence. As such, extensions of responsibility constitute another potential source of competitive tension between peers. Other intangible resources that add to one supervisor's power relative to her colleagues' include ready entree to the boss, access to scarce organizational information, or responsibilities that for whatever reason enhance her attractiveness to others.

Increasing her influence relative to her colleagues is a significant practice task for the supervisor. To be able to do so with a minimum of destructive tension (in contrast to the constructive tension that is frequently required to promote a desired change) is an important aspect of supervisory skill that we address more fully in Chapter 8.

Cooperative Relations

To this point we have emphasized the competitive aspects of the mixed organizational game; obviously, however, relations would not be mixed if there were not strains mediating toward cooperation as well. Next we identify two of the factors that encourage collaborative interactions: organizational and professional norms and common organizational interests.

Organizational and professional norms exert a powerful influence on the behavior of organizational actors. The culture of a human services organization is dominated—at least on an explicit level—by the service ethic. Rooted in the ideologies of equity and human dignity, the ethic prescribes how human beings should interact with one another. The centrality of themes in social work such as self-determination and empowerment, respect for the needs and interests of others, openness and mutuality, all constitute examples of this broadly accepted value orientation. In part because of the infusion of these professional norms and in part because of the mission and culture of human services organizations, the norms of conduct designed to guide professional behavior toward service recipients are generalized to suggest standards of conduct among the service providers as well.

Expectations, therefore, that professionals will treat each other with respect, will be open in their communication, and will be supportive of one another are part of the normative culture. The primacy of the organization's mission to serve clients is interpreted to mean that personal gain, interpersonal conflict, and parochial worker interests should be set aside to maximize the organization's ability to serve its clients.

In short, the norms and culture of a social agency dictate that its staff cooperate to achieve the agency's mission. These norms are sufficiently powerful in most social agencies to regulate public definitions of intent—if not always the private purposes of interprofessional interactions. Supervisors who seek to be accepted or influential will strive to function in ways that appear cooperative and collegial, and to the extent that competition between them is visible, they will justify their actions by their commitment to better serve their clients or to other ideological factors.

Organizational norms encourage cooperation in another way. Appropriate behavior between subordinates and superiors is in part prescribed by rank. Prescriptions regarding relations among peers, on the other hand, are more flexible. With peers, the rules of behavior largely grow out of interaction, and because there are more opportunities to give and receive feedback, they are subject to ongoing revision. Research on conformity to behavioral rules supports this position. Reardon (1981, pp. 178–189) found greater rule conformity, for example, in instances in which organizational members responded to superiors and subordinates, whereas in responding to peers, they were guided by their own preferences. It is true, of course, that the increased give-and-take permitted to peers can serve to encourage either cooperative or competitive interactions. We suspect, however, that the frequency and informality of these lateral communication patterns incline the participants to get along. In any case, however, informal and frequent interaction predisposes cooperativeness when it is combined with elements of commonality among supervisors.

Just as divergent goals, ideologies, or differences in technology predispose competition between colleagues, so do common goals, values, and technology encourage cooperation. Supervisors need one another for social and emotional support. Although this is the case with staff on all hierarchical levels, it is nowhere more so that with middle-level personnel. Those with supervisory rank are neither part of management nor part of the practitioner group, and work-life sustenance is found by turning to one's peers. It has been argued, as a matter of fact, that one of the ways in which individuals temper their commitment to an employing organization is through the compacts they make with their peers for support. In effect, they relinquish some independence from their peers to gain some independence from the organization (Strauss, 1978, p. 35).

With common goals, values, and technology, supervisors' instrumental and affective concerns are served by collaboration. To achieve one's ends, promote one's value system, or encourage the ascendancy of one or another technology, middle-level supervisors are usually required to work in concert with others. Even in instances of functional independence, supervisors frequently need the help of their colleagues to gain or avoid the adoption of overall agency programs or policies that affect their units in a like fashion.

At Carswell Community Services, for example, whatever the tensions among the six supervisors, they were united in their desire to increase the availability of housing for homeless people. Partners in Homelessness, an advocacy organization, had engaged in a series of protest demonstrations against public officials because of their perceived inaction. Carswell had been asked to co-sponsor the demonstrations, and in this case, Jill and her colleagues banded together to attempt to get Tom and the board's sanction for the agency's participation in the effort. Occasions such as this, when unit supervisors have common cause and work collectively to achieve it, are undoubtedly as frequent as those occasions when their interests diverge.

Frequently, too, subgroups of supervisors with common interests stand together, not merely to persuade the executive but also to overcome opposition from colleagues who are not similarly minded. This, of course, is the basis for the formation of cliques and factions. This dynamic is most readily observable in organizations with varying professions and established professional "pecking orders." Thus when social work is an ancillary service in a host organization composed largely of other, more powerful professionals, social work supervisors are more prone to band together and to cooperate with one another for mutual protection and support. Whatever the basis of their commonality, however, when opposition is intense, like-minded colleagues not only cooperate but often develop intense loyalty to one another. Their loyalty tends to reach beyond the issues on which they agree, to encompass other, more neutral matters.

In sum, the press to find support from one's colleagues and the standards for behavior inherent in the service culture of the social agency constitute a dynamic that predisposes cooperative relations between organizational peers. But the strains toward competition are also great, thus posing a key dilemma for many supervisors. Depending on the agency, the issues, and the preferences of superiors and peers, the supervisor's interests place her in competition with colleagues, while at the same time she is constrained to cooperate with them. Faced with this dilemma, what should she do? In our view, if she is wise, she will engage in interventions that promote her own objectives, objectives that to some degree differ from the intent and interests of others, but she will do so in a way that appears to be consistent with the norms of cooperation that are dominant in social agencies.

Relations with Superiors: Another Mixed Game

Cooperative and conflictual strains also typify supervisor-superior relations. The critical structural variable in these relations, of course, is the authority of the boss and the consequent fact that he enjoys disproportionately formal power in relation to the supervisor. The boss plays a significant role in the satisfaction the supervisor derives from her work, and she also needs his support in the conduct of her unit. Potentially, too, he may be a significant influence on the direction of her career. In this context, their disproportionate power is a critical factor indeed. The disparity between them furnishes the context for their interactions, frames the relationship, sets the norms for appropriate behavior, and provides the grounding for choices of one or another type of intervention.

Individual differences do, of course, alter the effects of the power dimension in a supervisory-superior relationship. Those supervisors who by nature are uncomfortable in relation to authority may find that their private reactions or public demeanors predispose a bias of support or opposition to the executive, quite apart from the substance of particular issues. Similarly, the personality of the executive may be such that he de-emphasizes the authority components of his role and establishes relationships that are more collegial than hierarchical in nature. Indeed, as we discussed earlier from the perspective of the supervisor relating to her staff, a wise superior will exert authority as unobtrusively as circumstances permit.

Whatever the individual differences, however, there are structural factors that mediate how these differences are enacted. To the extent that structural factors generate differences between the parties in the goals they pursue, the tasks they must accomplish, or the responsibilities they carry that generate the potential for friction, some tension is inevitable.

Divergent Perspectives

Location at the top of an organization imposes a unique set of concerns. Upper-ranking staff are responsible for the overall functioning of the organization, and they are therefore more likely to see the organizational whole than the supervisor whose perspective is limited by her attention to unit concerns. It has been suggested that the higher an administrator is in the hierarchy, the more diverse the elements he must accomodate in making decisions (Merton, 1968, p. 272). This dynamic helps to explain the relative conservativism of upper-ranking members compared to lower-ranking ones and the apparent unwillingness of executives to take risks that the staff may deem appropriate. The case of Carswell Community Services illustrates the point. All six of the supervisors wanted the agency to participate in protest demonstrations against public officials for failing to provide sufficient housing for homeless people. Tom, the agency executive, was unwilling to do so, however, although he had no lesser commitment to expanding the housing stock than they, nor did he hold any contrary judgment regarding the inadequacy of the officials' effort to secure shelter for the homeless. Rather, the agency received financial and program support from these public agencies. In his day-to-day dealings with the officials, Tom was acutely aware of their intense negative reactions to the demonstrators and therefore the real risk to Carswell's financial stability that the agency's participation in protest would entail.

Like Tom, all administrators carry responsibility for satisfying external constituencies, and their need to manage these constituencies gives them a different stake in issues than that of the supervisor, whose interests tend to be oriented internally. The supervisor at Carswell who complained to Jill that Tom did not understand the pressures faced by supervisors on the line was reflecting her internal orientation in contrast to his external perspective. Often, the tension between satisfying external constituents and attention to internal program matters is defined in terms of commitments to service and professional standards. The matter then takes on an overlay of moral righteousness. In the view of the supervisor, the executive is disinterested in the needs of clients; in the executive's perception, the supervisor is unrealistic, blind to the fact that no service is possible unless the agency maintains itself as a viable entity. The problem is confounded by the fact that each of them pays lip service to the other's view. Thus the executive will underline his commitment to service, while the staff will argue that they understand the risks to the agency. Their agreement is then often followed, however, with a *but* that qualifies the other's meaning so broadly that it denies the need for the action the other is espousing. When such a contest takes place, the supervisor most often occupies the moral high ground (i.e., client needs), while the director has to fall back on practicalities such as the agency's needs for funds. Even so, of course, the executive's additional power suggests that he will win the day, if not the moral argument. (As we suggest in our discussion of interventions in the two chapters that follow, unless the supervisor decides that there is a reason to encourage an executive's guilt, she will be more likely to achieve her objectives if she frames arguments in the context of the executive's interests).

The accountability of the executive for the entire organization generates other potential sources of tension between supervisors and executives. The executive's overall perspective leads him to downgrade the importance of decisions that affect only one unit or program. When those decisions, however important to the individual supervisor they may be, cost him something in time or energy, his disinterest may be apparent. One of the oft-heard complaints among staff and supervisors relates to the time lag in the agency in obtaining the response to a memo or the request to move ahead on some initiative.

For similar reasons, executives ordinarily have less stake in the struggle among supervisors and units over the distribution of influence or other resources. More than the competitors, the executive is likely to react to the substantive content of the conflict. But clearly, his decision to accomodate the needs of any particular supervisor almost ensures tension with other supervisors seeking similar satisfaction. Inevitably, then, as the executive garners the support of some supervisors, he risks conflict with others. It should perhaps be noted that, owing to the strain that executives experience in resolving conflicts between subordinates, when two supervisors are in an ongoing struggle, the one who makes fewer appeals for adjudication to the executive is the one more likely to be favored—all other things being equal.

Mutual Dependence

Supervisors and executives are, in some measure, mutually dependent. In the supervisor's case, her dependence is obvious. A supervisor needs her boss's support to guide unit operations; she needs the various resources that he controls; his approbation and positive evaluation are important to her success on the job and to her career. Though less apparent, the executive is dependent as well. He counts on his supervisor to conduct her unit effectively and to interpret and implement his policies accurately and with sensitivity. As his "eyes and ears" at the service delivery level, her feedback is important to his own ability to function properly. Further, her interactions with her peers can contribute to smooth or ruffled operations within the overall department or agency.

In considerable measure, the interdependence of supervisor and executive encourages cooperation between them. For obvious structural reasons, in supervisor-executive relations the strain to compete is less likely to occur than in peer relations. To the extent that an upper-ranking member is sensitive to his need for a supervisor's support, he will accomodate to a supervisor's interests if circumstances permit. And because of his higher rank, accomodation by an executive is valued currency for a supervisor, who will behave in ways that incur his obligation. Of course, the extent to which such cooperation is real—or merely *appears* to be real—is influenced by the similarities and differences in their goals, values, and professional orientation.

But their mutual dependence can create tension as well, even when their orientations are similar. A case in point is the executive's need for information and the supervisor's function to provide it. Although an executive requires the data that supervisors supply, when the information is negative, he may be understandably ambivalent about hearing it— problems that are not brought to his attention do not exist, and therefore the agency appears to be operating effectively. Those problems about which an administrator feels he can do little, for which the price of a solution seems more costly to him than living with the problem, or are the direct result of his own actions and hence seen as evidence of his failure are most likely to be avoided.

Yet it is the supervisor's function to convey bad news. Unfortunately, the onus for bearing bad news commonly falls on the messenger, and the supervisor who brings problems to her boss courts the risk of appearing to be unable to handle the problem or, even worse, responsible for its existence. The fact that the risk is real is supported by a study of fifty-two middle managers which found a high correlation (+.41) between upward work-life mobility and holding back "problem" information from the boss (Wilensky, 1967, p. 43). Empirical data on organizations consistently show that good news travels up the hierarchy more than bad news, and that all news takes on a rosier hue as it reaches the organization's upper levels (Katz and Kahn, 1966). To the extent that a supervisor takes the informant aspects of her role conscientiously, she courts the potential for strain or conflict with an ambivalent boss.

In the final analysis, however, disparate power is the critical structural variable. It engenders both cooperative behavior and tension between the parties. On the one hand, supervisors understand that their boss expects cooperation and if they do not cooperate, or appear to, he may reward or punish them accordingly. On the other hand, professionals are expected to be self-directing and to seek to enlarge their autonomy—a dynamic that runs counter to the executive's ultimate accountability and consequent need to control agency operations. It may be that one of the functions of norms prescribing proper hierarchical behavior is to ease some of the stress inherent in superior-subordinate relations. An agreed-upon set of rules, even when there are tacit understandings that some of the rules may be stretched, does much to maintain orderly relations.

An identifiable set of norms govern hierarchical relations in formal organizations. For the supervisor, the assessment of the norms that are operative in her particular setting is important in developing an effective working relationship with the boss. Sometimes the norms are implicit and not easily determined through direct exploration; thus sensitive observation and inductive judgment may be required to obtain an accurate reading. But unless she observes these norms—or *appears* to—she will not represent her unit or herself as effectively as she might.

Although norms governing hierarchical relations vary between agencies and individuals, some generalizations are useful to serve as guideposts. We cite three of the more common ones. Because, in greater or lesser measure, they reflect themes of authority as they occur within bureaucracies, the three overlap.

Chief among the expecations guiding superior-subordinate relations is a *norm of loyalty*. This norm constitutes a compact that is reciprocal in nature; each party is obliged to support the other in dealing with outsiders or lower-level staff. Essentially, the prescription calls for each of them to protect the image and interests of the other. In cases in which one has erred or made an unpopular decision, the appropriate person "takes the heat" rather than blames the other. Or they decide together who might most easily bear the onus for an unpopular action—taking both personal and organizational imperatives into account (ordinarily, the onus falls—or should fall—to the boss). It is also expected that each will publicly interpret the other's acts as positively as possible. In one case, for example, an executive acted in a way that agency workers knew their supervisor could not credibly justify. Provocatively, one of them asked her what she thought of the boss's behavior. Her reply that "I expect that he will be sorry about what he did" met the test of loyalty, for it was a graceful way of registering her opinion under difficult circumstances while casting the most benign light possible on the executive's act.

Protecting the other's image and interests, it should be noted, does not necessarily require that they agree on all positions at public meetings. Ordinarily, an executive and supervisor who work well together try to find some common ground on a controversial issue before going public. Or, depending on the issue, one will accomodate to the other's positions on some occasions and the reverse will occur at other times. Because of their respective ranks, however, the executive's views are likely to prevail on issues of importance to him. But loyalty to the supervisor requires that he accept her silence on an issue rather than require her to uphold a position with which she disagrees. On the other hand, her loyalty to him prescribes that if they have consulted on the matter in advance, she not "double deal"—that is, agree privately with him but express disagreement to others.

Although the norm is reciprocal, it is complicated by the power discrepancy in hierarchical relations. Although the supervisor is expected to protect and promote the interests of her boss, she does not have equal weight in shaping his views or guiding his actions. Because of this, the executive's loyalty to the supervisor is much easier to proffer than is the reverse. And the consequences of violating the norm is much greater for the supervisor.

To the extent that the supervisor feels supportive of her boss and what he stands for, the norm is not likely to be onerous. The supervisor's support or expressions of loyalty may engender negative reactions from other organizational actors or may require that she engage in activities that are technically unfamiliar to her, but her loyalty will not be at the expense of her personal values. The difficulty occurs when the supervisor is, in fact, ambivalent or her support is qualified. Under these circumstances, the potential conflict between her own commitments and the boss's expectations may be intense. If the conflict is profound, the supervisor could go so far as to leave the agency. More often, it will lead her to play a mixed game.

Although the supervisor may not fully follow the loyalty norm internally and still avoid grievous consequences, its violation with outsiders is considered a serious breach of faith. For example, one supervisor who told a site visitor from a funding source that she did not receive sufficient backup from her superior was warned that such an infraction would not be tolerated a second time. The threat of firing, or firing itself, is not atypical in such cases.

Another norm that guides hierarchical interactions is that of *respect for position*. We refer here to the expectation that each actor will respect the prerogatives and boundaries of the other's role—that neither will engage in activities that might be interpreted as the responsibility of the other. As with the norm of loyalty, the norm of respect for position is reciprocal; in view of the power discrepancy in the relationship, it holds more significance as it relates to the prerogatives of the executive than those of the supervisor.

Respect for position on the part of the supervisor implies that she accept the legitimacy of the superior's authority and act accordingly. If there are differences between them, the supervisor is expected to carry out his wishes, once a decision has been made. When she does have a disagreement with him, or unsuccessfully seeks his support, she must not go over his head to someone in a higher position; to do so would constitute a serious breach of organizational manners. The norm also prescribes that she consult her boss before making decisions about matters that he would define as within his purview and important.

In reverse, the superior is expected not to supervise members of his supervisor's staff, nor to delegate responsibilities to them without prior discussion and clearance with her. He is also expected to consult with the supervisor on matters that affect her interests and to avoid interfering—or at least, not to interfere inordinately—in the supervisor's day-to-day operations and decision making.

In contrast to the loyalty norm, which tends in large measure to transcend individual differences, respecting the prerogatives of the other's role varies significantly with the management style of the executive. Some develop highly interdependent relationships with their supervisors and tend toward informality in their dealings with others. These executives are likely to pay considerably less attention to their own prerogatives, while the supervisors who work for them tend, in turn, to be less concerned when their superiors deal direcfly with their staffs. On the other hand, executives who delegate little and maintain tight control of operations are likely to be sensitive to issues of role boundaries. These differences aside, however, a concern that the supervisor and executive do not "bump into each other" in the conduct of their respective jobs typically frames the relationship. The potential for tension when the norm is breached in either direction is apparent.

The final norm guiding hierarchical relations is the *norm of deference.* This refers to the expectation that subordinates will comport themselves so as to communicate the disparity inherent in the respective roles of superiors and subordinates. The very words *upper* and *lower* as used to describe their organizational level—or *superior* and *subordinate*—suggest that deference is an issue. But because ours is an egalitarian society, to act deferentially or to receive deference may seem to the actors untoward or may create feelings of discomfort. This does not, however, eliminate the norm. Instead, the deferential behavior tends not to be labeled as such, and its manifestation is often subtle and indirect.

Organizations—as the "property" of their upper-ranking members—collude to reinforce the norm. Those in executive positions are given considerably more perks than supervisors. The size of the office, for example, (or its more lavish furnishings) is designed to signify the executive's "superior" status and influence and to indicate that deference is

organizationally supported. (Indeed, bureaucratically sophisticated oper-
ators often try to work this for themselves; i.e., they go after the trimmings
in the knowledge that a fancy office and other perquisites help to define
the significance of their status and influence in the agency).

Sometimes the deference is so ingrained in organizational practice that
it is not recognized as such. For example, in meetings between a supervisor and an executive, irrespective of who was the initiator of the meeting or for whose benefit it might have been convened, neither party gives
a thought to where the meeting will occur. The supervisor always knows
to go to her boss's office, and he always knows to expect her. Or the
deference may be even more subtle and individually rooted. If the supervisor laughs a little harder at her boss's jokes than they deserve, for
example, if she is more responsive to him than would be appropriate
under different circumstances—or than she would like to be—she is
behaving deferentially, however the behavior might otherwise be labeled.

Unlike the norms discussed earlier, the deference norm is clearly uni-
directional; that is, it reflects an expectation of the subordinate's behavior
toward the superior and not the reverse. For the reasons cited above, its
behavioral manifestations are also more ambiguous than the norms of
loyalty and respect for position. It often must be enacted more by implication than by direct reference, and the norm is unlikely to be the subject of
open discussion between the supervisor and her boss. There are exceptions, of course, but executives ordinarily expect that supervisors will get
the message regarding appropriate deferential behavior without their having to request or direct it. If, for example, a supervisor waited for a few
hours to return a director's call, he might be edgy about it if he knew she
were available. But it is unlikely that he would raise the point unless there
were significant instrumental agency consequences in her being late in
returning his call. He could hardly have objected on the grounds that he
was too important to be treated so casually by her, though he might in
fact feel that way. As a matter of fact, in the case of a less than interper-
sonally adequate executive whose expectations for deference are not being
met by the supervisor, trouble between them can become chronic without the executive's ever finding the way to express the source of his
dissatisfaction.

The norms of loyalty, respect for position, and deference exercise a
cumulative effect in predisposing cooperative interactions between the
supervisor and superior, and this may be the intended function of such
norms. Perhaps the point should be put differently. The norms may be
quite effective in ensuring the *appearance* of cooperation. When they are
breached by either party, or if their behavioral manifestations are unclear

to either of them, tension may result. When there are significant substantive differences between executives and their subordinates, the norms may serve to paper over their differences. Conversely, when there are substantive differences, supervisors may feel that the requirements of loyalty, respect for position, and deference constitute additional pressures that infringe on their authenticity and create a further source of tension between the executive and themselves.

In sum, organizational roles and structural patterns lead supervisors to experience a mixture of some elements of cooperation and some elements of tension in their relations with both colleagues and superiors. As a fact of organizational life, then, their professional interactions range on a contiuum from those marked by collaboration to those entailing conflict or pressure. Factors affecting where on the continuum these interactions fall are important in informing supervisory practice, and we conclude this chapter by reviewing them.

Factors Affecting Organizational Interventions

For conceptual purposes, we identify three modes of intervention that range along the continuum. They have been called (1) collaboration, (2) campaign, and (3) contest (Brager et al., 1987).

In collaboration, problems tend to be stated as such rather than as solutions; information regarding the perspectives of the parties is widely shared; and a climate of openness typifies the interaction. Collaboration includes such activities as problem solving, joint action, education, and mild persuasion. Problem solving involves the supervisor and others with whom she is working in the mutual search for data, ideas, resources, and models that best fulfill commonly derived criteria to solve a problem. Joint action denotes teamwork to implement a proposed solution, program, or policy. Education refers to the sharing of information not available to others, the intent of which is to inform rather than to convince. Finally, in mild persuasion, the supervisor attempts to convince the other party through the spontaneous expression of ideas and arguments.

Campaign interventions fall at the midpoint on the continuum between collaboration and conflict and contain some elements of both. They are the interventions used most widely in mixed games, and include hard persuasion, negotiating, covert maneuvering, and mobilizing pressure. Hard persuasion involves advocating a position tailored to appeal to the other actor, in which the supervisor consciously selects (or excludes) facts, values, and emotional content to make the most convincing case.

Covert maneuvering implies a secret exercise of influence; distinct from the open communication of collaboration, maneuvering entails the *appearance* of openness or the guise of common purpose. Negotiations involve the sequential exchange of resources, sanctions, accomodations, and rewards toward the end of reaching a mutually acceptable outcome. The exchange may be implicit or explicit, but it ordinarily takes place by making requests or demands, arguing them, and then conceding and accepting some part of the other's position. Finally, the mobilization of pressure, either overtly or covertly, refers to garnering additional support to impel the other's acceptance of the supervisor's goal.

Contest interventions carry pressure a considerable distance further and involve public conflict. They include virulent clashes of position (through no-holds-barred debates and public manifestos), the violation of normative behavior (e.g., moving out of the bounds of organizationally proper behavior through activities of provocation or protest), and in the extreme, the violation of legal norms (e.g., illegally halting agency operations). For reasons that are apparent, contest interventions are not usually practiced in internal agency operations. We mention them only to note the full range of theoretically possible modes of intervention.

The four primary factors that influence one's choice of collaborative, campaign, or contest interventions are the degree of goal commonality shared by the actors, the relative power of each, the nature of their relationship (Brager and Holloway 1978), and the larger organizational climate. We briefly summarize below the primary issues related to these factors as they affect the supervisor in her dealings with colleagues and superiors.

As discussed in the prior section of this chapter, the goals of the supervisor and the goals of colleagues or executives are sometimes the same and sometimes diverge. The greater the goal congruence, the more likely are the parties to act collaboratively. And the more disparate their ends, the less likely or appropriate is collaboration. Thus in the Carswell case Jill and the other supervisors joined together to try to convince their executive and board to participate in demonstrations in which they shared a common objective, to increase housing placements for homeless people. They caucused, decided together which arguments might be most persuasive, and agreed that all of them would play a role in their meeting with Tom. Jill was designated the lead-off person at the meeting; although it was unstated, the choice of Jill as initial spokesperson was based on the collective perception that she might have more influence with Tom than the others. The supervisors collaborated on this issue because of goal consensus, but in their stance with Tom, they engaged in a campaign mode, because they anticipated he would be likely to hold a different position than theirs. Conversely, on the issue of training unit staff, the other supervisors held different goals than Jill, with the result that they were minimally cooperative. Here, Jill and Tom, in common cause, were the collaborators.

Essentially, it is the *perception* of goal commonality and difference that drives one's behavior. Thus a supervisor's accurate assessment of the goals and interests of her peers or executive—and how *they* perceive the situation—is key to the effectiveness of collaboration. If, for example, the supervisor perceives goal commonality with these other organizational actors but they define the goals to be divergent, she is at a disadvantage. The fact that she has chosen collaboration while they are being overtly cooperative—but all the while maneuvering covertly—is likely to result in her lesser effectiveness. On the other hand, if she perceives other parties to have different ends than hers when in fact the differences are small or nonexistent, and thus chooses campaign or contest interventions, she risks alienating them by what may be viewed as inappropriate behavior on her part.

The relative power of the actors is a second factor relevant to the choice of interventions. As we suggested in our discussion of the supervisor's relations with her executive, he has the resources to ensure her compliance, because the power discrepancy between them is likely to be significant. In effect, high-power people can require low-power actors to accept their goal and cooperate. The low-power person has one of two choices—to submit or to attempt to accomplish some measure of his or her goal by engaging in campaign interventions. It is not unusual for some supervisors to use hard persuasion, covert maneuvering, negotiation, and—where possible—mild (if invisible) coercion to affect an executive's decision in matters of importance to them. The game must match the stakes, however, because the risks of exposure and its concommitants may be costly.

Because of power discrepancies, only rarely do supervisors engage with a superior in the contest interventions we have described. They do so, however, under some circumstances. When their differences and anger are so great, a supervisor may lose control—although, needless to say, this is hardly an intervention in which effective practice is an issue. Or she may join with others when virulent negative reactions about the executive's behavior are pervasive throughout the agency. Supervisors may also enter into conflict with superiors when their value or career referents are outside of the agency and they view their tenure there as less than critical to their interests. Or contest may be engaged if, for some reason, the supervisor is out of reach of the executive's retaliation. This occasionally occurs in organizations, for example, when staff have strong protections such as those of civil service or a tenure system or when the supervisor has a significant constituency (e.g., a funding source) so that the discrepancy in their relative power is not as great as the formal system would have it. Except in unusual cases, however, contest with the executive poses such significant dangers as to be most often avoided.

When there is a mutually recognized parity in power, as is often the case among colleagues, and goal commonality also exists, collaboration is likely to take place. On the other hand, if the power of two or more supervisors is relatively equal, but there are goal differences, the parties are likely to turn to campaign interventions. Indeed, as we have already suggested, the effective supervisor should be on the lookout for the ways in which she can increase her power relative to her peers. Often, this leads to covert maneuvering.

As with goal commonality and difference, an accurate assessment of the actors' degrees of power is critical to effective organizational practice. Clearly, one wants neither to overplay nor underplay one's hands, should power be one of the elements influencing a particular decision. And as Pfeffer (1981) notes, "Skill in diagnosing power can help one line up on the winning side of issues, thereby giving the appearance of being powerful by being associated with victories. Knowledge of the distribution of influence can provide insight into which issues hold a chance of winning, and therefore, where effort should be expended, as well as which issues are hopeless and thus should be ignored" (p. 132).

Pfeffer (1981, pp. 133–134) cites a study that supports the importance of the accurate assessment of power factors. One of three variables investigated by the study was the accuracy with which a university department head assessed the relative power of the departments within the organization. The accuracy of his power perceptions had a significant effect on the department head's ability to influence the distribution of university resources. Interestingly, knowledge of the power distribution was most important for the effectiveness of the least-powerful departments—a particularly notable finding for social workers who are often in lesser positions of influence in interdisciplinary settings.

The relationship with her peers and superiors is a third factor that has implications for how a supervisor approaches agency issues. Two interdependent aspects of relationships are worth noting in this regard: one having to do with the prior experience of the parties in working together and the other relating to the intimacy of their connection.

Supervisors, in dealing with unit or other professional issues, take into account their prior interactions with another party. Over time, each develops expectations regarding the interests and behavior of the other, and their current interaction is inevitably colored by their past association. It is logical to suppose that the number and strength of cooperative bonds enhances present cooperation while "experiences of failure and disillusionment in attempts to cooperate make it unlikely" (Deutsch, 1969, p. 27). When past interaction has been cooperative, differences in points of view may be experienced as minimal, whereas if the relationship has been troubled or distant, even commonalities may be perceived with suspicion. The supervisor's understanding of this point importantly shapes the ways in which a supervisor presents her ideas to the colleagues or superiors she hopes to influence. For example, with a suspicious partner, the supervisor must take particular care to moderate her arguments, eschew obvious exaggeration, and avoid the appearance of misstating.

Too readily presuming the reaction of another on the basis of past experience is sometimes a mistake. The supervisor might, in this instance, perceive her goal as dissimilar, when in fact it meets the other's interests. Or she could react the other way around, assuming similarity because of past agreement when their current goals are actually in conflict. Although it is appropriate to form a hypothesis about how another will react as a result of prior contacts, a supervisor needs to feel out her assumptions before she behaves as if the other's position is known.

Obviously, the closer or more intimate a supervisor's relationship has been with a peer or executive, the more it is incumbent on her to limit herself to collaborative actions. This is the case even when their goals in a particular instance are divergent. Their friendly relations make campaign or contest interventions unacceptable, because, in our value judgment, few issues are as important as the character of a close ongoing relationship.

What, in fact, does a colleague have a right to expect of a friend when they disagree on an issue? The case of Sandra, Jill's friend at Carswell, is instructive. Sandra felt that she could not support Jill's training program. Jill had discussed the idea with her before their staff meeting, but Sandra had been noncommittal. As a friend, Sandra owed it to Jill to raise whatever objections she might have had at that time. Later, Sandra did fulfill friendship norms by remaining silent at the meeting. Later too, when the program was adopted, Sandra demonstrated her friendship by offering Jill suggestions about how to enhance its effectiveness. Had

Sandra tried to generate opposition to the plan before the staff meeting or if she had otherwise engaged in covert maneuvering following its adoption, in our judgment, their friendship would be at issue. Of course, close colleagues have to decide together on the importance any particular issue holds for them. In some instances—usually on a noncritical matter to one or both of them—public disagreement is acceptable and may sometimes even be strategic. If a matter is critical to both, they may have to agree to disagree and do all in their power to win the day. There is no question, however, that such a contest will cause strain—sometimes considerable strain—to their relationship, depending on the importance of the issue to them. In Jill's case, the program was considerably more important to her than opposing it was to Sandra, and thus their modus vivendi worked for them.

Strain also occurs between close colleagues as a result of conflicting self-interests—for example, when both want to receive a choice assignment and it appears that the game is zero-sum. The pursuit of one's own interests, even when they conflict with a friend's, is ordinarily perceived as legitimate. Discussing the matter openly is the ethical stance and is more likely to preserve the relationship as well. Occasionally, accomodations can be found such as sharing the assignment, taking turns, or withdrawal, having determined that one has considerably less stake in the matter than the other. Short of that, each will have to weigh the importance of her interests against the importance of the friendship, or they may find that it is possible to acknowledge their respective interests, agree to play fair, and not personalize the contest.

A converse circumstance also occurs, although probably less frequently. Sometimes the relationship between a supervisor and one of her colleagues is so strained that joining together to work for a common end is less important to one or both of them than the maintenance of relational distance. In one organization with which we are familiar, for example, two supervisors had developed a finely honed emnity over the years. With the arrival of a new executive, they found themselves on the same side. One of them, then, quickly withdrew—she was too uncomfortable to be seen as associated with the other.

Even in cases considerably less fraught with antagonism, a supervisor may hesitate to engage in collaborative activities with an estranged other for fear that the other cannot really be trusted. Essentially, she makes the assessment that the other's stake in preventing her from achieving her objective is greater than the other's stake in a common goal. The latter is perceived as prepared to sabotage the collaboration to ensure that the former is thwarted, even if this compromises her own interests in the process. Although we do not view this as a frequent or rational response, it is not unknown for some organizational actors to engage in self-defeating behavior of this sort.

One final comment about the impact of relationships on interventions has to do with the supervisor's image. Any practice decision to advocate for or influence an organizational issue must be weighed against its consequences to the worker's reputation with her colleagues and superiors. Of course, those who use campaign interventions skillfully—or sparingly—are unlikely to suffer image problems. Too, there are occasions when a supervisor is unconcerned about how an intense persuasive attempt or a covert strategem might bear on her relations with others, so important is the issue to her. But if her action risks a great deal in her relations with her superiors—or with colleagues—she might choose to forego the attempt in favor of their more positive definitions of her.

The final factor to consider when choosing collaborative, campaign or contest interventions involves the larger organizational context in which the interactions occur. In a sense this consideration is related to the normative and image concerns mentioned previously. The exact same activity—for example, the obvious and aggressive pursuit of a goal—may be viewed benignly and as legitimate or pejoratively and as illegitimate, depending on how the intervention fits the prevailing mood or climate of the organization at any given point in time.

In part, it is the organization's structure and culture that determines what may or may not be deemed acceptable or feasible as an intervention strategy. We hypothesize, for example, that an agency's predominant decision-making style may influence an organization's tolerance for one or another type of intervention. If rational decision making is highly valued—whatever the objective reality of how decisions are made—the supervisor must engage in, or appear to engage in, problem solving, joint action, and education. If, on the other hand, decision making is viewed as ad hoc and properly responsive to the pushes and pulls of a variety of interests, she can persuade, negotiate, and even mildly pressure without unduly negative judgments on the part of her organizational co-workers. Similarly, when the control of decisions is highly centralized, there is more incentive for her to cooperate with colleagues and to risk campaign tactics with administrators—and therefore a more general acceptance of such practice. To cite one final example: in agencies in which rules and routines are consensually shared as appropriate to effective service provision, the supervisor violates the rules and routines at some risk to her reputation. But when the means for effective service are ambiguous or subject to widespread disagreement, her latitude for maneuvering without cost to her image or reputation is considerably enhanced. Whatever the case, the important point is that some agencies permit a wide range of organizational interventions without significant risk, whereas in others campaign or contest interventions pose considerably more uncertainty in the supervisor's relationship with others.

In addition to the effect of an organization's culture on definitions of what is an appropriate intervention, the agency's current circumstances are also a factor. Research studies have demonstrated, for example, that under threatening social conditions, people are more likely to judge identical interactions harshly than they are when social conditions are positive. During difficult times—for example, when uncertainty exists regarding important leadership transitions, if there are potential funding or other crises, or when staff members are faced with new and impossibly demanding workloads—a supervisor's actions may be viewed with a harshness that simply would not occur at other times. If her activities are perceived as unresponsive to these circumstances, she courts particular trouble with superiors and probably with colleagues as well. If, on the other hand, these same activities are viewed as redressing the organization's stress, she will be judged as helpful.

We conclude this chapter by noting that much of what occurs in an agency, of course, is beyond the supervisor's ability to control. A set of forces stemming from the environment, the organization's structure and culture, the actions and reactions of other organizational actors, all impact on agency events, including her unit and its services. Nevertheless, one important element that influences these forces—and hence agency events—is the supervisor's ability to represent her unit's (and her own) interests. To do so with maximum effectiveness requires that she has the political skills necessary to shape some outcomes and to avoid others.

Persuading and Negotiating

A predominant theme in organizational life, we have said, is the mixed game, including some elements of cooperation and some elements of competition and conflict. In such circumstances, contending actors attempt to get others to accept their perspectives on organizational events. The very choice of organizational problems, the terms of the debate, the symbols and lessons from the past that are called forth, are all influenced by the fact that different actors have different stakes in defining the agency's problems and thus affecting the resultant actions (Yates, 1985). When there is resistance or opposition to one's favored ends, and these ends are important, actors are likely to bring to bear whatever influence they have to shape the outcome.

The skills one brings to defining problems and influencing actions may be said to be political skills—if one accepts the view of organizational politics as the term has been used in this book. With Pfeffer (1981, p. 7), we hold that political behavior "involves the exercise of power to get something accomplished, as well as those activities which are undertaken to expand power already possessed . . . " Theorists have noted that there are three major strategies in the effort to win an outcome or increase one's influence—persuasion, negotiation, and the mobilization of support— for it is principally through persuasion and negotiation that organizational decisions are made (Bucher, 1970, p. 30). We devote this chapter to a discussion of the techniques of persuading and negotiating, but first comment briefly on the supervisor as a political actor.

The Supervisor as a Political Actor

A precondition for effective persuasion or negotiation, as well as for other political interventions, is how the supervisor handles her organizational role and how she is perceived by others in the agency. We have, especially in Chapter 3, discussed aspects of the supervisor's practice intended to extend her influence. Among these aspects are exchanging resources with others, enhancing the perception of one's competence, assuming a proactive stance, and representing subordinate interests with others in the agency. Because the practice is intended to increase her influence, these efforts meet our definition of political behavior. We now bring the subject front and center and expand on the characteristics and skills that make for effective political intervention.

A survey of managers to assess their perceptions of the personal characteristics of effective political actors is instructive (Allen et al., 1979). The surveyed managers did not, by and large, choose characteristics that we would associate with backroom wheeler-dealers, as is the stereotype of many social workers about political actors. The two most-cited characteristics were articulate and sensitive (both 29.9 percent), the third was socially adept (19.5 percent), with competent and popular following next (17.2 percent).

A major interest of the study for us is that articulateness and sensitivity are mentioned a significantly greater number of times than any of the other characteristics. This conforms to our own view that these are important attributes for political practitioners and are also qualities of particular significance for skillful persuasion and negotiation. In our discussion of articulateness, we broaden the reference to encompass communication skills generally.

It is perhaps obvious that an articulate supervisor can be a more effective advocate for her position. Convincing others to accept her view is achieved, in part, by how well she selects, presents, and develops her definitions of events. Collecting credible data, making thoughtful presentations, and choosing appealing arguments help to convince others regarding the substance of her case. But it does more, too. In making an effective, "rational" argument, it allows those who want to go along with her for other reasons to do so with greater legitimacy. Furthermore, being articulate (and sensitive) helps the supervisor to present herself as she would like to be seen.

Supervisors may be uncomfortable with the notion of their contriving an image. But, as has been pointed out, "even the presentation of the no-nonsense, honest, natural side of one's character *is* a presentation; it may be the 'real self' but it is also a controlled, projected image which the actor wishes to have taken account of by others" (Mangham, 1979, p. 53). And Goffman, in a classic work, has effectively argued that the basic underlying theme of all interaction is the desire of each participant *"to guide and control the response made by others present"* [italics added] (Goffman, 1959, pp. 3–4). The very notion of "the conscious use of self" in professional social work implies interaction that is contrived, in this instance, to elicit maximally helpful responses from clients. To try to influence the judgments of others about oneself to obtain desirable organizational ends is simply another application of this social work precept.

Communication skills are similar in both clinical and political interventions. Gummer has noted that the ability to use words for the purpose of conveying ideas and sentiments and the ability to focus attention on what people say and do as a basic source of information are central to both. He has remarked that " 'listening with the third ear' is as accurate a description of how politicians go about eliciting and identifying the interests and intentions of their friends, foes and constituents as it is of the social worker's approach to probing the thoughts and feelings of clients" (Gummer, 1983, p. 25).

Effective communication entails not only being articulate, but also knowing what *not* to say and when *not* to say it. As in poker, not tipping your own hand while knowing what cards your opponent holds is crucial in negotiations and other political encounters (Mangham, 1979, p. 103). Indeed, as we have already said, to be in control of information—or at the center of a communications network—is a source of considerable power in organizations. We should caution, however, that in maintaining secrecy, the supervisor must not appear to be playing things too close to the vest. If information is withheld from colleagues or one's boss consistently or as a matter of style, it is almost sure to be noted. The reaction of others, then, may be that she cannot be counted on or, worse, that she is not to be trusted.

Making an appealing or precise case is one skill, but making an ambiguous case, when the conditions call for it, is probably as important. Communicating implicitly—simultaneously saying and not saying—is a significant talent for use in political encounters. We develop this subject further in our discussion of negotiations later in this chapter.

The second attribute of effective political actors that scores highly in the managers' survey is sensitivity. By sensitivity, we mean the ability to recognize the thoughts and feelings of others, along with one's own. Sensitivity is important in political and other interventions, because interaction is a mutually influenced behavior; each of the parties must take into account what the other says and does—as well as appreciating their subtle meanings—as they respond to the other. The supervisor who can identify the interests of others, understand their value commitments, and recognize how they perceive her and themselves possesses significant data to move the interaction in desired directions, whether the interchange is cooperative or conflictual.

Self-awareness, a prized characteristic in clinical work, is also important in political engagements. If we are right in suggesting that the presentation of self serves as a grounding for effective intervention, the awareness of how one thinks, feels, and acts serves as a central element of that image making. When supervisors are in touch with how they react in particular situations—and are sensitive to how others respond to them— they are more likely to shape and discipline their responses effectively. Interestingly, research suggests that people who have a high capacity for self-monitoring are more accurate in identifying the attempts of others to deceive them than do low self-monitors (Snyder, 1974, pp. 525–537). Because some colleagues and superiors are likely to be deceptive in conflictual situations, identifying if and when they shade the truth is a relevant skill indeed.

Sensitivity to self and others allows a supervisor to choose to adapt her style in persuading, negotiating, or otherwise intervening in specific situations. Schutz (1970), has identified three interpersonal *needs*: inclusion, control and affection. Inclusion refers to the extent to which an individual needs to be included in a group, to belong; control connotes assertiveness and the degree to which one needs to carry authority or to dominate; affection is concerned with warmth and liking in interaction. Mangham suggested that, rather than needs, the three dimensions of behavior can be viewed as aids in influencing. A sensitive practitioner can decide with whom and in what circumstances being "one of the 'boys'" might suit her purposes, when a show of unwillingness to brook disagreement might work better, and when displaying warmth might impel others to respond in a like fashion (Mangham, 1979, p. 89).

We would add one caution. In organizations, one's behavior needs to be moderated by the fact that there are both a history and a future to one's interactions. Consistency—or at least its appearance—is necessary, and it may be difficult to display affection on Monday and be authoritative on Tuesday. Nor is the display of warmth or the penchant for belonging likely to accomplish one's purposes when it is served up only when one wants something. Once that is said, however, it is worth noting that varying one's approach or style to fit particular people or circumstances or to advance particular ends is politically useful.

Accurately interpreting behavior requires that the supervisor stand outside herself, observing her own and the others' responses as she engages in political encounters. Factoring in her experience with the other, along with the interests that stem from their organizational roles and function, is important as well. Close attention to the details of an encounter or event—what is said and not said, done and not done—both as it occurs and afterward is also highly useful. The review of details often uncovers meanings that would otherwise have remained obscure.

Finally, the supervisor may refine her interpretations by sharing her observations of interactions with astute and sensitive colleagues to elicit feedback. Two conditions are necessary to ensure the usefulness of their feedback in checking her impressions. One is that the supervisor report the interaction with as little perceptual distortion as possible, so that the colleague has a relatively unbiased description as a basis for judgment. The other is the supervisor's openness to hearing opinions that run counter to her own and her encouragement of the colleague to share opinions of that kind.

People differ, of course, in the degree to which they can view events from the perspectives of others or accurately identify their own ideas and feelings. As with other skills, however, these can be acquired with practice. But even when a supervisor is able to make these assessments reliably, she must also be willing to put her awareness to use—to intervene in organizational contests of significance to her staff and unit. Putting some of the principles and precepts of persuasion and negotiation to use is a condition of effective intervention.

Persuading

Effective practice in organizations entails the management of meanings—for the meanings events hold for people motivate them to act or not. Persuasion is, of course, a significant way in which meanings are shaped, strengthened, and revised, and extensive research has been undertaken on its techniques. By and large, the research has emphasized three components: the communicator, the message and the audience or target of the persuasive attempt. Insufficient attention has been paid to situational factors (Reardon, 1981), and there has been little study regarding persuasion in organizations. We intend here to draw on the persuasion research as we discuss the communicator and what makes for effective arguments in agencies. To relate the research to an organizational context, however, we first cite an example of one supervisor's attempt to persuade.

Sue, the supervisor of the outpatient services department (OPD) at the Heights Mental Health Service Program, has been interested for some time in relocating one of the four neighborhood units in her department. She believes that the Heights disproportionately serves middle-class clients, and she would like at least one of her units to be located in a predominately low-income neighborhood. Herb, the Heights' executive director, also feels that it is important to attract a larger number of low-income clients to the agency. When Sue broached the possibility of moving one of her units to another neighborhood, however, he thought the idea was untenable. There was likely to be an outcry from the neighborhood that would lose the service, and moving the unit would also be costly to Sue's relations with her staff.

Prior to coming to the Heights, Sue had worked in an agency with a large child-abuse caseload, and she had developed a reputation for expertise in that area. She was mindful that although the incidence of child abuse had risen markedly in the community at large, the Height's caseload did not reflect this growing problem. She has not raised the issue of serving abusing families with Herb because she believes he would be cautious about a program that might pose political problems for the agency. Any move by the Heights in this direction might be viewed by some of its board, staff, and clients as a redirection of the agency's basic mission to help rehabilitate the emotionally vulnerable.

Sue's OPD provides direct counseling to individuals and groups. There are three other departments at the Heights: a community treatment program, with responsibility for a day program and community residences for the mentally ill, headed by Jim, a pyschiatrist; a community consultation unit, offering consultative services to community groups, directed by Will, a social worker; and a research department run by Elias, a sociologist. Herb meets with these department heads regularly as a management team to gain their advice with regard to program and policy development.

A contact of Sue's in the department of social services (DSS) has informed her that DSS is planning to contract with some agency to develop a program to work with abusing parents in Southpart, a low-income neighborhood, and that an innovative component of the program will be to design a computerized tracking system to identify variables that make for success and failure in work with these clients. DSS is interested in the demonstration potential of the program, and expects that the tracking system may ultimately be used by other contract agencies. If the Heights is interested, Sue is told, it would have the inside track on obtaining the contract.

Adding a fifth unit in OPD at Southpark, with emphasis on child abuse, would meet Sue's two major objectives for the agency—to increase services to low-income clients and to move into the child-abuse area. She is aware that the program would be a visible and high-risk endeavor, and that Herb may be reluctant to approve it. In addition, unlike many other agency executives, Herb has not been particularly interested in expanding the agency. Sue hopes that her relationship with him will help in gaining his approval—because Herb sees her as a competent and loyal supervisor.

Sue expects that Herb will consult with the management team before making his decision. She decides to ask Elias, the research director, for "advice," because he is the management team member who is most likely to be supportive of the new direction. She proposes that the tracking system be located in his department. Although she is not quite as certain of Will, of the community consultation unit, he is a fellow social worker with similar perspectives on the field as hers, and he has at times expressed some frustration about the "elitist" nature of the agency's program. Among the team members, she is most concerned about Jim, whose interest is in the chronically mentally ill to the near exclusion of other client populations. Her unit and Jim's are the two largest and most powerful units of the Heights, and Jim, she adjudges, views her as overly ambitious. Her relations with him have always had elements of underlying tension.

If Herb is ambivalent about her proposal, she presumes that it will be necessary for Elias and Will to be strongly supportive and for Jim not to be adamantly opposed. Although Sue was unaware of it, there is research to support that presumption. One study found, for example, that when an executive's lieutenants are supportive of program innovations, the likelihood of their adoption is greater than when the executive alone holds change-oriented values (Hage and Dewar 1973, pp. 376–378).

Sue followed a prudent process by discussing the matter with her natural allies first and only later opening the subject with others who might be either tentative or negative about the initiative. She began with Elias, whom she assessed would favor the program, then moved to Will, the next most likely supporter. Thus when she spoke with Herb, she had already garnered the backing of those members of the team. She approached Jim in an attempt to neutralize him only after Herb had placed the item on the team meeting's agenda.

Sue was successful in gaining approval for the DSS program, although earlier she had been unable to accomplish her goal of increasing the agency's low-income census. As has frequently been observed, it is considerably easier to innovate when increased resources are available—in this case, funding from DSS—than when resources are fixed. Nevertheless, she achieved her goals also because, as we shall see, she was persuasive in her interactions with Herb and her colleagues.

The Supervisor as Communicator

Credibility has been the most frequently studied characteristic of the communicator in persuasion research. More immediate attitude change takes place when a message has a high credibility source (Hovland and Weiss, 1951; Hovland, Janus, and Kelley, 1953). Credibility, however, is a multidimensional concept that may include such components as expertise, trustworthiness, and lack of bias. It is also situational and affected by the relations between the communicator and the target of the persuasive attempt.

In our example, Sue's relationships with the four actors to be convinced had already been established, as is usually the case in organizations. Her arguments, we may suppose, would be more credible to Herb and least credible to Jim, and her message to each of them did, in fact, reflect this difference.

Credibility decreases when a supervisor is perceived as arguing in her own self-interest or in the interests of her unit. When she is perceived in that way, others often assume bias—and expect selective interpretations or perhaps less-than-complete candor. Sensitivity to the ascription of self-interest can help to close this credibility gap.

If a supervisor's argument includes advantages to herself or unit but there are other cogent reasons for making the argument, she should acknowledge her interests and move on to make the substantive arguments supporting her case. When the other actor is either unsympathetic or is knowledgeable about the issue under discussion, the supervisor must transmit self-evidently unbiased messages. If, on the other hand, the supervisor's argument appears to be in her unit's interest but is not, the point should be clarified. Finally, if a position is *against* her interest, much should be made of the fact, because credibility is increased if she is arguing against her own interests (Brager et al., 1987).

Sue took the position with Herb that the DSS program was a significant opportunity for the agency, even though she was reluctant to expand her unit any further. It was an argument that he would be likely to believe, because she knew that he felt that way himself with regard to the agency as a whole, and it might suggest to him a lesser self-interest on her part. With Jim, however, she indicated that although the new program would add staff to her department and therefore it was in her interest to move forward on it, its other benefits—aid to children, the agency's image— were really much more important to her than any turf advantage. As a matter of fact, she said to him, she had initially been uncertain about whether she would recommend the program to Herb for it had its pros and cons. Although there was the potential for a high programmatic and public relations gain for the agency, it would be difficult to launch and was a high-risk endeavor as well. But, she concluded, on balance, the scales tipped in a positive direction.

As shown, Sue used a soft-sell with Jim. Studies of attitude change suggest that moderate presentations are most effective with those who are suspicious of the speaker's angle, or when the speaker has limited credibility and the issue is one of importance to the audience—all of which were relevant to Sue's relations with Jim (Aronson et al, 1963; Whittaker, 1965).

When speakers have high credibility, on the other hand, or when their listeners are predisposed to their positions, forceful advocacy is likely to move the audience in the speakers' direction. To be credibly forceful, supervisors must believe what they are saying. But because people are usually more likely to pay attention to facts that support their views and to forget those that are contrary, it is not overly difficult for many of them to convince themselves of the truth of their positions. And even half-truths are more credible when a one can bring oneself to believe them before engaging in an interaction.

The most convincing communicator may be the one who does not try to convince at all. This was Sue's approach with Elias, whom she asked for "advice" rather than tried to persuade. Because his department stood to gain from the DSS program, the assumption that he would support it was a fair one to make. And the very fact that she defined him as a supporter probably aided in reinforcing his position. Attributions create perceptions and expectations that often influence attitudes, and fixing a label on others or imputing a role to them is thus a technique for changing their behavior. For example, an experimental study showed that the attribution of neatness to school children was more successful in influencing neat behavior than attempts to convince them to be neat (Miller et al., 1975). Labeling others as supporter, friend, opponent, and the like and acting toward them in that fashion encourage them to act supportive, friendly, or oppositional in turn.

By not trying to convince, the communicator's presumed lack of stake in the outcome apparently enhances her credibility. Experiments have even shown that conversations that are overheard accidentally are more persuasive than those intended to convince the hearers, even when the messages are identical. Audiences are also disarmed when communicators are not trying to convince them. Not having to resist an assault on their beliefs, they are more open to hearing the message. Some theorists believe that message recipients tend to engage in selective listening when they expect to disagree with speakers, often tuning them out. Under these circumstances, listeners also unconsciously conjure up counterarguments. Persuaders are advised, therefore, not to forewarn their audiences of potential disagreement. "You may not totally agree with me, but . . ." is a poor way to begin to make one's case. Audience counterargument may help to explain why distractions—albeit pleasant ones such as a joke or poignant anecdote—increase the effectiveness of a persuasive attempt. Presumably, one of the reasons for this is that the audience is distracted from mustering its silent rebuttal (Brager et al., 1987).

Although the precept does not apply in the Heights example, supervisors sometimes need to line up someone else to make the case for them when another worker would make a more credible persuader. The other worker might be someone whose previous interaction with the person to be persuaded has engendered trust or someone whose position on the issue appears more disinterested or even less expected than the supervisor's. By and large, when someone unexpectedly favors a position, he or she is likely to be more convincing. Similarly, the less familiar or stereotypical an argument, the more persuasive it is. Experimenters report that people who *expect* an unfamiliar argument are more persuaded than those who expect a known case to be made—regardless of the actual argument itself. (Sears and Freedman, 1965).

In the final analysis, the most persuasive communicators are probably those with formal or informal power, because they are often prestigious— and the prestige of the communicator is a significant factor in one's ability to persuade. Powerful communicators are also more persuasive because others are dependent on them and they have the ability to apply sanctions, if only implicitly. Furthermore, they are in a position to mobilize the support of others in the agency and thus make effective advocates. Had Sue been certain that Herb would champion the DSS program, the backing of her colleagues would have been unnecessary.

One final point in relation to the supervisor as communicator: When she and her colleagues have common values, she is better positioned to convince them, regardless of the particular viewpoint she may be espousing. It is, of course, rare that some common values can not be found. Insofar as it is possible for her to underscore the similarities of their values without being overly obvious about it, it is well to do so. Establishing agreement with an audience on one topic promotes its acceptance of a speaker's other positions (Weiss, 1957).

When Sue talked to Herb, therefore, she made an initial connection by saying that he had been right to veto her proposed relocation of one of her units—because now they could achieve their shared goal of increasing the agency's low-income cohort without the costs that the change in location would have entailed. And in Sue's discussion with Will, she subtly appealed to their commonality as social workers committed to reaching the underserved. She also referred approvingly to his perception of the agency as elitist, and she indicated that the DSS program would impel the Heights in a different direction.

Effective Arguments

To craft a convincing message, communicators need to know—or to infer—the goals and values of those they are trying to persuade and what underlies their attitudes and actions. In organizations, an awareness of the criteria that are used to reach a decision, as well as how their own objectives correspond to these criteria, provides supervisors with meaningful data for making an effective argument. They can then selectively stress those aspects of their case that appeal to the target's underlying beliefs or makes the best agency fit. Anticipating potential responses give them the advantage of rehearsing their arguments or counterarguments in advance of the exchange.

Sue reviewed the grounds on which Herb and the others might support or oppose the DSS program before she approached them. Herb believed that the Heights was a sufficiently large agency already, so she would avoid what otherwise might make a natural point to an executive— namely, that the agency's resources in money and personnel would be increased by the proposed program. On the other hand, the Heights's reputation was important to Herb; his own self-esteem and the esteem of others was in part related to positive perceptions of the agency. Second, Sue knew that Herb would assess the potential reactions of various of the agency's constituencies to the DSS program—and although some of the staff, including Jim, might be troubled by it—and perhaps some members of the board would be troubled, too—there were other staff and board members who would favor its adoption. Lastly, there was Herb's sense of social responsibility, a factor that would encourage his support of Sue's position. (It is worth noting that one could predict most of Herb's criteria for decision making from his *role* as chief executive. With the exception of the issue of agency expansion, his interests conform with those of most executives. The mix and priorities undoubtedly vary among executives, but we suspect that the order of importance for many executives follows the order in which we have presented them).

In reviewing where Jim might stand, Sue judged that the *real* issue for him would be the competition between her department and his for agency ascendancy. But the matter would never be framed in those terms. Rather, if Jim decided to oppose the program's adoption, he would be smart enough to do so by referring to the agency's mission. He might argue, for example, that the new program constituted a social service rather than a mental health initiative and was therefore deflective of agency purposes.

Sue made a strong pitch for the program with Herb. She relied on his concern about the agency's reputation, saying that the Heights could feel proud of DSS' confidence in the agency. The program was important to the department, and turning to the Heights was a measure of the agency's reputation for excellence (not incidentally, although unstated, it was also a recognition of Sue's reputed expertise in child abuse, a factor she hoped would not be lost on Herb). The program would have high visibility and therefore might further redound to the agency's credit. Because the problem of child abuse was receiving so much attention in the community, it would be unconscionable for the Heights not to move into the area. Mindful of his sensitivity to the agency's constituency and his social conscience, she asserted that she did not see how people could really oppose the agency's involvement in an area in which the need was so pressing. Indeed, if the agency did not, it might appear to be behind the times or unresponsive to a central community concern.

In the course of their conversation, Sue also found the occasion to say that although some of the workers might define the program as a social service and thus inappropriate for a treatment-oriented agency, the point was a weak one. The line between the two was too thin and the boundaries too unclear. Workers who made such a point, she said, would probably also be opposed to the goal she and Herb shared together of increasing the number of low-income people who were served by the Heights. Besides, at the regional mental health conference she had attended in May, other clinics reported that they were increasingly offering services to children and abusing families.

One factor affecting how moderate or extreme an argument appears to be is whether it contains opposing points of view. One-sided communications—those that omit opposing arguments—are more effective when the recipient is already predisposed or likely to accept the speaker's position. Two-sided communications—in which the speaker apprises the recipient of alternative arguments—are more convincing to those with less-favorable initial attitudes (Brager et al., 1987, p. 355). Anticipating that Jim would react less favorably to the DSS program than Herb, Sue's argument was two-sided, and she expressed some uncertainty about the program to him, whereas she was considerably more forceful in presenting it to Herb.

It is clear that Sue put her knowledge of Herb's goals, values, and interests to use in constructing her case. His concern about the agency's reputation, his interest is not arousing the agency's constituents, and his sense of social responsibility were all touched on, directly or indirectly. Two other aspects of her presentation are worth further mention. One is her passing reference to the regional conference; the other is her assertion that some staff might define the DSS program as inappropriate for a mental health clinic.

Referring to the regional conference accomplished two purposes. By citing the experience of other agencies, Sue hoped to suggest a lessened risk for the Heights. Implicitly, too, her comments were designed to reap the benefits of whatever agency competitiveness Herb, as an executive, might feel. Two generally effective arguments—that a proposal reflects the traditional values of the agency or closely conforms with its current directions—could not credibly be made in this instance. One advantage of these arguments is that conformance with tradition or current direction implies that the new program is predictable. Sue's reference to the experience of other agencies was the closest to this assurance she could come.

When she noted that some workers might define the DSS program as inappropriate for a mental health clinic, Sue was trying to put some distance between their values and Herb's. Implicitly, her reference was to Jim; she was hoping to "inoculate" Herb against an argument she thought he might hear from Jim. McGuire (1961, 1964) has postulated a "germ theory" in regard to attitudes. Just as the body can be immunized by small doses of a virus, or allergen, so too can people's attitudes be protected from an opposing argument if they have been primed to counter it through hearing the contrary view. Studies have explored the relative effectiveness of supportive and refutational arguments. In the supportive argument, the speaker takes only one side of a position in the hope that reinforcing the listener's bias in favor of the position will engender resistance to the contrary view. In the latter, the negative side of a position is presented—in a weak dose—and then refuted, much as Sue did. The aim is to prepare listeners to resist arguments to which they may subsequently be exposed (and incidentally, to demonstrate that the speaker has taken these opposing arguments into account before reaching a conclusion). Some support for the germ theory is suggested by the fact that refutational presentations are generally more effective than supportive ones. But most persuasive of all are the two together.

Because Sue was espousing the DSS offer, she needed to take immediate and decisive action. Had the offer not been made and had she been interested in finding a way for the agency to move into the child abuse area in any case, her approach would have been different. With no specific program to vote up or down, there are advantages to offering a range of alternatives, while at the same time giving prominence to the proposer's most desired outcome. For one thing, posing alternatives is a useful device for obtaining expressions of interest and assessing the commitments of a boss or colleagues, thereby allowing a supervisor to revise her ideas with their preferences in mind. The proposal can be shaped to depart from current agency practice to a greater or lesser degree; its scope may be broad or narrow; it may represent a partial or incremental step or go the whole distance to achieving a desired end—all depending on initial reactions. For another, offering alternatives gives the appearance of openness and moderation, and when a supervisor is unsure of where other actors stand on an issue, featuring these characteristics is advisable. Further, presenting a series of alternatives gives others some feeling of choice, which sometimes generates greater "ownership" of the proposal on their part. It has been suggested that commitment is strengthened when three conditions prevail: (1) there is a perception of freedom to choose from a number of options; (2) the chosen behavior is made public; and (3) the person's actions are irreversable (Pfeffer, 1981, pp. 291–292). Finally, suggesting options not only increases another's choice, but limits the likelihood of a flat rejection; that is, in an uncertain field, a range of alternatives increases the chance that one of the alternatives will be accepted, thus keeping the process alive for future advances.

As it was, however, there was an advantage for Sue in making her case to Herb with conviction, quite apart from the content of persuasability of her argument. Executives factor the importance of an issue to their staff into their decision making. To accede to their views serves as a reward for competence if the decision would not otherwise be costly. Further, when there are equal contenders on each side of an issue and a decision could go either way, the strength with which the positions are held affects the outcome. With Sue strongly committed to the program, for example, Jim only mildly opposed, and all other things equal, Herb's predisposition would be to favor Sue's position.

Two other components of message are worth noting here. One is the order in which the arguments are made. The other is the threat-arousing potential of the message, that is, the reference in a communication to the adverse consequences that will follow if the speaker's recommendations are ignored.

Considerable study has been conducted on the effectiveness of the order of presentation of arguments—whether to put one's strongest arguments at the beginning of a presentation or at the end. The results have been equivocal, with neither order found to be consistently superior. Both, however, are superior to placing one's best case in the middle of the message. A communicator must, first of all, capture the attention of the audience—and a dramatic beginning may be called for to assure the listener's interest. If listeners are expected to be positively disposed, the stronger arguments go first. Similarly, the stronger arguments lead off when it is anticipated that the listener's interest may flag. If, on the other hand, the subject is of interest to the audience or it is likely to question the speaker's position, holding one's best case to the last is recommended (Robertson, 1971, p. 153).

To try to persuade by making a direct assault on another's beliefs is more likely to incur defensiveness than attitude change. But there are times when arousing fear or anxiety may be useful. The occasions in which a supervisor can exert the leverage of a threat with colleagues or superiors is limited, but they do exist and can sometimes be invented. It is well to observe certain guidelines, however.

It has been found, for example, that some intermediate level of anxiety is generally more effective than no anxiety or high anxiety arousal (McGuire 1973, p. 234). This is probably so because people faced with a strong threat have an incentive to withdraw from the situation if they can or to deny its validity if they cannot. A mild threat is particularly more effective than a strong one when a message has high salience for the audience (Levanthal, 1971)—perhaps because the subject generates greater anxiety than messages dealing with matters of lesser consequence. Finally, when threats are used, they are most effective if the arousal of anxiety is followed by prescriptions for action to reduce the threat.

Ordinarily, making a direct threat to a colleague or superior in an organization is viewed as heavy-handed and may violate one of the organization's norms. Because, as we have said before, organizational participants "live together" for extended periods of time, direct threats can seriously endanger relationships. By and large, therefore, threats must be made indirectly or implicitly. We deal with this matter in greater detail in the following section of the chapter.

Negotiations

Negotiating is pervasive in social interaction. It may happen informally and go unrecognized as such by one or more of the parties. But it occurs in families, with clients, among friends, and in the corridors of every agency. Behavior in organizations is especially marked by an ongoing process of negotiation, one in which agreements are continually created, sustained, and overturned as staff members interact (Mangham 1979, p. 75).

Two organizational issues most commonly subject to negotiation have to do with turf and role making. Participants view the protection or expansion of their territory as vital to their interests, and when these interests vie with the interests of other participants, as inevitably they must, negotiations frequently ensue. Negotiations also take place as staff members strive to define their organizational roles. Although much behavior is prescribed by the role a person fills in an agency, roles are ambiguous as well, and their boundaries are unclear. They are shaped by situational requirements, social pressures, and personal needs and are subject to shifting demands. Because individuals can only partially control their own role's definition, a give and take occurs with others to define a satisfactory role repertoire (Reardon 1981, p. 187). For example, the social worker in a hospital who tries to shift from discharge planning as her primary task to performing other health care functions engages in a role-making process. She puts out feelers, argues, wins adherents to her position, and negotiates to define her role.

But whether the subject for negotiations is intended to promote the supervisor's interests or those of her unit, improve services, or resolve organizational difficulties, every facet of agency life is touched by the process. And it takes place at all levels of an organization's hierarchy: workers with supervisors and executives, supervisors with their staff and superiors, and so on. Sykes has even reported on implicit negotiations by such disparate hierarchical groups as prison guards and prisoner-leaders who surreptitiously worked together to maintain institutional discipline (Sykes, 1958).

Most of the research and writing about negotiation has been about its formal and explicit manifestations such as collective bargaining and conflict-resolution techniques. Negotiations that are informal and implicit, on the other hand, have received scant attention in either the social work or organizational literature. Yet implicit negotiations are undoubtedly the most relevant for supervisors and other practitioners, because they occur with considerably greater frequency than the formal and explicit variety and are such a potent influence on the workings of the agency. Our focus, therefore, is on implicit negotiating, although the overlapping boundaries of implicit and explicit negotiations should be recognized.

Implicit Negotiation

Negotiation, by definition, means to confer with another so as to arrive at the settlement of some matter . . . to arrange for or bring about through conference, discussion, and compromise. Whatever the type and structure of a particular negotiation, some give and take on the part of both parties is entailed—the exchange of resources, reward, and/or sanctions as a means of reaching agreement. The process also involves persons whose goals are both shared and divergent.

By implicit we mean any negotiation in which one or both of the parties are unaware that a deal is being forged or in which, although consciously negotiating, the parties either individually or jointly share an interest in not openly acknowledging that a negotiation is taking place. Because implicit negotiations wear different guises, it is not always apparent that negotiations are occurring at all.

Consider the following. An executive has been considering a shift in the administrative responsibility for his agency's drug hotline from its outpatient department to the inpatient unit. Before making a final decision, however, he wants to assess the strength with which the inpatient unit supervisor might oppose the idea. At their meeting the supervisor resisted the change with considerable intensity, citing a number of professional and personnel problems that such a departmental move would cause. She also said that he knew that she has always worked much beyond the call of duty, and hinted that the change might force her to rethink her role in the agency. The supervisor's response carries an implicit threat, and she is counting on the credits she had accrued as a result of her widely recognized competence and her extra-official role representing the agency with a variety of important publics. Although the executive was planning the change in location because it would increase the potential for raising funds for the hotline's support, he has decided to postpone making a decision. Although neither the supervisor nor the executive would have acknowledged it in those terms, their conversation was a negotiation.

Why Implicit? There are a number of reasons why one or more parties to a negotiation may prefer that the encounter not be defined as such. One such circumstance is when the organizational rules or role prescriptions of the parties define negotiating about certain issues (or even negotiating at all) as illegitimate. This is frequently the case when the encounter occurs between individuals of unequal rank. Organizational norms dictate that subordinates take direction from superiors, and when the two engage in open trading, that authority system is, to some degree, undermined.

A supervisor who initiates a negotiation with an executive about whether to perform some ordinarily appropriate facet of her work may be viewed as overstepping the bounds of proper organizational behavior. Because it might not look or feel right to either party—but both wish to explore the issue nonetheless—the two collude to define it as a conversation rather than a negotiation, though they may, in fact, be bargaining implicitly. There is a considerable advantage to the supervisor interested in influencing a high-power participant in gaining that definition of the exchange. It permits the softening of what might otherwise seem a demand and mitigates the potential charge that the worker is too pushy. More important, when a negotiation remains implicit, a high-power person (or any involved party) is more able to accede without appearing to lose face. Even when a capitulation is obvious, the damage is limited by the implicit and private nature of the interaction.

When a negotiation is implicit, it also has the advantage of giving a supervisor room to maneuver. Through a process of sounding out, in which positions are indirectly or inferentially tested, supervisors can assess preliminary reactions to their objectives—where others stand and what they may be able or willing to trade for their agreement. What the supervisor can reasonably hope to accomplish and what stance might best achieve the result can thus be modified before either party moves to a fixed position. Because stated commitments intensify the commitment of speakers to their point of view, it is good organizational practice for a supervisor to forestall the expression of an opinion or decision until there is some indication that the response will be a favorable one. Furthermore, the sounding out in implicit negotiations allows the supervisor to make a graceful exit if it appears that destructive conflict will ensue, that her minimum objectives cannot be achieved, or simply if the timing seems to be wrong. When demands are only hinted at, they lend themselves to deniability.

Finally, two other conditions suggest the usefulness of negotiating implicitly. The first is when the process in which the parties are engaged might be endangered if others became aware of the negotiation. In the second, one or both parties may wish to avoid a fixed agreement because of the expectation of changing conditions or additional data, and an ambiguous negotiation may encourage an ambiguous outcome.

The following description of an implicit negotiation between two colleagues shows some of its advantages, as well as illustrating a typical process of negotiation. The two, José and Myrna, are supervisors at the Family Support Center, an agency specializing in domestic violence. The center provides services to an extremely difficult population and an extensive training program for graduate students in social work. The center is affiliated with a school of social work. Its executive is an adjunct professor at the school, of which he and many others on the staff are graduates. They take considerable pride in the center's reputation as a desirable site for student interneships.

José heads a service unit and has supervised graduate students for the past three years. His job has become increasingly demanding, and the fact that his most recent student was weak made the job feel even more pressureful. Although José finds student supervision professionally stimulating, he has decided that he will not supervise a student next year unless he can attest to the student's ability to work effectively with the center's population. Only if he can interview the student candidate(s) in advance, he believes, is there any assurance of the student's appropriateness for the placement. He is aware that interviewing candidates for field placement is against school policy.

Myrna is a unit supervisor and also serves as the agency's coordinator of student placements. As José knows, Myrna is under pressure from their executive to secure the requisite number of student assignments to fulfill a commitment that he made to the school. Other supervisors have, like José, responded to the added pressures of their jobs with increased reluctance to supervise students.

When Myrna calls José to discuss the next year's placements, he informs her that he is unsure that he can accommodate a student because of increasing job demands and the fact that, in his view, the placement can work "only if we can be sure of the student's effectiveness in working with the center's difficult client group." Myrna indicates that she "really needs the placement" and that she is sure she can convince the school's fieldwork department to choose a strong student for him. José knows that Myrna has denied the requests of other supervisors to interview prospective students and, even assuming she could induce the school to grant an exception, that she would be under considerable pressure from them to do likewise. Nevertheless, he counters Myrna's offer by stating that he cannot risk leaving the assessment to the fieldwork department. "It takes a special kind of person to work with our clients; since the field work people haven't worked with violent families, they are not in a position to make an accurate assessment," he argues. "I'd like a student," he continues,

"But I'm afraid I'll have to forego the opportunity if I can't judge the student for myself. Give it some thought, Myrna," José concludes, "You and the fieldwork people may be able to figure out a way." Myrna responds by indicating that José's request places her in a very difficult position and that she knows the executive will be distressed if he is informed that the agency cannot meet its student quota. José hears an implied threat in Myrna's statement, but he holds firm. He suggests again that Myrna think about it and get back to him if she has any ideas.

Myrna calls back a week later with an idea. Each year the fieldwork department holds briefing sessions for students to inform them about placement possibilities. Myrna indicates that she always makes a presentation at the session, and "If you were to join me there, I could highlight the work of your unit and introduce you. Then if students wanted more information about the unit, they could discuss it with you after the session. Whatever you chose to work out with interested students insofar as further discussions were concerned would, of course, be your own business. While you know I can't give you a guarantee about getting a student of your choice because it would upset the other unit supervisors, your preference will be a major factor when assignments are finalized."

José accepted Myrna's proposal. Essentially, she was promising to set the stage for him to interview and honoring his preference from among the students he would meet—as long as he agreed not to characterize the arrangement as a preplacement interview and to keep it quiet.

Both parties were clear in this instance that a negotiation had occurred. But its implicit character was advantageous to both of them. Their initial conversation, tentative and conditional in nature, permitted each to sound the other out. Not having flatly refused to take a student without an interview, José could wait to see what Myrna proposed as he maintained flexibility regarding his final position. Ambiguity served Myrna in turn. She hoped that her implicit threat to inform the executive of José's possible refusal to take a student might generate some anxiety, while she was left free to explore options. In addition, José was essentially asking Myrna to violate an organizational policy—that of respecting the school's rule of not interviewing prospective students. By doing so implicitly, he increased the likelihood that his position would be defined in terms other than rule breaking.

The Negotiation Process

Skill in implicit negotiations is allied to skill in other interventions. The ability to persuade, for example, is a requisite for effective negotiating.

And the dynamics of negotiating implicitly are in many ways similar to explicit negotiation. In turning to a discussion of the negotiation process, we emphasize those practice issues especially relevant to implicit negotiation, although many of these issues are applicable to practice generally and to negotiating in its explicit manifestation.

For purposes of presentation and analysis, we characterize the negotiation process as consisting of four phases: assessment, initial engagement, exchange, and settlement. In the assessment phase, the actor identifies an objective that may not be totally compatible with that of another party. He or she must then make an assessment to determine the goals and interests of the other, their respective resources and potential for applying sanctions, and the costs and benefits of negotiating versus finding another means of resolution. The next phase, engagement, refers to the start of the interchange—the initial presentation of interests and/or positions and the beginning exploration of the issues. The exchange phase involves the sequential modification of positions and the exchange of threats and promises as the search for a satisfactory outcome progresses. Finally, a settlement—a deal—is struck.

To illustrate with the case of José and Myrna, the initial engagement phase of the negotiation occurred when Myrna asked José to take a student, and José responded that he might not be able to accommodate her request. In that conversation, Myrna made clear that she could not sanction an interview, and José demonstrated his commitment to making a personal assessment of the potential student. In the exchange phase, Myrna offered to have the school's fieldwork department do the assessment for José, made a thinly veiled threat to incur the displeasure of the executive if José did not cooperate, and agreed to explore alternatives. José for his part, displayed the firmness of his position, threatened not to take the student unless his conditions were met, and offered the suggestion that Myrna explore alternatives as a way of not prematurely locking the two of them into a struggle from which one would emerge the "winner" and the other the "loser." In the final phase, Myrna essentially offered José a means of access to the students and promised to implement his preference in placing a student. José, in turn, agreed not to define the arrangement as an interview and promised to keep the exchange private. On those grounds, the matter was settled.

To some degree, these phases of implicit negotiation are arbitrary. As is the case with any practice that evolves in a phased progression—or indeed, with all social processes—movement between the phases is not linear. Although an initial assessment is essential for appropriate positioning in a negotiation, assessment is ongoing and occurs in each phase of the process. Similarly, one person's assertion of a position during the engagement phase may be sufficiently compelling so that the other capitulates on the spot; in effect, elements of all phases of the process may have been included in the beginning interchange. Nonetheless, it is helpful to view practice processes from the standpoint of beginnings, middles, and ends, because useful distinctions can be made about the strategic concerns and practice tasks that are likely to be appropriate to different phases of a process.

Assessment. The primary task of the assessment phase is to gather preliminary information, organize available data, and analyze its meaning. The task can be more or less elaborate, ranging from considerable exploration before the negotiation commences to a "quick-and-dirty" judgment on the spur of the moment. But whether the information and analysis are cursory or elaborate, the implicit negotiation itself must usually appear natural and unplanned to be effective, seemingly intrinsic to the broader set of interactions that are occurring between the actors.

Prior to any negotiation, effective political practitioners will be generally knowledgeable about particular aspects of an agency's functioning. They will recognize who has power in the organization and in regard to which issues. They will have a feeling for the styles and quirks of the principal actors and other players, along with notions about their organizational interests. They will broadly understand the agency's decision processes, those that are formal and legitimate as well as the ways in which decisions are actually made. They will know the agency's policy and procedures, something about its past history and disputes, the organizational or professional norms that shape the behavior of its participants, and the roles of various constituencies (Yates, 1985, p. 21).

In the assessment phase of a negotiation, the information must be specific and focused to the matter at hand. Two elements are of particular importance: the interests and stakes of the parties regarding the issue to be negotiated and the respective resources for influencing that each brings to the encounter.

The meaning that an issue has for actors, the degree to which it has personal or professional consequences for them, and the extent of their investment or stake in a particular position critically influence the outcome of a negotiation. Although the significance of an issue may stem from any number of specific or idiosyncratic factors, the source of its significance is often either the actors' ideology, their self-interest, their concerns about the perceptions of others, or some combination thereof. Whether issue significance is rooted primarily in one or another of these factors suggests differential pathways to the resolution of the negotiation.

Ideological commitments often serve to rationalize instrumental interests, but whether they serve that function or some other, deeply held values are core elements of an individual's sense of self. As such, they are typically closely guarded and dearly defended. Potential conflicts that assault one's ideology are difficult to settle when a compromise of these values is required for the resolution of the issue. By its very nature, negotiation suggests some give-and-take, so that supervisors will find that negotiations assaulting another's belief or value structure to be problematic at best. Variations occur, of course, depending on the centrality of the beliefs in question, the role that ideology plays in the self-image of the actor, and the degree to which compromise is required to achieve a satisfactory outcome. In the main, however, when ideology is a deeply rooted source of one's position, generally only two alternatives are available. Occasionally—but only occasionally—the actor may be persuaded that the supervisor's proposed resolution does not compromise his or her values. Short of persuasion, some form of coercion is the other alternative. In view of the significance of ideology to one's sense of self, there is some advantage to being "forced" into a resolution that is inconsistent with one's beliefs. When a value compromise is defined or experienced as being beyond one's control, it may be more acceptable psychologically than would otherwise be the case. Clearly, though, coercive solutions are costly to the supervisor in the lingering hostility that they can generate.

The position of an actor frequently appears to be a matter of ideology when, in fact, the real concern is something else—for example, the interpretations that *others* might make regarding the potential compromise. It is not unusual for negotiators to be speaking as much to third parties who are not present at the negotiation as they are to each other. Although actors sometimes represent their resistance as a matter of principle, the principle is not always the actor's own. Skillful exploration by the supervisor, however, often allows her to ascertain whether the issue is one of personal ideogy or of the damage to the actor's credibility associated with compromising the ideological commitments of others. One may assume the latter when interest is expressed in a resolution that lends itself to a private understanding or when an acceptable public definition can be found. The exploration may be implicit—for example, a general discussion of the value of confidentiality or a review of the possible reactions of others to a proposal. But the exploration may also be as explicit as a direct question, depending on the supervisor's relationship with the person with whom she is negotiating.

Finally, issue significance rooted in self-interest suggests its own probable pathway to resolution. Following an initial assessment or an exploration (overtly or covertly) of the precise nature of the interests at issue, the supervisor seeks resolutions that are responsive to some dimension of the actor's interests and/or begins to barter sanctions of equal or greater significance to the actor in exchange for his or her cooperation.

Closely related to the source of the parties' investment in an issue is the degree of that investment. When the investment of the parties is unequal, particularly when the difference is visible to one or both of them, the cards are stacked against the one for whom a resolution of the matter is more important. Thus in our example of José's and Myrna's negotiation, it was clear that Myrna's stake in the student placement was greater than his; indeed, she very nearly made it explicit with her comment that she "really needed the placement." As a result, José could more comfortably remain firm, and the burden for finding a solution became hers. Had the importance of a resolution to each of them been reversed, the process and outcome are likely to have been different. Obviously enough, the respective stakes in an issue determine what "quid" can satisfy which "quo."

The supervisor must thus measure not only the other's investment, but her own. Clearly, in organizational bargaining, an issue of not-great moment to the supervisor can be used to pay off a prior obligation or be a throwaway in exchange for good will regarding a subsequent matter of greater significance. Depending on the nature of the process and the relationship of the parties, the supervisor may not want to acquiesce too quickly or easily or do the other a favor too lightly. Any concession or favor is likely to be more valued in direct proportion to the perceived difficulty in proffering it. A stance such as "I'll really try but I don't know if I can swing it" thus increases the desirability of an action.

In addition to an assessment of the potential significance of the issue, the supervisor must have some estimate of her power relative to the other party as she enters a negotiating process. The process of a negotiation and its outcome are often determined by the balance of power of the parties. Negotiations can only take place when the party with disproportionate power is willing to engage in the process. The boss may or may not be willing to play the game, for example, because he ordinarily has the resources to achieve a goal without having to offer something in return. Nevertheless, bosses find it advantageous to negotiate on some issues, and the efficacy of the supervisor's resources for influencing him—or her own colleagues for the matter—are, of course, closely related to the agenda of the negotiation and the intensity with which the other parties are committed to their position. Put differently, the supervisor's ability to influence does not have to be strong when an issue is not perceived by others as particularly critical. As its salience increases, however, the supervisor's resources for influencing must increase as well.

The fact that influence is issue-specific permits maneuverability and calls for both careful assessment and a "fine-tuned" balancing between the supervisor's demands and her resources. For example, the supervisor who resisted her executive's intention to move the drug hotline from her department to another had the resources to prevent the move—the credit she had accrued as a result of her competence and her extra-official role in representing the agency with important others, which she implied that she might forego. Her investment in maintaining the hotline under her aegis was sufficiently important to her to "call in her chips" on the issue and risk the executive's displeasure. On other issues, however, this configuration of investment and influence might well have led to a different outcome.

Essentially, then, the assessment task is to collect the information necessary to inform the negotiation that is to take place. Gathering information for use in implicit negotiation is difficult, however, because supervisors may need to be discreet until they have enough data to chart a course. As we implied earlier, to some degree the information is at hand, and politically sensitive supervisors are alert to organizational currents. After all, the supervisor has often had prior experience with the persons she hopes to influence or opportunities to observe them in practice. She has also undoubtedly been a party to agency gossip, and gossip is the currency that allows information to circulate. Supervisors who are well plugged into the agency's informal network are analogous in this regard to information bankers. Although the credibility of gossip must be carefully evaluated, its contribution to the matter at issue may be significant.

Contacts with members of other social networks are frequently another source of data. Supervisors whose contacts cut across diverse cliques are especially favored, because they are privy to information from one camp that might otherwise remain a secret to members of another camp. The information may have to be elicited with caution and tact (i.e., implicitly), however. One technique to avoid a direct question is to steer the conversation to the particular subject in the hope that someone may volunteer to shed some light on it. Another technique is to assert a position to encourage the person to reveal his or her stance on the position and perhaps occasion additional data.

But often collecting important data must await the engagement phase of the process. An initial assessment concludes with a tentative decision about the advisability of proceeding with the effort. If the decision is affirmative, the supervisor develops some beginning ideas about how to go about it. If in her judgment, however, the position of the other party is too firmly entrenched, if that party has access to significantly more resources than she, or if the agency climate is such that it bodes ill for the encounter, she may decide to postpone the effort or forego it altogether. On the other hand, one advantage of an implicit negotiation is its very ambiguity. Thus if she is uncertain about whether to proceed, it is possible for her to "talk around" the issue during the engagement phase to test further the other's resolve. Technically, the undecided supervisor is undecided only in her assessment and may proceed if she chooses without appearing to do so. If the discussion suggests there is merit in moving forward, she does so. If not, she continues the conversation as a chat, connoting that a negotiation has been neither anticipated nor engaged.

Prior to engaging the other party, a well-prepared supervisor will have reviewed her own goals and, ideally, developed a number of options to accomplish them or to move incrementally toward their achievement. It is ordinarily useful to have identified a best possible outcome and a minimally acceptable outcome—a bottom line—below which she is not prepared to negotiate. There is some risk in entering a negotiation with a fixed bottom line, because it can inhibit the supervisor's flexibility, her ability to benefit from what she learns during the negotiation. On the other hand, unless she has identified alternatives to coming to an agreement at all, she may be *too* committed to a settlement with the other, and her overcommitment could be a liability in achieving an advantageous outcome. Although preparation is an advantage in a negotiation—and in implicit negotiations, it is ordinarily the initiator who is so favored—the preparation must not act as an impediment to the supervisor's listening actively and responding spontaneously as the parties interact.

Initial Engagement. As stated previously, an implicit negotiation is one in which one or both parties are unaware that the negotiation is taking place or in which the parties are aware that they are forging a deal but do not wish to acknowledge the interchange openly as a negotiation. The initial engagement phase signals the beginning of the interchange. It may consist of "testing the waters," or if may represent an invitation to negotiate. Depending on the circumstances, opening communications may be direct or indirect. When indirect, it ordinarily commences with a benign conversation that is labeled or experienced as an information exchange, as a review of a recent organizational event, or even as plain gossip. The supervisor then unobtrusively focuses the subject of the conversation to the topic that concerns her. As the topic comes into focus, ambiguous language is used if the supervisor desires maneuvering room to exit from the exchange or to reshape the discussion if need be.

Once the supervisor decides to move ahead, her primary task in this phase of the process is to communicate her goal or position with sufficient clarity to obtain a reaction from the other party that can provide information about where he or she stands. This initial dialogue serves as an assessment tool for both of them—because how each responds to what the other puts forth provides important clues about the aspirations and investments of both. The supervisor tunes into not only the positions others are espousing, but to what may be behind those positions. Often, too, what is *not* said or why someone is *not* taking a particular position is as revealing as what is said or the position that has been taken.

Although drawn from explicit negotiations, there are studies suggestive for practice in beginning the process. These studies point consistently to the tendency for an initially established pattern to persist over the course of an interaction. Thus whether each party's stance is initially cooperative or competitive strongly influences whether the entire process will be characterized by a win-win or a win-lose approach. As one might anticipate, an early initiation of cooperative behavior tends to promote the development of trust; early competitive behavior, on the other hand, induces mutual suspicion. And when a cooperative climate has been established, introducing an obvious competitive note is more harshly viewed than if the pattern had been competitive from the start (Rubin and Brown, 1975, pp. 263–265).

Shaping one's expressions of initial positions to appeal to the underlying beliefs and values of the other party is as effective in negotiating as it is in persuasion. Furthermore, it is ordinarily advisable at the start for the supervisor to put forward her goals or interests, rather than a fixed position—if the context of the interaction permits it. There are often a number of paths available to achieving one's ends, and being open and receptive to a variety of possible solutions both enhances the supervisor's appearance of cooperativeness and increases the likelihood of arriving at a satisfactory outcome. Essentially, she engages the other in problem solving with her. She, in turn, takes the interests of the other party seriously and tries to find a positive outcome for him or her as well.

With initial engagement, the stage is set. An invitation has been proffered, interests put forward, and initial reactions obtained in ways that preserve room for maneuver. The next step is the exchange phase, the core of the negotiation.

Exchange. In the exchange phase of negotiations, the parties modify positions, trade resources, and, if necessary, imply or threaten sanctions.

The factors that influence the character of the exchange are many, but one important element is the indirection of much of the communication. Although communicating by hint or indirection is not always called for, it is ambiguous communication that most distinguishes implicit negotiation from formal negotiations. Indeed, indirect communication is appropriate in all phases of the process.

Supervisors find a number of ways to express themselves ambiguously as they offer concessions, make promises and threats, or sometimes bluff another party. One way frequently employed by social workers in client interactions, as well as with colleagues, is to substitute a question for a statement. Thus one *wonders* about an issue as opposed to asserting a position. A second often-used technique is a game that might be called *not-me-it's-them*. Other persons—who may be named or nameless—are reported to believe or feel something that, in fact, represents the supervisor's own thoughts and feelings. Suggesting that someone else holds a view that the supervisor also holds allows her to avoid asserting her position unless she gets a compatible response. A variation of the *not-me-it's-them* game is to refer to people in general. Framing a discussion in the context of unspecified others permits both parties in a negotiation to talk around an issue while making their positions clear, thus preserving the definition that a negotiation is not taking place. A sample dialogue might go something like this:

Supervisor A: Changing the intake procedure doesn't seem particularly controversial to me. I can't think of any reason why other people in the department wouldn't support it, can you?"

Supervisor B: "No, unless they thought the matter wasn't important enough and didn't want to be bothered . . . or they wanted to push something else that was preoccupying them. Gloria's asked me to work with her to try to get part-time psychiatric help for the clinic; I doubt if you could count on her to do very much about the intake problem."

Supervisor A: "Well, I'm not so sure I want to deal with the intake issue myself—but if I do decide to push it, I'd certainly offer her my assistance on getting the psychiatrist. I think we could use more psychiatric help around here too."

It is obvious that a trade is in the offing, although neither party has yet made a commitment, and ostensibly a negotiation has not occurred. Essentially, maneuverability has been preserved by talking in generalities about others.

Another form of the *not-me-it's-them* game occurs when the supervisor is ostensibly or actually representing others as well as herself. Then, if she feels unsure about a proposal or wants to buy time for other reasons, she can use her accountability to these others, indicating the need to check matters out with whomever she is perceived of as representing. Or she can go into the negotiation with her authority apparently restricted. This permits an assessment of the give in the other's position without having to make any concession in her own. If the other party does not agree to the supervisor's terms, she still has recourse to introducing newcomers into the process, particularly those with higher authority or special interests in the issue (MacMillan, 1978, p. 35). Depending on the situation, the introduction of newcomers or appeals to higher authority may serve as an implicit threat, as it did in the case of José's and Myrna's interchange.

A third means of maintaining ambiguity is the *yes-but* technique. In this instance, the supervisor frames the discussion in conditional terms. She may express uncertainty, as supervisor A did in expressing doubt about whether she was interested in pushing the intake matter when she was really quite prepared to do so. Or she may imply a set of conditions to gain the other's support, as in the following conversation between two supervisors. This dialogue follows an earlier exchange in which supervisor B had solicited supervisor A's opinion about a policy change, and supervisor A inferred that the question was a bid for her help in seeking the change.

Supervisor A: "One of the things that galls me about this agency is its lack of collegiality."

Supervisor B: "What do you mean?"

Supervisor A: "I feel that I often go out on a limb for others, but I don't see them reciprocating. Just last week—you remember—at the staff meeting, I raised the issue of our being unable to take compensatory time for overtime. Hardly anyone in the group supported me. When I can't count on the support of others, I'm not very inclined to extend myself in pursuit of their concerns."

Supervisor B: "You're right. You know, I didn't speak up at the staff meeting because I didn't think the timing was right. Perhaps we should work on this together."

By ultimately bringing the conversation around to the agency's lack of collegiality, supervisor A was implicitly communicating her terms for cooperation. She had suggested the possibility of her support in conditional terms (i.e., why should she support others unless they . . .), and she could now assess the other's willingness to deal. When supervisor B suggested that they work together on the matter of compensatory time, she was in effect agreeing to the terms. Yet no trade had ever been proposed.

Obstacle setting is another ambiguous communication gambit. In this technique for discussing a trade without apparently doing so, the supervisor alludes to the barriers or problems for her in another's proposal.

When, during the exchange phase of a negotiation, an executive or colleagues indicate what he or she desires of the supervisor, and the latter does not want to communicate her "price" directly, she may assert her interests in the form of a problem to be solved. Such a response might sound like this: "You know, I think you're right about the importance of going after that proposal, but right now my unit is so overburdened with extra cases that without some relief I doubt that I will be free to help very much." Such assertions set the stage for the other actor to offer ways— hypothetical or real—to solve the problem being posed. If the terms offered are sufficiently attractive, the supervisor settles. If not, she explains why the proposed solution is not satisfactory. Thus in the example of José's and Myrna's negotiation, José responded to Myrna's request to take students with the problem that his experience had taught him that students were often insufficiently prepared to be of use to the unit. With this, Myrna began to offer solutions to the problem. Knowing his leverage was great, José explained why the various solutions would not work until Myrna reached one that met his criteria for settlement.

Another means of indirectly introducing one's interests into a discussion might be called the *woolgathering ploy*—that is, purposively communicating in a fashion that does not respond to the other's subject. Seemingly not paying attention or misunderstanding can carry an implicit message. One is that the supervisor wants to avoid the subject altogether; in effect, then, the negotiation cannot continue. Or when one actor is attempting to promote an exchange and the other actor responds in ways suggesting preoccupation in regard to the matter, the latter may be inviting the former to explore the bases for the latter's preoccupation. After all, if a colleague is typically sharp, but all of a sudden seems dense, there are grounds for wondering. If the promoter then begins to probe the grounds for the woolgather's preoccupation, and the preoccupation is indeed related to their exchange, the stage is set for them to pose their respective interests in ways that facilitate a settlement. A primary advantage of the preoccupation maneuver is that it does not require the supervisor to find an unobtrusive way to introduce her interests into the negotiation—rather, it forces the other party to discover the issue and to find ways to assist her. The supervisor does not, in short, have to take accountability for raising the matter.

One form of indirect communication that does not entail direct discussion at all is the sending of messages by third parties. The supervisor may assert a position or opinion to some third party in the expectation that the third party will pass the word along. This ploy depends on the willing or unwitting cooperation of the third party. It is done all the time, of course, but it is particularly useful in negotiations. Thus one supervisor who was negotiating a salary increase with her executive was concerned that he might not meet her minimum demand. If she threatened to resign, she risked the hardening of his stance and the possibility that she would have to leave the agency before she was prepared to do so. Instead, she asked the associate director, who was her direct supervisor, to write a reference to place in her file "in the event that I need it," fully expecting that the executive would get word of her request. Others often see through these gambits. Their advantages must therefore, be measured against disadvantages of their potential transparency in specific cases.

Ambiguity is sometimes useful even when both parties are aware of exactly what is occurring, for an ambiguous communication tends to soften the character of an assertion, giving it a somewhat lighter touch. To "wonder," even when everyone knows that the question is more of a statement than an actual question, communicates that the speaker is not likely to pursue the matter without the assent of a positive response from the other. It permits *both* parties to leave the subject without the discomfort that an assertion might have occasioned. For example, if a supervisor would like a colleague to do her a favor but does not want to put the colleague on the spot, a hint or indirect request allows the colleague the option of not catching on—so that the colleague has more leeway and both are protected from the embarrassment of a direct refusal. In other words, recognizably ambiguous communications sometimes display a concern for another's sensibilities.

There are some disadvantages to obvious ambiguity, however, particularly in a negotiation. In signaling a lack of readiness to assume responsibility for her position (e.g., "so-and-so thinks it would be good to . . . "), the supervisor could appear more timid than tactful. Also, a desire for deniability may seem like deviousness. In the latter instance, such an impression obviously counters the attempt to gain the other's confidence or to build trust. But it is the former—timidity or its appearance—that poses the major danger to a satisfactory outcome. If the supervisor appears to be timid but is not, she transmits the wrong message—that she can be made to "sell" more cheaply on an issue than would otherwise be the case. As suggested earlier, assertion is important in organizational practice—but it is especially so in negotiations. However much the negotiation may rely on inference by either or both parties, undergirding inferences are positions that are understood by both. Unless the inferences are clear, they are irrelevant to an influence attempt. When they are clear, inferences are assertions masquerading in indirect garb. Although the masquerade is often preferable, frequently an inference will be taken further or not taken further, and it is the assertive worker who has the advantage in the exchange, because she is more likely to be able to impose her interpretations of events.

It is often advisable for supervisors to be direct and candid about their own goals and interests. This may seem anomalous advice following a discussion of some of the techniques of indirect communication and our earlier injunction regarding the requirement of secrecy, but it is not as contradictory as it seems. Secrecy is often useful when pursuing a clearly oppositional strategy, or on those occasions when a situation is emotionally charged. It is also sometimes necessary when circumstances entail an outcome in which one party must lose if the other party wins. At other times, however, there are a number of reasons why directness and honesty may be the best policy.

Directness is often appreciated as connoting trust, and as we have suggested, sharing with others encourages them to do the same and facilitates problem solving. Even in cases of some contention, the truth, because it is unexpected, may be disarming. Reactions to statements or events are in good measure determined by one's expectations regarding the positions and behaviors of those who are involved in the situation. Violating expectations has the advantage of being attention getting, in addition to other advantages. There is empirical evidence too that if expectations are violated in a negative manner, negative judgments will be more intense than if there had been no expectations at all. But if, on the other hand, they are violated in a positive way—as in credible truth telling to an adversary—the positive reaction is also all the stronger (Miller and Burgoon, 1979).

Beyond the tactical implications of truth telling, there are broader concerns of relationship that inform practice in negotiating. Because organizational negotiations occur between persons who share organizational space over time, supervisors must take into account their relationships with all other parties to a negotiation. One may, as a matter of fact, conceive of a negotiation as being composed of two themes: the substance of the particular issue and the relationship of parties to the encounter. Both are of concern, and substance and relationship usually get intertwined as bargaining takes place. Most often, it is unwise to approach an issue in such an excessively goal-oriented or single-minded manner that the parties' ongoing relationship is overlooked. On the other hand, a supervisor who is concerned primarily about relationships may be vulnerable to another party if the latter does not play by the same rules. Obviously enough, the supervisor must decide whether the issue or her relationship with the other is the more critical factor in any particular instance.

No matter which is more important, it is well in any case for her to consciously keep relationships in mind as she trades, threatens, or promises. This is one of the advantages, of course, to an implicit encounter—the ambiguity of the interaction softens the edge of otherwise negative content such as a threat. And it is another reason why an expert organizational negotiator expends considerable energy in finding a solution that is satisfactory to the other party. Or why, if a satisfactory solution to the other is unattainable, she helps the other find a face saver to smooth matters over.

In the example of José and Myrna, we may assume that José's having been so hard-nosed could have cost him something in his relations with Myrna. She might well have resented his apparent unconcern about the tough spot she was in, although because of the favorable outcome of the negotiation, the feeling would probably have been temporary. José's relationship with Myrna may not have been high on his list of priorities—in which case her possible ill-will would have been unimportant to him. We may presume, though, that she will be less likely to extend herself in the future when he needs a favor. He could have left himself in a better position, though, had he thought to praise her for her creativity in getting them both out of a bind.

Few organizational negotiations start with a clean slate, of course. The next time José and Myrna negotiate, for example, they will have some additional measure of what to expect from each other. Even people who are unfamiliar with one another provide important clues to their attitudes by how they move into the negotiations and the offers and concessions they make—how tough or flexible they are, how reasonable or emotional, and the like. Nevertheless, the prior experience of the negotiators with each other—whether it has been in negotiations or otherwise—strongly influences their encounters. Obviously enough, when the relationship is positive, the parties' mutual trust facilitates trading, and their understanding of one another reduces any potential misunderstanding of their implicit communications. When the relationship has negative overtones, on the other hand, negotiations may be impossible. Even though both parties might benefit, their suspicion of one another may prevent the attempt or make a settlement unreachable. Sometimes the importance of a negotiation between agency opponents rests in the very fact that it demonstrates that the two can work together.

If someone is perceived to be intransigent, there is little incentive for anyone to accommodate to that person. Supervisors are sometimes aware that no matter what they say or do, certain organizational colleagues will cast their words and acts in a negative light. Essentially, these colleagues have relinquished any hope of influencing her, because she is unlikely to modify her responses in the face of excessive or frequent suspicion. Similarly, if the supervisor views an executive in inherently negative terms, there is little reason for him to behave other than as typified. If one believes there is no hope of winning, one will not try, and the grounds for negotiation do not exist.

Supervisors with long-range perspectives should be mindful of how they are perceived today affects dealing with tomorrow's issue. A supervisor who is identified as a member of a particular clique, for example, both gains and loses from that identification. The gain, of course, is the support of the clique in regard to most substantive matters; the loss is the supervisor's isolation when the support of other factions is necessary. Shifting alliances with the issues is probably helpful if the agency is not organized into semi-armed camps or if shifts take place in moderation—it suggest rationality and demonstrates that the supervisor is not predictably in anyone's pocket. To withhold support from a friend, however, may risk the friendship (although the meaning of the issue to the friend is a factor in this regard). The way a supervisor withholds support may also raise issues for others of her trustworthiness. To maintain a consistent and credible image requires that she not be privately disloyal—people assess whether to trust another's positive responses toward themselves by observing how they behave toward others. A consistent and credible image is required for effective organizational influencing in the long term; it constitutes a further reason for largely honest dealing.

Depending on the nature of the issue and the relationship of the negotiators, the substance of the offers and counteroffers made in the exchange phase of the negotiation may be sufficient to lead to an agreement. Often, however, influence must also be brought to bear in the course of these interchanges. The sources of power enumerated by French and Raven (1959) and the resources that are required to influence others, to which we referred in Chapter 3, are particularly relevant in a negotiation context.

In putting forth offers and counteroffers, the supervisor makes use of resources that help to move the other party toward an accommodation. She may rely on the norms and values that she shares with the other, or she may attempt to call forth feelings of solidarity (French and Raven's referent power). If they share common opponents in the agency, solidarity is enhanced by calling attention to that fact—if her intention in doing so is not too obvious (Rubin and Brown, 1975, pp. 260–262). Resources such as access to superiors or to social and political alliances in the organization are also bases for referent power and may be implicitly proffered or withheld in exchange for the other's responsiveness or its lack.

Expertise is another tradeable resource. Its use requires a degree of trust, because the supervisor must convince (or have already convinced) the other actor that she does possess superior knowledge or ability in regard to the matter at hand or has access to others who can provide it (Raven and Kruglanski, 1970). Information may serve a similar purpose, particularly when the information (agency rules, laws and regulations, resources in the community and the like) is necessary for other parties to perform their tasks adequately. Information and expertise are also useful in negotiating when they permit the supervisor to point out contingencies in various offers about which the other party is not aware or when they can be used to make a persuasive case for or against a proposal.

Legitimate power may be called on in negotiating as well. Practice in this case is to convince the other party that the supervisor has a right to make a particular offer or demand. Her legitimacy may stem from the supervisor's role or function; for example, the supervisor who heads an intake department in an agency is viewed as having the right to influence intake policy. Or one might have a claim on legitimacy by calling forth precedent, norms of reciprocity, or simply fair play. It has been suggested, as a matter of fact, that a negotiator can shame another into acceptance of an offer by pointing to the other's dependence or lesser knowledge and ability regarding the issue (Rubin and Brown, 1975, pp. 260–262).

French and Raven's final two designations are *reward* and *coercive* power. In a bargaining context, these translate into any promises the supervisor can make that the other party desires or any threats that he or she wishes to avoid. The supervisor may implicitly promise that, in exchange for today's cooperation, she will support other actors in areas of interest to them in the future. Conversely, she may implicitly threaten future noncooperation in these areas of interest. The content of promises and threats is probably as varied as there are agencies, issues, and staffs. Some examples: promising to keep some information private when that is the others' preference or threatening to go public; promising to avoid future activities that are counter to the others' interests or threatening to pursue just such activities; and facilitating or withholding social or political access to important others.

Research evidence supports what we might expect in any case—namely, that promises are likely to be more effective than threats in inducing another's cooperation and accommodation. It has been found that negotiators who transmitted promises were not only more cooperative than were those who threatened, they were also more effective bargainers as well (Cheney et al., 1972). The magnitude of the promise or threat must also be considered. It has been noted, for example, that whereas a small promise may be interpreted as a measure of liking for the other party, too large a promise may seem like a bribe. Similarly, a small threat might make others feel that they can be too easily made to submit, whereas a larger threat might connote more respect for them (Raven and Kruglanski, 1970).

In any case, promises and threats should be used sparingly, and only if other forms of influence are unavailable. It is true that when conflicts of interests between parties are relatively small, promises and threats have been shown to be effective (Deutsch and Lewicki, 1970). But when negotiators are positively disposed toward one another, threats and promises are unnecessary, and when their conflicts are large, promises may be seen as bribes and threats become "gateways to the use of punitive power" (Rubin and Brown, 1975, p. 288). The supervisor's threats—if not also her promises—should be sufficiently ambiguous so that they can be credibly denied if she is directly confronted. And in any case, as we have said, implying rather than directly asserting something coercive significantly lessens the force of the threat and makes it more acceptable to the other.

By the time the supervisor has reached the exchange phase, she should have assessed her own and other's resources for influencing with some degree of accuracy. As the parties make offers and concessions and then attempt to influence each other, the preferences, degrees of investment, and cards held by each of them become clearer. Errors in estimating these factors are costly. Underestimating her own resources, compared with the resources of the other, leads a supervisor to a perception of relative powerlessness and may predispose her to act in that fashion, thus contributing to her lesser effectiveness. On the other hand, overestimating her resources risks loss of face or worse. The need to find the correct spot of the fulcrum of leverage between the two parties is a compelling reason for any negotiation to remain implicit.

A final observation about techniques useful in the exchange phase relates to the issue of the spacing of encounters—that is, taking a break during the process. It can be done as José proposed to Myrna in our earlier example. In suggesting that they both "think the issue over," José provided Myrna with the time to explore ways of meeting his conditions. This technique has the effect of emphasizing the negotiator's firmness (whether such is real or simply a bluff) and, to some degree, places the burden of resolution on the other actor's ability to meet his or her conditions. Taking a break in the process may have advantages for both parties. It allows time for consultations with others, it may be useful in garnering additional support, and at the least, the pause in negotiating permits the private exploration of possible solutions. It also holds the possibility that if an agreement appears unreachable, the parties can simply fail to resume the discussion, so that neither loses face or takes accountability for obstructing a resolution of the issue.

Settlement. Negotiations conclude in one of three ways. First, parties may terminate the negotiation when they realize that a mutually acceptable resolution seems unreachable. Second, an agreement may be concluded that falls somewhere between what each party maximally hoped to gain. Or finally, the outcome may meet the full needs and interests of each party. The third outcome may occur by a change in the initial perception of the issue through processes of problem solving, persuasion, external intervention, shifts in context, or the discovery of new resources. The parties may, for example, have learned in the exchange that their interests are compatible; their goals may change as a result of the interaction; additional resources may become available; or any number of other events may take place that restructure the terms of the negotiation.

A compromise settlement, in which each party wins something and loses something, may be satisfying to both, in which case it constitutes a fully acceptable conclusion to the encounter. But a settlement in which all the interests of both parties are wholly met is clearly the more attractive alternative. It is likely, in that event, that the parties will not only be satisfied with the substantive solution to their differences, but the relationship between them will probably have been enhanced.

The ambiguity of implicit negotiations sometimes poses a unique problem in regard to a final agreement. As we have suggested, practice in implicit negotiations hinges on a subtle paradox. On the one hand, the supervisor is clearly interested in cutting a deal, and wants the outcome to be sufficiently well understood so that she can rely on the other's implementing the agreement. On the other hand, her form of communication may be sufficiently ambiguous so that it is subject to misunderstanding.

Negotiations may, of course, conclude with an explicit agreement, or some of its terms may be explicit and others merely understood. This occurred in José's and Myrna's exchange. She explicitly agreed to invite him to the student briefing, and he agreed to go. However, she did not directly state that she would implement his recommendation regarding student placement—though he could fairly infer that she would. On his side, the assurance that the arrangement would remain secret was understood by both, even though it was not explicated.

Whether resolutions are stated or implicit, it is critical that they be honored. Respecting an agreement that is implicit may be even more important than an explicit one, because implied agreements hold greater potential for deniability and thus depend on the parties' trust of one another to a greater degree than explicit settlements. People who believe that an understanding has been reached and are then let down will strongly resent having been betrayed. At the most, they will find ways to retaliate; at the least, they will avoid similar encounters in the future.

We conclude this chapter by underscoring a point that is central to this volume—namely, that effective supervision requires that just as supervisors attempt to extend their influence with staff, they also approach their relations with superiors and peers from a political perspective. When a person offers support, helps a colleague, proffers or withholds approval, extends one's network, and the like, he or she ordinarily does so because the support is deserved, the colleague is worthy of help, and so on. Although these acts may be performed for their intrinsic value, they are also performed for the advantages that accrue to the performer—to incur an obligation, to gain support in turn, to garner influence from the other, and the like. It is a mistake to ignore the fact that they have these extrinsic benefits and consequences. Indeed, it is only as supervisors are sensitive to these dynamics that they can develop the political mind-set that is a prime basis for supervising effectively in an organizational context.

Group-Based Politics:
Using Coalitions

Supervisors who wish to influence agency decisions or extend their power among peers and superiors must be adept at mobilizing support as well as skillful in persuading and negotiating. Informal groups that serve instrumental ends play a significant role in advancing the interests of organizational participants, and working with them effectively is central to garnering support within an agency. To represent her unit adequately and encourage the loyalty of her staff, a supervisor must not only be effective in influencing individuals in the agency, but must manage group-based politics as well.

We need only reflect on our experience in any social service setting to appreciate the importance of instrumental informal groups in influencing opinions, behavior, and the distribution of resources in an agency. Frequently, race, ethnic, and gender factions exercise significant leverage on agency policies and personnel actions related to the interests the caucuses represent. Similarly, groups comprised of like professionals such as physicians, psychologists, or social workers often informally coordinate efforts to increase their impact on agency practices in regard to issues that affect the joint interests of these professionals. Further, workers within similar occupational categories and hierarchical ranks such as case aides, supervisors, or administrators join together in common causes regarding matters of shared concern. Other common interests such as ideology or animosity toward particular persons or subgroups also precipitate the formation of coalitions. Indeed, it is not unusual for informal alliances to be forged between members of an agency and individuals or groups outside the agency in a collective effort to shape organizational events.

Thus influencing agency decision making and increasing a supervisor's power often entail dealing with informal instrumental groups that diverge from the formal organizational structure.

Definitions of *coalition* vary. By and large, the term has been used broadly to refer to an alliance of persons or parties committed to achieving a common goal. There are shades of difference in definition among coalitions, interest groups, social networks, and factions. But these finer distinctions can be ignored for practice purposes, because practice prescriptions hold for the most part, irrespective of the distinctions between these terms. Our reference in this chapter, then, is to any informal network that is primarily instrumental and among its purposes seeks to influence aspects of an agency's functioning.

Supervisors often have varying degrees of choice regarding whether to join or avoid an existing agency coalition. They also have decisions to make regarding how active or peripheral their participation will be. Sometimes, too, they must consider whether to form an alliance to pursue some end or organize one to counter group interests that are antagonistic to their own. And when joining or forming a coalition, they must give thought to how the group may be strengthened or strategies devised to win the day. Our discussion in this chapter is designed to inform these supervisory choices.

To Join or Not to Join?

The primary function of a coalition is for its members to generate sufficient clout, through the power of numbers, to enhance their influence and gain their ends—because individual supervisors do not ordinarily have sufficient resources to achieve many of their desired goals alone. Members of organizations are used to working together, and as they interact, they informally make judgments regarding the commonality and differences of their own interests with those of others. They form or join coalitions to pool resources and strengthen their positions.

More broadly considered, coalitions of supervisors may have the effect of empowering supervisors as a class. When one contrasts the relative influence exerted by the supervisory—or middle—level in agencies without supervisory coalitions with that exerted in settings in which there are active supervisory alliances, it is clear that the collective influence of supervisors is greater in the latter instance. As we have said earlier, each level of an organization experiences a particular set of concerns from which it gains perspectives unique to that organizational level. In instances in which top managers do not usually involve supervisors in overall agency decision making, the increasing of supervisory influence through the use of coalitions—thereby pressing the agency to take supervisory perspectives more into account—is likely to be constructive in its impact on agency policy, as well as benefiting the supervisors themselves.

Coalitions also provide a neutral setting for supervisors to engage in reality testing and to consider possible individual actions. On occasion, it is imprudent for a supervisor to discuss sensitive issues with her superiors, and in such instances friends in the coalition may offer supportive consultation. Indeed, it is advantageous and sometimes necessary for individual supervisors to map out a strategy with others before they engage in political interventions. Coalitions also provide a safe and effective vehicle through which a supervisor can raise areas of agency problem to heighten agency consciousness and/or dissatisfaction with the current state of affairs. Spreading dissatisfaction with things as they are is often a first step in moving to change an agency procedure or policy, and the existence of an informal network advances the potential for creating the necessary climate for change. Beyond setting the climate, of course, coalitions actively intervene to press for common goals. It is not unusual, for example, for coalition action to alter executive behavior successfully, to confront or prevent discriminatory acts, and even to isolate or constrain destructive peers.

Although the raison d'être of coalitions is enhanced organizational influence to accomplish a supervisor's goals, they serve other purposes for her as well. High on the list is the ability of coalitions to meet affiliation needs. To know that there is a group of friends at work who share a common—or at least a nonantagonistic—organizational view is an important source of support. Participation in the group's activities often leads in time to in-group feelings that are more intimate than occurs with peers in general. Nowhere is this more the case than when the participants have common adversaries.

Identity needs may also be met through participation in an informal instrumental group. In a setting with considerable diversity, in which there are a range of strongly held views, professionals find comfort and assurance in having access to a group of like-minded individuals. In effect, the group validates the perspective of the individual supervisor. The more diverse and controversial the views within an agency, the more significant this function of coalitions is for many of its participants. Coalitions also provide special status opportunities for supervisors who might otherwise be "status deprived" in the larger agency setting. To be a valued member of a coalition in an agency in which social workers are insufficiently appreciated, for example, aids in buttressing the worker's feelings of professional self-esteem.

Implicit in much of this discussion is the presence of potential adversaries. We may presume that when coalitions form, countercoalitions are also likely to develop. Although one consequence of participating in a coalition is to increase cooperative bonds and collegiality among members of the group, another potential consequence is a heightening of competitive and even hostile linkages with members of opposing factions. It is here, then, that some of the costs of joining an alliance must be balanced against its benefits.

There is the risk that in-group versus out-group attitudes can distort organizational reality and institutionalize agency conflict. The more elaborated and broad-based a coalition, the more dependent its members are on the subgroup for mediating organizational life. Members consult about the meaning of events and collaborate in formulating hypotheses about what is and what is not occurring within the agency. As this process is routinized, participants typically increase interactions with one another and reduce interactions with members of opposing or unrelated factions. The result is a kind of hothouse effect in which a flurry of speculation following an ambiguous event leads to the construction of a reality that is often overdetermined, more reinforcing of the members' views than an accurate depiction of what has occurred.

To the extent that this takes place, participants develop a skewed perception of the system that to be effectively influenced must be accurately understood. Worse, with time the misperceptions can create a self-fulfilling prophecy, ensuring the accuracy of a reality that has been only perceived. By reacting politically to benign occurrences, participants force the politicization of increasingly wider arenas of organizational life and intensify the tensions or conflict that are a normal part of an organization's processes. In that instance, not only does intense conflict inhibit the organization's ability to achieve its objectives, but the tensions that protracted conflict generage are costly in energy and job satisfaction on the part of individual participants.

Another cost for supervisors, particularly newcomers to the agency, in participating in a coalition is the potential it holds for labeling them in the eyes of other organizational actors. The risk of labeling is greatest, of course, in settings in which alliances are relatively stable, consistent with respect to membership, and predictable in their positions. In effect, because observers believe that the positions of the coalition members are well understood, the newcomer is perceived as holding a similar set of positions and defined as one of *them*. Although there are frequently advantages to a supervisor in being labeled, the supervisor's tasks of image management can become unduly complicated by labeling, or her ability independently to find her own pathway through some of the minefields of agency relations can be made more difficult.

The labeling effect is often so pervasive that once a new supervisor develops a reputation by association, she is dismissed by nonmembers as someone whose positions and loyalties are presumed to be predictable derivations of those of the coalition's leadership. In an agency with which we are familiar, this process was so pronounced that one newcomer complained bitterly that, as a result of her friendship with a powerful and mischievous leader of a well-differentiated faction, members of opposing factions so type cast her that she was prevented from demonstrating who she was in her own right. To the extent that persons are subject to stereotyping, the chances are increased that they will be ignored or that when they state positions, they will fail to be convincing.

Finally, another cost to the individual supervisor of participating in an agency coalition is the flip side of its positive effect on her interpersonal relations with other group members. As we have said, coalition membership engenders cooperative bonds and affective support, as well as help in the pursuit of specific outcomes. But because coalition relations are essentially those of social exchange, there is often a cost for membership. The question, of course, is whether the cost is a reasonable one or too high for the anticipated benefits. A likely cost is constraint of the supervisor's maneuverability, her freedom to take independent action. Participants in a coalition are expected to conform with the positions that are seen as important to its interests. It may be a problem for some supervisors to do the coalition's business in specific instances, and sometimes deviations from this loyalty norm can incur a cost in their relationships with colleagues in the group.

We suspect, too, that many actors assess their potential power *within* a coalition, even if only informally, before they commit themselves to active participation in it (Caplow, 1956). Thus although a supervisor's purpose in joining may be the power that membership brings over those *outside* the coalition, she is likely to be mindful, too, of her own place in the internal scheme of things. Therefore, we can expect the vying for position within a coalition may generate interpersonal tensions within the group. To the extent that internal tensions are widespread or intense, of course, the coalition is weakened in its contention with other factions. Nevertheless, it is not unusual in a coalition, as in any other group, for some of its members to compete for status and leadership—often at some cost to the individual participants and the coalition's effectiveness.

Although supervisors must weigh the advantages and disadvantages of allying themselves with a specific alliance or deciding whether they want to join an informal instrumental group at all, their choice is ordinarily circumscribed. Newcomers may, of course, steer clear of alignments early in the game. But it would be unusual over the long term for a supervisor to have an impact on agency policy—much less develop a comfortable place in the agency—without developing a constituency or associating with some informally organized grouping. The question, then, is not so much to decide whether to join a coalition, but rather, how to maximize the benefits and minimize the costs to her as she participates in one. It is sometimes possible, for example, to reduce the negative consequences of labeling or to extend the opportunities for independent action, even as one maintains relatively good relations within and outside of the alliance. We offer some advice in this regard in subsequent sections of this chapter.

The Formation and Maintenance of Coalitions

How a supervisor relates to, aids, or counters coalition activity is partly shaped by her understanding of some of the characteristics of coalitions, the circumstances that encourage their formation, and the factors that make for effective alliances.

Coalitions vary along several dimensions, one of the more significant being their degree of permanence. Two types of alliances are found at either end of a continuum: standing and ad hoc. The ad hoc coalition is organized on a one-time basis to address a specific issue. It is often the outcome of a spontaneous reaction to an organizational event and persists only until it either achieves or abandons its effort to influence the event or issue. Individuals group and regroup into ad hoc combinations when past conflicts fade and the issue of the moment becomes primary. Thus ad hoc coalitions tend to be fluid and are not necessarily composed of like-minded people (a point that is insufficiently appreciated by supervisors who seek support only from friends). All that is necessary for an ad hoc coalition to come together are participants who are like-minded with respect to the question at issue. Their perceptions of their interests on other organizational matters can—and indeed, often do—differ widely.

Standing alliances, on the other hand, persist over time and may cover a broad range of issues. Sometimes they are so informal that they are barely recognizable as coalitions, and their manifestation may be no more than a predisposition of members to agree on organizational positions or an implicit understanding that they will avoid public disagreement. Wax (1971) has observed that a standing alliance is something like a credit card, in that the member can borrow the influence of the coalition in service of some desired end. Standing alliances often start with affective relations among their members or, if formed as a reaction to an event or issue, when the members are sufficiently homogeneous in their interests and ideology as to develop friendships as they work together. Standing alliances may become embedded in an organization's culture. The events or issues that precipitated their formation fade or are forgotten, but the alliance holds together, ordinarily with some turnover of membership. New members who were not among the coalition's founders are recruited, enlarging the group or replacing those who have left. The coalition persists, even as participants and agency concerns change.

The degree of permanence of a coalition is interdependent with other coalition characteristics. The extent to which coalitions are composed of participants with similar or diverse interests and ideology is one such variable. Whether their membership is constant, involving the same individuals over time, or there are shifts in membership is another. A related dimension is the permeability of the coalition's membership and the degree to which its members are visible as participants in the group's activities. The members of a coalition may be more or less identifiable among the subentities in an agency's sphere of informal relations. For example, some participants may be so far on the fringes of the group that their membership is uncertain, both within and outside of the alliance. Or it may serve a supervisor's interests (and her coalition's) for her to *appear* to be a neutral rather than a committed constituent. Indeed, sometimes a coalition is itself relatively invisible as an entity in the organization as a whole. Just as there are occasions when it is advantageous for individuals to exert influence unobtrusively, so, too, can unobtrusive influence work to the benefit of a coalition. On other occasions, a reputation for power—for either individuals or coalitions—is a resource that increases influence, because visibility that comes with such a reputation can give the parties additional leverage to achieve their ends.

The primary bases for a coalition's formation are twofold: a precipitating issue and the existence of affective relations among people who are interested in shaping organizational events, but there is more to the story. Dynamics relating to both elements that lead to a coalition's formation—its utilitarian or instrumental purpose and its affective or expressive source—determine whether a potential coalition will, in fact, come into being and how effective it will be.

By and large, for an issue to precipitate the creation of an alliance, it must meet two criteria. The first is obvious: the issue must have sufficient meaning or intensity for the actors to impel their coming together. More importantly, it must be perceived of as something that can be won by concerted effort. The less powerful a supervisor is in her agency, the more attractive coalition membership may be as a means of extending her influence. But the coalition must be sufficiently effective so that it provides payoffs that the supervisor could not otherwise gain, or else its ability to sustain itself is seriously undermined. The need for a coalition to accrue power—and to achieve shared ends—is thus critical to both its formation and its survival.

We would expect, therefore, that a coalition is likely to form and persist when its propsects for generating influence are high. To some degree, contextual factors—factors such as an agency's structure allow supervisors and other organizational actors to exert a greater or lesser impact on agency policy and practice, and thus encourage or discourage their grouping into coalitions. Although it is beyond the scope of this chapter to detail the impact of various organizational structures on the distribution of influence, we cite one structural variable for illustrative purposes.

In decentralized settings, those in which decision making is widely dispersed, one may anticipate considerably more coalition activity than in centralized structures. The more power and authority that is delegated to the lower reaches of the organization, the more effective will be the efforts to influence those in the upper levels of the hierarchy—and thus the more likely that coalitions will form. In contrast, in centralized structures in which the top managers tend to control the decision-making process, the bosses are less likely to respond to coalition efforts unless extensive pressure is mounted. The requirements of mounting a successful pressure campaign may then be so costly as to discourage the attempt except in unusual circumstances. Furthermore, when peers have more power, as they do in decentralized structures, they not only become attractive coalition partners, but they are also potential targets for influence efforts. When they have little or no power, their value as coalition members is minimized, and efforts to influence them are less important.

A clear example of the relationship between decentralization and coalition formation can be observed in university settings. Highly decentralized in their governance, universities are known as hotbeds of political activity. One major reason for coalition activity in such settings is the dispersion of power. Because peers collectively hold the power to have an impact on most decisions in the organization, or *believe* they do, the value of their participation in a coalition is enhanced. And to the extent that faculty and administrators are not themselves active in a coalition, they are the likely targets of coalition activity by others because of their own influence in the setting.

An agency's relationship to its environment is another contextual factor that affects the ability of participants to shape agency directions, thereby encouraging or inhibiting coalition formation. We hypothesize that the *degree* to which an agency is independent of or dependent on its environment affects the extent of coalition activity within it. Some organizations are relatively independent; for example, those with a significant endowment or those that, although receiving external support, are not regulated by their funding source. Similarly, agencies with discrete and delimited functions and those in low-controversy service areas enjoy a benign, relatively independent relationship to their external environment. Internal coalitions are probably discouraged under these conditions, for the agency's independence gives internal participants less leverage to make an impact on its policies. Whether this is, in fact, the case, certainly agency independence from its environment limits the development of coalitions with external parties. When an agency is embedded in its environment and its staff has the potential for access to external actors, these staff members have a potent resource for influencing and therefore have a heightened incentive to join in an alliance with outsiders. Because a supervisor's participation in an alliance with outside parties sometimes represents a high-risk activity, we devote a subsequent section of this chapter to the issue.

Another contextual factor that influences coalition formation has to do with agency management, specifically the degree to which executives are subject to influence by supervisory and other staff. There are many elements that make up an executive's amenability to influence. One, of course, is his personality. To choose only one example: if he appears indecisive or ambivalent about issues, he encourages or unknowlingly gives permission for others to try to mold his thinking. (We note parenthetically that the same dynamic occurs between the supervisor and her staff if she is an ambivalent decision maker). Another element is the executive's style of management. If he seeks the input of his staff and has a participatory orientation to administration, he encourages coalition activity by increasing the success of staff groups in pursuing their common interests. Another executive characteristic that encourages coalition behavior is his training or experience. An executive who is a member of the same professional group as the supervisory staff is more prone to be responsive to their positions than if he were from a different profession, because he and the staff are more likely to share norms in common and to have similar reference groups.

Executives are often constrained in their decision making by agency structure or circumstances—the tenure of faculty in a university, civil service requirements, the presence of staff members with independent constituencies, or the existence of strong staff factions, for example. Depending on power balances within the agency, it is conceivable that top administrators may informally ally themselves with line staff in order to increase their influence over middle-level personnel. Various combinations of alignment among the different hierarchical levels are possible (e.g., line staff and supervisors versus upper-level managers or upper-level managers and supervisors versus line workers) and these often do take place. The point here, however, is that many executives whose influence is constrained play the political game by surreptiously or otherwise aligning themselves with other participants. In seeking their support, the exeuctive encourages and/or legitimizes the coming together of these participants in an alliance. To the extent that he is then viewed as a member of a coalition or predisposed to favor one, he probably induces heightened attempts to form countercoalitions.

If the prospect of successfully achieving some instrumental outcome is critical to a coalition's formation and maintenance, how does one explain the existence and endurance of losing coalitions? Nonwinning coalitions may form for a number of reasons. One is the inadequacy of information available to the participants—predicting who will win or lose is an uncertain business at best. Secondly, winning or losing may not be dichotomous variables in some circumstances. Thus a loss in a current effort may constitute a step in the direction of ultimate progress toward achieving longer-term goals. Or participants may view a setback as minimizing what might otherwise have been an even greater loss. It is also conceivable that although a coalition may incur a defeat, it nevertheless sees itself as narrowing the power differences between it and some other faction (Bacharach and Lawler, 1980).

These reasons are probably insufficient to explain why some losing coalitions persist, however. In an organization with which we are familiar, one such group has endured for many years with committed constituents and highly visible activities, even though the group rarely achieves its objectives. The fact that its members have similar ideologies, have developed affective relations, and have come to define others in the organization as adversaries is, we suspect, the basis for the coalition's survival in the face of its utilitarian failures. There may be other reasons as well. When people believe they are right and others wrong, there is a potential psychological gratification of persisting, even in a losing struggle. More significantly perhaps, the losing coalition may serve the function of allowing members to justify their own behavior and/or to deflect criticism of their performance.

Thus although the instrumental grounds for coalition formation and activity are significant, coalitions also form because they serve important expressive functions. A study by Lawler and Youngs (1975) is instructive in this regard. They explored the effects of three variables on a person's choosing to join a coalition: (1) the expected payoffs (or significance of particular issues to the parties), (2) ideological similarities among the expected participants, and (3) the probability of the coalition's success. They found that all three contribute to a coalition's formation, but that, interestingly enough, attitudinal or ideological similarity is more important as a reason for joining than the coalition's expected payoff. Although attitudinal or ideological similarities may, of course, advance common instrumental interests, they are clearly a factor in promoting affective ties as well.

It is necessary to consider more than ideological similarity when selecting partners for an effective coalition. Obviously, members who have bases of power contribute more than actors with lesser resources for influencing. Diversity of resources is also important. Participants with differing sources of information, a variety of types of expertise, and links to other constituencies in or outside of the agency make a more potent combination than coalitions in which the members' information channels, experience, or informal relations are merely additive. Nevertheless, the more powerful a potential actor—and therefore, the more desirable as a coalition member—the less likely she is to join, because her ends can be accomplished without being a member. Similarly, the more powerful the potential actor, the higher will be the price she can demand for her participation. For example, a coalition that is organized to press for hiring a new staff member will have to weigh whether to involve an additional supervisor, however much influence with the boss she may have, if the supervisor is set on finding someone whose expertise is viewed with question by the group. (A common accomodation in such a situation is for the coalition to try to keep its aims sufficiently general to attract the supervisor as a member without committing itself to her demand for the specified expertise.)

Just as diversity in resources for influencing adds strengths to the group, so too does heterogeneity in the attitudes and ideologies that are represented in it. The more unexpected the combination of these differences among members, the greater the coalition's chances to reach its goal.

When persons with known ideological differences join together, their coalition attracts more attention and is more persuasive. Such a coalition cannot be neatly pigeonholed and is therefore more difficult to dismiss. It is often assumed that, in light of their wide divergencies, they must be "right" about an issue about which they agree.

There is inevitable tension, however, in a coalition that includes people with sharply differing beliefs. Diverse positions inhibit consensus and cohesion, which are important for successful political engagements. Furthermore, people are considerably more likely to join a coalition composed of others with common attitudes. Valuable in this regard are boundary-spanning members, those whose attitudes and values bridge differences among participants. These are persons who represent particular interests or points of view with a sufficiently broad perspective to be able to connect with those whose interests and positions are related but more circumscribed. At the very least, coalition members who disagree in private must preserve a common front in public. But cohesion and a united public stance are considerably more difficult to achieve in an ideologically heterogeneous group.

Thus trade-offs are required in matters relating to power and ideology—as indeed they are in much of organizational practice. A single intervention often simultaneously carries both benefits and costs. As we have seen, one may want to recruit a powerful staff member, but the price of obtaining her participation has the potential of distorting the coalition's aims. Or taking a person into a coalition whose values differ sharply from the values of other members can add credibility to the group, on the one hand, while at the same time reducing its strength by generating tensions within it, on the other. The task then, is to decide which is more important in a specific instance and/or how one may maximize benefits while minimizing costs.

Coalition size is also a factor for which trade-offs may be necessary. According to some coalition theorists, smaller coalitions are more effective than larger ones (Riker, 1962). Because generating support from others often involves supervisors in a further trade—sometimes with payments required at some later time—coalition building can be conceptualized as incurring future costs that supervisors must be ready to pay. In addition, the larger the number of resources necessary to influence an action, the more complex the system of exchanges (Clark, 1966). One would, therefore, wish to keep the use of resources to accomplish a goal to the minimum necessary.

Smaller size appears desirable on other grounds as well. Larger coalitions tend to be more difficult to organize or maintain than smaller ones.

Further, larger coalitions are likely to have more problems of coordination and frequently have to resolve complicated conflicts of interests among potential participants (Bacharach and Lawler, 1980). In addition, the smaller a coalition's size, the less likely that the views of its members will diverge and that the supervisor will have to concede some part of her objectives to obtain a consensus.

But there are also distinct advantages to larger coalitions when one considers an organizational context (Pfeffer, 1981). If a supervisor wants to get as many organizational interests as possible behind a decision, she should consider the expansion of the group beyond the minimum number of people necessary to accomplish its goal. Very often the implementation of a decision in an agency is at least as important, if not more important, than making the decision itself. Sometimes, therefore, it is adviseable to enlarge an agency coalition to the maximum size possible rather than maintaining it at a minimum. Furthermore, so-called standing coalitions deal with a diversity of issues, many of them transitory, and having a greater number of participants ready to plan or take action adds to the potency of the coalition in the agency. Indeed, the mere existence of a large and watchful group undoubtedly influences how others in the agency will act and what positions they will espouse.

Some of the elements of an effective coalition that we have suggested, and the trade-offs that are necessary to put it together, provide a critical underpinning for recruiting participants to an alliance.

Recruiting Members

Often an explosive issue impels the formation of a coalition, almost as if by spontaneous combustion. One such issue might be the promotion of an unpopular male who is perceived as considerably less adequate than an available female. Under these circumstances, considerations regarding whom to recruit to the coalition or how to recruit them are of limited relevance. To some degree, the coalition forms itself, and who will participate is determined less by conscious choice than by how the issue affects particular staff members.

Frequently, however, to put together an effective coalition the supervisor must be cognizant of elements that influence a coalition's functioning and consider them in the context of the agency's particular circumstances and the short- and/or long-term objectives of the budding alliance. She must, first of all, be able to assess the distribution of power in her agency. Who, for example, has sufficient power to make an impact on the program or policy she wishes to influence? Here, she is mindful that different colleagues may be more or less influential with respect to different issues. She must have some sense of whether the values and interests of these powerful others are compatible with her own or the budding coalition's goals. Are they, for example, likely to be responsive to the issue as it is currently defined, or will the issue have to be redefined to gain their attention or support? Further, what price will have to be paid to elicit participation, and is it worth paying? How might the participation of certain colleagues affect the participation of others, either in attracting new or important constituents to the effort or making them wary about joining the group?

Much of what has been written in earlier chapters of this book can be put to use as the supervisor responds to these questions in recruiting members to a coalition. Particularly pertinent is our review of the techniques relating to persuasion and implicit negotiation. For example, as a supervisor explores the reactions of colleagues to specific issues or the willingness of colleagues to join in a particular effort, she may do so indirectly—if it is important not to reveal where she stands too early in the game or if she is unsure of the price that she is willing to pay for the other's backing. Similarly, she will consider how to shape her arguments to reflect the underlying values of potential participants or to make her case to them with maximum credibility.

By and large, the process takes place informally. There are likely to be some differences in approach, depending on whether one is recruiting for an ad hoc or a standing alliance. When issues are at stake, one of two ways is usually employed. In the first, individual members consciously lobby potential collaborators on an initiative that the coalition wishes to promote. The strategy here is to select the supervisor who has most influence with the desired recruit. The choice may be based on their relationship, ideological compatability, or because the two have discussed the issue in the past. A particular coalition member may be selected because the potential recruit wants or owes something to the member, and it would be difficult for the recruit to turn her down.

A second way in which an issue-oriented initiative occurs is in a "spontaneous" exchange—which can be actual or planned—at an informal gathering. For example, someone at the gathering complains that the boss rarely involves the supervisory staff in agency policy formation. The boss is expected at the next staff meeting to announce plans to launch a new program, despite prior staff expressions of concern about it. Another supervisor proposes that the group speak against this plan, and they agree to make a motion at the meeting that the idea be deferred for further study by a task force. Although the above often takes place in an impromptu fashion, such an event can also be planned. In the latter case, core group members of the coalition will have already spread dissatisfaction about the matter, so as to encourage a receptive response when the plan of action surfaces. Indeed, some individuals may have been primed to comment at the informal get-together in an attempt to create the right group climate for action. With widespread and strong feelings expressed, others are more easily swept along.

As we have suggested, affective relations play a role even in many issue-oriented and ad hoc coalitions. Thus the supervisor must be cognizant not only of the self-interests and ideologies of those whom they wish to engage, but of the pattern of needs that potential members bring to the group. Colleagues have pronounced needs and feelings to look good, capable, and wise—or at least not incapable, weak, and foolish—in the eyes of other colleagues. These needs and feelings act as potent levers when supervisors know how to use them. Further, group activities may be structured to meet these needs, such as invitations to periodic lunches or "debriefings" following staff meetings in a member's office.

Obviously, affective concerns are more significant in the case of a standing alliance. Here, matters of friendly relations and value compatability are critical. Because power varies with issues and over time, the right mix of resources for influencing that members may contribute and the extent of ideological diversity that can be accomodated are less clear. Whereas in ad hoc coalitions it is sometimes appropriate to limit the group's size, this is hardly ever the case in coalitions that are designed to persist. Indeed, for reasons cited earlier, hitherto neutral staff often make highly desirable participants. When numbers are helpful, or at least not contraindicated, even weaker members make beneficial recruits, and their participation entails minimal costs. Weaker members are more prone to join a coalition than are powerful ones and are more likely to devote their energies to its goals. They are, in addition, unable to exact a price for participation which more powerful actors can demand. Among the staff who are ready candidates for recruitment are workers who have recently been hired, because it usually takes some time before they are sufficiently integrated to be able to make much of an impact on the agency.

This raises a significant question for a new supervisor. As she is solicited to become a member of one of the agency's coalitions, what ought her response to be? Clearly, joining up has several advantages, although there are cautions to be observed as well. We have noted that it is an asset for a newcomer to have access to a seasoned veteran or organizational mentor. When one or more such individuals are also active participants in an agency alliance, the new supervisor is likely to feel that she has happened upon a network of colleagues who have a genuine interest in helping her become comfortable in the agency. The new group thus offers support at a time of heightened insecurity. Standing alliances, in contrast to ad hoc ones, also offer ongoing protection against adversaries in cases of conflict.

But the new supervisor is wise not to become more than peripherally involved in a coalition too early in her tenure—at the very least, not before there are indications that joining up serves her instrumental interests as well as meeting her sociability needs. It is true that in highly politicized agencies, her choice is limited. In such settings it is not unusual for there to be a prevailing attitude that "if you ain't for us, you're against us," and noninvolvement thus exacts a cost. Even so, neutrality is advisable until she has gathered sufficient information to be relatively comfortable in making a preliminary assessment of the various players and forces at work in the setting.

Two factors are particularly important in reaching a judgment. One has to do with the values of coalition members and the extent to which they conform to her own. Obviously, an alliance in which others have similar values and beliefs is more satisfying than the reverse and is more likely to reflect her interests as well. Even as her interests shift over time, she is more likely to find common ground in responding to these new interests with ideologically compatible partners.

A second factor in considering whether to join is the relative power of the coalition. A coalition's power may be less obvious than its ideological leanings, but this only makes it more important that the new supervisor assess the coalition's place in the agency scheme of things as accurately as is possible. The advantages of belonging to an influential alliance are obvious enough—some part of its influence rubs off on her; the coalition is in a better position to protect her if protection is called for; and by definition, the coalition will be more successful in achieving its ends, including those of concern to the new supervisor.

Conversely, if she locks herself into a consistently nonwinning coalition and is labeled as one of its members, she may close herself off from the agency's more influential members. Reaping the worst of both worlds becomes a distinct possibility. The new supervisor risks the disadvantages of coalition membership cited earlier—negative prejudgments, constraint in pursing attractive activities out of group loyalty, and pressure to support positions with which she is less than completely comfortable—all without the influence and protection that a powerful group provides.

Indeed, in some settings, she incurs suspicion, if not emnity, from these important others. Thus if the new supervisor has not initially done an accurate assessment of agency forces, some months afterward she may find that she has undercut her ability to promote the interests of both her unit and her own interests.

Usually, joining up occurs without forethought. One enters an agency and experiences an affinity for an individual or group, and when the latter are active participants in a coalition, the new supervisor is slowly inducted into the group without full awareness of the political implications of her participation. When her new friends ask her to support a particular position or to vote in a particular way, a sense of obligation and loyalty predisposes her conformance.

Staff who extend themselves to a new supervisor may do so quite naturally, without ulterior motives. But often, too, their friendliness is consciously intended to recruit the new supervisor into a coalition. We do not mean to suggest that when the recruiter is acting consciously she is ill-motivated or that her friendliness is deceptive. Rather, active coalition participants believe strongly in their issues and objectives. Knowing that newcomers feel uncertain in the early days of their tenure in the agency, old-timers offer assistance and access to their networks to educate the new supervisor about the agency, its issues, and politics. When the newcomer is responsive, the old-timer feels that she has found a kindred spirit and that the supervisor's joining is an informed choice.

But until the supervisor has some clear idea about such issues as the character of her relations with top administrators, the degree and nature of coalition activity in the agency, and a coalition's potential import for her relationships with significant actors and effect on collegial interactions, she is well advised to move cautiously in affiliating. It is, of course, possible to modify political alliances, but the process can cause bruised feelings and a residue of ill-will. Further, supervisors who appear to be inconsistent or unreliable in political interactions risk not being trusted, even by friends.

This issue transcends the accurate assessment of power relations, however. The same concerns affect knowledgeable and experienced participants as well. Even standing alliances are somewhat fluid. A supervisor's interests may shift over time; other groups may offer her more attractive inducements; changes in staff may alter the direction of the agency, precipitating changes in the direction and composition of the coalition. Any of these circumstances may require some change in a supervisor's relation to a coalition.

Managing Coalition Relations

As in the case of recruitment to a coalition, managing ongoing coalition relations requires two perspectives—one, from that of the coalition's leaders; the other, from the perspective of a less centrally involved member. Because the roles of leader and member differ, their interests—and practice behaviors—vary as well.

Actually, there are many levels of membership in standing agency coalitions. Because coalitions are so informal, the existence of these levels may not be obvious. Nevertheless, one may observe four gradations of participation along a continuum. At one end of the continuum is the core leadership, constituting the coalition's steering committee. It consists of a small number of committed and influential members, the ones who most tend to shape the character, content, and decision making of the alliance. The leaders' lieutenants constitute the next place on the continuum. Lieutenants are active in pursuing the coalition's initiatives and conduct much of its business; they may or may not be members of the steering committee. Lieutenants are intensely committed, but less influential; their task is to cajole, argue, and lobby, primarily at the behest of the core leadership. A third group might be termed occasionals. As the term implies, they are actively involved in coalition campaigns only sporadically, with much depending on the specific issue or the agency's political climate at a particular moment in time. Finally, there are peripheral participants. Peripherals do not, by and large, engage in coalition activity, but they can be counted on to support the coalition's positions and to behave in the right way as an occasion demands.

Effective coalitions do not require that all members be similarly committed or involved. Core leaders who are aware of this do not expend useless energy in trying to induce full participation and are not judgmental with respect to those who take less central roles. Indeed, judgmentalness can be self-defeating, because it may lead to sermonizing, and the explicit or implicit chiding of those who do not give their "all" to achieve group purposes risks their disaffection.

Three important tasks of a leader in managing coalition relations are worth noting. One is to ensure that those on the coalition's periphery will be available when their support is needed. Another is to encourage consensus within the group, and the third is managing conflict with adversaries. Managing these tasks skillfully is the key to the maintenance and effectiveness of the coalition.

Obviously enough, support can most readily be gained when a member's connection, either to the leader herself or to a subgroup of the alliance, has been cultivated between campaigns. The "care and feeding" of occasional and peripheral members is accomplished in a number of ways. One is as simple as the leader's extending herself socially, making sure to include the occasionals in the group's coffee klatches and gossip sessions. Trading inside information helps others to feel like insiders and serves also to generate information in return. Another way, similar to the supervisor's work with her staff, is to express appreciation and approval of the others' positions whenever approval can be legitimately proferred. Still another useful investment in the future is to seek ways to offer help to members on the coalition's fringe, because it is expected that they will return the favor. The old adage that it is better to give than to receive, if not true in all circumstances, is true in organizational politics.

Leaders try to protect or promote the interests of other coalition members with agency administrators or other staff members in order to build or maintain a constituency. For example, a leader might mediate for a fellow supervisor with an executive, "confidentially" informing the executive about the supervisor's concern about some organizational issue and urging ameliorative action—as a favor to both the executive, who might want to have the information and advice, and to the constituent.

Encouraging consensus is another task of a coalition's leadership. It is true, of course, that when important staff interests are at risk, minor disagreements among the coalition's members are likely to be discounted. Consensus then evolves naturally, and there is little more for a leader to do but underline the commonality of the risk to their interests. This occurs, too, in crisis situations and when strong feelings are shared with regard to some issue or adversary. Normally, however, coalitions face peculiar constraints in gaining a consensus with regard to important decisions. On the one hand, the issues with which coalitions deal have political significance for many of its constituents; on the other, the lack of standing meetings, formal procedures, and often little or no face-to-face contact by members of the entire group pose a dilemma for decision making. The question, then, is the extent to which leaders should make decisions which they then try to "sell" to less active constituents versus the extent to which they broadly involve lieutenants, occasionals, and peripherals in the decision-making process as a means of ensuring consensus and commitment. Errors can be made by moving too far in either direction. At one extreme, alienation rather than consensus may be the outcome, whereas at the other, a weak, least-common-denominator position may result.

Coalition leaders manage the dilemma by consulting with their colleagues, at times directly, at times tentatively, and sometimes by using the techniques of persuasion and implicit negotiation. As core actors and lieutenants are involved in the consultations, the leadership's position takes shape and is modified. Although some actors are considerably more influential than others, the impression (or reality) of a collective judgment is created. Awareness that consultations are taking place encourages consensus, but even when consensus cannot be achieved, the process of polling members increase the acceptance of the decision as a representative one.

As positions and plans for action are formulated, the tasks of involving, informing, and coordinating with occasional and peripheral members are necessary. The danger of garbled messages—or worse, undelivered messages—is great and can have highly deleterious effects. Coalition activities sometimes expose participants to risk or embarrassment and need to be coordinated effectively to reduce the potential for dissent or disaffection. Leaders must stay close to their lieutenants to make certain that requisite communications have been sent, processed, and responded to.

The sophisticated leaders of coalitions find opportunities to increase the agency influence of trusted lieutenants or even peripheral members and friends. This is accomplished in a number of ways; for example, by publicly complimenting their work, calling attention to their competencies, suggesting their names for significant assignments or committee work, and helping them to expand their network of contacts. A supervisor who has influence with top administrators enhances the power of her own network, for example, when she helps to get allies promoted or placed in key units. Interestingly enough, if the appointment is controversial, her power is even further enhanced. For a reputation for influence generates more influence in turn, and the controversial appointee is likely to be a more reliable ally.

Conversely, sometimes leaders of standing coalitions can be tarred with the gaffes of their lieutenants—often through no fault of their own. The two, leader and follower, are closely associated in the minds of other agency personnel and may not always be perceived as totally independent entities. When this occurs, the leader tries to work with the lieutenant to improve the latter's political performance—but because they are in fact independent personalities, the follower may or may not follow a leader's advice—or indeed, may be incapable of doing so. If the political costs of having an inept lieutenant begin to outweigh the benefits of her support, the leader has little choice but to attempt to distance herself from the offending lieutenant. She may do so by finding issues of minor import about which to publicly disagree with the follower. Or she may privately and casually communicate her upset to others about the latter's ineptitude.

A final task for a coalition leader is dealing effectively with adversaries. Decreasing the influence of other factions is a long-range goal and calls for the opposite of the interventions with respect to coalition members. One would, in other words, look to decrease the power of adversaries. This goal may be advanced by challenging the adversaries' legitimacy— that is, their appropriateness, expertise, or objectivity—to participate on certain committees or to be involved in decision making regarding partic- ular issues. Pointing out the inadequacies of members of the out-group to important actors in the agency is useful, although denigrating out-group members must be credible and must not appear to be part of a campaign. Adversaries sometimes unintentionally collude in this effort by extreme or irrational behavior, thereby making themselves easy targets. To the extent that a prominent member of a countercoalition behaves in this way, other members of the countercoalition are disadvantaged as well, because their association with the extremist actor is often obvious and may, in any case, be highlighted.

In trying to win over the hearts and minds of other agency staff in conflict situations, coalition leaders are better positioned when they ap- pear to be responding to an attack rather than seen as the aggressor in the conflict. Studies of conflict suggest that when disagreement is protracted, as is frequently the case between standing alliances, the disagreement becomes highly personalized, and differences tend to be defined in strongly moral terms (Coleman, 1957). Noncombatants who observe this phenomenon are likely to make judgments based on the reasonableness, rather than the virulence, of one side or the other. The leader who is aware of this dynamic and can maintain sufficient discipline to moderate understandable emotion is more likely to be perceived favorably. In other words, moderation—or at least its appearance—is strategic in dealing with adversaries.

Whereas coalition leaders seek to increase membership loyalty and participation, individual supervisors are sometimes best served by taking advantage of offers of friendship and assistance from established actors without becoming overinvolved in the political commitments of their faction. Newly hired workers are most likely to be permitted a free ride on this, because when there are competitive groups, there is often a norm that permits newcomers some leeway before requiring that they align themselves. This allows the new supervisor some time to assess the re- spective power positions of the groups and the critical issues for which each stands. Her predilictions tend, nevertheless, to be scrutinized, and assessments are made about her potential for membership. She will thus need to proceed cautiously until she has gained sufficient information to decide where she wishes to locate herself on the political landscape.

As she interacts with the group with which she is predisposed to collaborate, she will also have to decide the level of her participation in the group. As time passes and her long-term interests become clearer, she may continue to adjust her levels of involvement commeasurate with her ongoing assessment of the advantages of moving closer to the coalition's core.

When the supervisor is a high power person, or when the coalition has a political stake in expanding its numbers regardless of her power, playing hard to get has political benefits. As long as the supervisor participates frequently enough for the group to believe that there are terms and issues around which her cooperation can be elicited, she will continue to receive direct or implicit initiatives designed to engage her cooperation. Maintaining a degree of distance while at the same time contributing to coalition activity from time to time (i.e., as an occasional or peripheral participant) increases her ability to gain accomodations to her points of view that might not otherwise be offered. It also permits her greater latitude to choose the issues she wishes to engage in. When she is not perceived as totally committed to the group—and therefore there are lesser expectations regarding her participation—pejorative judgments about her unwillingness to go along in a particular circumstance are likely to be muted.

Two qualifications are worth noting. When an issue is critical to coalition members and represents a position that is intensely held, a supervisor who is not supportive may be viewed negatively, at least for the moment, however friendly her prior experiences with coalition members have been. In extreme cases—typically when the group is engaged in a contest associated with some risk—backing off from an issue may well be perceived as a measure of cowardice.

Similarly, if there is strong emnity, or its undercurrent, between two standing alliances (an in-group and an out-group, say), the supervisor whose distancing moves her in the direction of the "enemy" will be viewed with suspicion. Because the negative sentiments toward the out-group undoubtedly reinforce the image and identity of the in-group, occasional or peripheral members who maintain more than superficial relations with out-group members challenge the integrity of the in-group, however unintentionally.

Although it is not required that the supervisor avoid informal contact with members of a competing faction, overt courting of its members is likely to be defined as signaling a realignment of her loyalties. By the same token, if the supervisor overplays her hand in playing hard to get, she risks being written off as a potential ally. The supervisor who chooses to maintain distance—but wants to remain on friendly terms with coalition members—must find occasions to participate in its campaigns.

Three of the more important determinents of the positions taken by agency staff are the extent to which it serves their self or subunit interests, its compatability with their ideological orientation, and who else among the other staff favor or oppose the position. Sometimes, then, tension is generated when one factor conflicts with another. For example, a coalition of friends—people whom the supervisor would ordinarily support—may engage in efforts that are counter to her unit's interests. To serve her unit, she must consider how she can reduce the potential disruption to her relations with allies.

A few simple prescriptions may be followed to permit a supervisor to pursue an independent action without its resulting in an undue cost to her relations with the coalition. For one, the supervisor should inform her colleagues in advance that she disagrees with their position. If the issue is a more significant one to other coalition members than to her, she may be asked—or volunteer—to remain silent when the matter is discussed at a staff meeting or with important others. She thus garners credit for being concerned about her relationship with them. If the issue is central to her own or her unit's interests and she feels that she must take a public stand or campaign against her friends, she is also well served by warning them in advance. Surprising them with her disagreement feels like a betrayal, whereas notifying them ahead of time suggests her integrity. Dealing with the matter as an issue of self-interest rather than trying to justify her opposition to their position solely on its merits is also advisable. Sophisticated colleagues usually figure that out in any case; because they are likely to understand a self-interest explanation, they will credit her with honesty for making it.

A rationale that rests on principle is also likely to be acceptable to colleagues as an explanation for a supervisor's unwillingness to go along with the coalition on a particular issue. A critical professional norm is that one acts as one's principles, however much the norm may at times be breached in practice. Because the situation may represent an instance in which adherence to one norm (that professionals act on principle) violates another norm (that friends remain loyal to one another), for a supervisor to use principle credibly as a rationale, she must be known as someone with integrity and the principle must be consistent with previous stands she has taken. But the supervisor must also keep her adherence to principle within normative bounds. For a colleague to communicate that she has higher moral standards than her peers does little to endear her to them.

External Coalitions

Coalitions may involve parties who are either inside or outside of an agency's boundaries. Although there is considerable theoretical similarity between coalitions composed solely of internal actors and those that include both internal and external constituents, there are differences between them as well.

External coalitions may serve to support an agency's or management's goals, as in the case of organizations that provide benefits or services to particular groups and reach out to those groups to help them to press for additional agency resources. Parents of school children who are organized to fight for increased allocations for school programs offer one such example. But external coalitions may be oppositional to agency management as well. An example is provided by mental health and social service staff who work for a governmental agency but who surreptitiously join with advocates of the homeless, sharing inside information to strengthen the advocates' campaigns against the laxity of public officials in dealing with the problem.

Both of these are examples of active mobilizing efforts to influence organizational program and policy. More relevant to agency supervisors in the normal course of their work perhaps are the external coalitions that come into being naturally, as an outgrowth of pre-existing networks. An example might be a group of professionals who share an interest in a particular problem area—for example, family violence—and who belong to a subcommittee of their professional association studying the matter. If two or three of them work in the same family agency and share their frustration regarding the agency's lack of interest in battered women, it is conceivable that the committee could formally press the agency executive to increase its efforts for that client group.

By and large, ties to an external constituency increase a supervisor's influence within her agency. At times the coalition—and her participation in it—is advantageous to the organization and otherwise is benign; that is, it serves to advance the interests of the executive and agency and poses no threat to upper-ranking personnel. The supervisor whose contacts with DSS personnel resulted in a funding opportunity for the Heights Mental Health Clinic in Chapter 8 constitutes an example. Her ability to garner desired resources made her more valuable to the agency and therefore made her a more influential staff member.

Prestige, credibility, and referent power ordinarily accrue to cosmopolitan supervisors who participate in a wider network of affiliations than their internal peers. Furthermore, when members of an external network take it upon themselves to influence agency policy, it captures the attention of the executive in a way that internal efforts may not. As stated earlier, executives tend to be more concerned about external judgments than internal ones, and if all other things are equal, they will be more responsive to external pressure.

There is, however, another side to the coin. The ideology of most organizations presumes a set of common goals held by organizational members. To participate in an alliance with external constituents implies that the overall interests of the organization could take second place to the interests of the supervisor's own unit or that her personal-professional values could take precedence over the agency's. She risks, in short, being perceived of as disloyal (Pfeffer, 1981).

Indeed, when a supervisor's external allies are significant to the agency—as in the case of supervisors with connections to a funding source or to important political others—an executive may feel discomforted or threatened by the implicit leverage over him that this permits the supervisor. Unless their relationship is a close one and she has demonstrated her commitment to the agency over time, he is likely to feel some edge of concern about her association with important outsiders as constituting a power center independent of his own.

But even when the supervisor's outside connections are not politically potent, the agency commitment of cosmopolitan workers may be subject to question. In their favor is that significant associations or high professional visibility can redound to the agency's credit. Nevertheless, if a supervisor's activity outside the agency is extensive, she may be perceived as more interested in professional activities (and perhaps professional advancement) than she is in the agency's services or its clients. Here again, an issue of loyalty may arise.

The juxtaposition of the potential for enhanced influence, on the one hand, and the risk of being viewed as disloyal, on the other, frames the issue of a supervisor's involvement in external coalitions. Although on the surface it appears to be a high-risk high-gain proposition, in practice many external associations are relatively risk free. The key is to develop relevant external affiliations over time so that the agency incrementally accepts the arrangement before any overt attempt is made to influence agency outcomes. As these affiliations take place, the supervisor must, through the normal course of her work, find natural and unobtrusive ways to make others aware of her outside activities.

As she is establishing a perception of herself as a participant in an external network, she must also consider how her outside activities can lead to benefits for the organization. This may be accomplished in numbers of ways. For example, if the supervisor is asked to participate in a conference workshop, she can promote the agency by featuring an aspect of its program and ensuring that, directly or indirectly, that agency officials hear about the presentation. Similarly, if she has been invited to participate in planning a program, she might consult with the executive about which staff should be included in the program as way of promoting the agency's interests and image within the community. In this way, over time she maximizes the view that her affiliations are an organizational asset.

Balance and sequence are important if her outside commitments cause inconvenience in the agency (e.g., when an outside meeting requires that she miss an agency event or if she must ask permission to work on a special project during agency time). Executives can accept minor inconvenience to accomodate a valued supervisor in any case, but they willingly do so when it is clear that the supervisor's associations represent a potential benefit for the agency. She should understand, however, that this equation is monitored closely, and the benefit-inconvenience balance must be perceived as clearly tipping in favor of the agency. Similarly, the degree and character of the supervisor's external affiliations must be kept within acceptable boundaries. If her external activities begin to detract from her agency responsibilities, the advantages that might accrue to her will be more than offset by resentment engendered by inappropriate priorities.

Once the supervisor has modulated the disadvantages of having external affiliations by developing a reserve of organization goodwill, she must communicate the fact that these associations come at the price of requiring a degree of loyalty to their constituents. Only then can she consider using those affiliations overtly to influence internal organizational events.

When an external coalition with which the supervisor is identified intervenes in an internal agency matter, attributions of disloyalty to the agency may be made. The risk is mitigated if the issue in question is not highly controversial and the coalition's activities are moderate. The more controversial the issue, the more her executive will expect her to support the agency view, and the more significant for him will be the meaning of her not doing so. Even when the issue is not highly controversial, the supervisor must not appear to have instigated the intervention. If she is defined as facilitating the coalition's acts, she brooks the risk of seeming to care more about the coalition's agenda than her agency's.

In any case, as the external coalition tries to influence the agency, the supervisor should frame the issue as the coalition's agenda, as opposed to one that is primarily her own. Depending on the issue and circumstance, she may attempt to create the appearance of some distance between herself and the acts of the coalition. Although this sometimes requires fancy footwork, her external colleagues will understand the risks for her in assuming a visible role. If she argues the case, she will emphasize the advantage to the agency of its being responsive and will underscore her own commitment to the agency as she does so. In effect, she assumes a boundary-spanning role. She proves her loyalty to the agency by visibly appearing to be interpreting the agency's stance to members of the coalition, while at the same time she interprets the coalition's perceptions and positions to agency officials.

Usually, this process presupposes that the target of the coalition's acts is the agency's top management and that the issue in question lends itself to collaborative or mild campaign interventions. But there are occasions—however infrequent—when a supervisor has the latitude to engage with outsiders regarding issues that are implicitly critical of the agency without causing highly negative judgments to be made about her. An illustration is a minority group supervisor who may be expected to represent minority perspectives in regard to some agency activities. Sometimes this is part of the price an agency pays for the legitimation it gains from having a minority group member fill a particular position. Employing a black supervisor to head an intake department, for example, projects an image of agency nondiscrimination; for the supervisor to engage with colleagues to work for improved services to minorities is hardly unexpected and is not likely to be perceived negatively.

Whether a supervisor who is a member of an external coalition behaves solely collaboratively depends, too, on the extent to which she has an independent power base. If she or her colleagues in the coalition contribute important resources to the agency (such as access to funding or the sanction of significant community influentials), she may be insulated from significant retaliation and thus moved to act with greater militance when the occasion demands it. Militance is also possible in any situation in which the cost to the agency of punishing the supervisor is greater than the cost of either acceding to the coalition's demands or ignoring them. A union shop steward, for example, can engage any number of outsiders in the union's campaign to achieve its goals and get away with it—if, as is usual, the union is prepared to protect her and settling with the union is more important to the agency than a protracted conflict with it. In sum, a supervisor's ability to get away with militant opposition depends on her power within the agency and her value to it, and we might add, the extent to which she is perceived as replaceable.

A supervisor may also behave more militantly if the target of the coalition's influence attempt is not the agency's management but some subunit of the organization. Indeed, her involvement of outsiders may be designed to provide the extra clout necessary to convince her boss to decide in her favor in a contest with peers.

By and large, however, supervisors who engage in coalition activities with external actors are constrained to act collaboratively—or at the very least, to appear to be collaborative and be able to carry it off with credibility. As in our example of the staff who drew on their contacts with advocates for the homeless, staff members who need to appear collaborative may choose to go underground and engage in secret maneuvers with outsiders, but internal secret maneuvering can entail significant cost if one is exposed. If a supervisor is seen as double dealing, she may win an issue, but her long-term interests will have been compromised. The risk in getting caught at secret maneuvering with external actors is all the greater.

A Final Word on Ethics

Although the foregoing discussion has focused on group-based politics, it is fitting that we close the chapter—and this book—with a cautionary final word about the ethics of political interventions. The word *political* conjures up an image for some social workers of deceit and trickery—and indeed, our own reference to double dealing supports the stereotype. Nevertheless, many of the interventions that carry a political label reflect largely candid and direct interactions. There may be little dissembling, for example, in persuading, negotiating aggressively, or trying to mobilize support—all of which are political acts. The study in Chapter 8 in which a large sample of managers characterized effective organizational politicians as sensitive, articulate, socially adept, confident, and popular supports the view that political actors are not necessarily perceived negatively—nor, in our judgment, should they be.

Nevertheless, political interventions may also entail covert maneuvering or the hidden exercise of influence. As such, they raise ethical issues. In our view, ethical behavior between colleagues can be monitored in two ways. The first is essentially pragmatic; the second is to be guided by a set of principles that inform the intervention.

To be effective politically, the supervisor must not appear to be manipulative. However she might wish to maneuver covertly in a particular situation, the very fact that her behavior may be judged negatively acts as a constraint. The cautions throughout this volume on the importance of being prudent when one goes underground have been offered in this vein. It is critical, we have suggested, that the supervisor be viewed in the agency as a committed and competent professional, one who is loyal to the agency and its administration, is concerned about the effectiveness of her unit, and cares about the needs and well-being of its clients. It is against this backgrop that specific political struggles must be assessed and interventions engaged or eschewed. Her credibility—and therefore her influence—suffers if her political maneuvering is seen to overshadow her commitment and expertise. To counsel political moderation, as we have done, represents a pragmatic attempt to monitor ethics. The core assumption is that if she is judicious in her use of covert political means, she is less likely to cross the boundaries of ethically questionable behavior.

Even so, there are often value issues at play, and the overarching principles of professional conduct serve only partially as a guide. Many ethical issues in social work are clear and direct. Professional misrepresentation, abdication of one's responsibilities to clients, and misappropriation of the work of a colleague are all examples of distinctly unethical practice. As is the case for other professions, social work's code of ethics was initially developed primarily to protect the interests of clients and to prevent their exploitation. This is appropriate in large measure because the vulnerability and dependence of the client on the professional suggests the need for protection. Quite properly, if there is a conflict of interest between client and worker, the interests of the client should be foremost. Thus guidelines provided by the profession's code of ethics are relatively clear in distinguishing between ethical and unethical behavior with respect to relations with clients.

The same cannot be said regarding the ethics of interactions between colleagues. Although the code of ethics now includes prescriptions to guide behavior between professionals, they are—perhaps inevitably— general and ambiguous. More than is the case with clients, the organizational base of practice interjects a powerful set of variables that complicate the precise application of fixed ethical guides between colleagues. Factors such as variety in patterns of authority, conflicts generated by role or structure, or significant power differentials between actors result in a shifting and less precise value definition in interactions between colleagues. Furthermore, because there is a lack of consensus on precisely what constitutes the core values of social work and even less consensus on what behaviors should be viewed as a rejection of those values, it is hardly surprising that ethical prescriptions regarding relations with colleagues are imprecise and subject to disagreement.

Nonetheless, it is useful to articulate guidelines for interprofessional behavior in political situations. As we have noted elsewhere, the ethics of political maneuver depend on the nature of the situation (Brager and Holloway, 1978). Three variables inherent in the situation are, in our view, of uppermost importance: the social purpose of the interaction, the relative distribution of power in the encounter, and the requirements of effectiveness in the practice.

Identifying the prime beneficiary is important in assessing the ethics of the intervention. When the supervisor's clients or staff (and, by implication, the workers' clients) are the primary beneficiaries of an intervention, its ethical implications are different than when she is acting solely in her own interests. This is not to say that the supervisor's interests cannot be coincident with client interests, for the two are often closely related. For example, when a supervisor is successful in expanding the staff allocated to her unit, and by so doing reduces the caseload of each worker, this action is also in the clients' interest, because they will presumably receive a higher-quality service. But the action also serves the interests of the staff by making their jobs more manageable *and* it serves the interests of the supervisor as well. When, however, there is little benefit to staff or clients from a covert intervention, the activity has considerably less ethical justification.

Discrepancies in the power of interacting colleagues also informs the ethics of tactic selection. When the supervisor is the one with lesser influence and her goal is not fully shared by more powerful participants, she is, in our view, quite within ethical bounds to use political maneuvering as a tactic if the goal benefits her clients or unit. When her influence is equal to another's, the ethical choice is less certain, and much depends on the significance of the goal and her relationship with the other. If, for example, the other party has or would deceive her, she is ethically more free to play by the other's rules, particularly in regard to issues of importance. On the other hand, when there is parity of influence between the supervisor and another and their relationship has been marked by trust, ethical behavior requires openness between them. Similarly, when she is in the one-up position, it is incumbent on her to eschew covert means.

It is important to add that assessments of power in given situations may be more complex than a difference in positional power would suggest. It is possible, for example, that the power of unit staff may be such that they could successfully subvert the implementation of a new policy. If the new policy would benefit the unit's clients, political maneuvering in effecting the policy change would be appropriate in our view, even though technically the supervisor holds more positional power than her staff. Even in the above instance, however, covert means are justified only after the supervisor has intervened directly and failed, or prior experience leads her to the conclusion that a direct intervention would be unsuccessful.

We are aware that these conditions justifying covert interventions could provide workers who have a manipulative bent with the moral license to be covert for its own sake. The unobtrusive exercise of influence is justified, however, only when other means would be ineffective. Stated differently, social work values suggest that supervisors operate directly and openly as the norm; only when political maneuvering is really necessary should it be considered.

We note, in concluding this discussion, that there are a wide range of behaviors that fall under the rubric of political maneuver and they represent acts of quite different moral orders. For example, a supervisor could secretly try to generate support to pressure her executive, and although the act would meet our definition of political maneuvering, it would not be judged negatively by most professionals (except perhaps the executive!). The supervisor might even obfuscate her role, if confronted, without necessarily being perceived of as unprofessional. And although such acts as withholding information, exaggerating, and distorting are often seen as violations of the social work norm of openness, they have a different ethical coloration than major misrepresentation or outright falsification. Although the latter are proscribed in any situation, the former must be evaluated by the context in which they take place.

In sum, pragmatic considerations are an important means of limiting excess in political maneuvering. In addition, a set of ethical principles related to specific situations also inform value choices in the political arena. In concert, they provide direction for the supervisor as she strains to balance the political realities of her role with the professional interests for which she stands.

References

S. Alinsky, *Rules for Radicals*. New York: Vintage, 1971.

R. W. Allen, D. L. Madison, L. W. Porter, P. A. Renwick, and B. T. Mayes, "Organizational Politics: Tactics and Characteristics of Its Actors," *California Management Review*, Vol. 22, 1979.

W. P. Anthony, *Participative Management*. Reading, Mass.: Addison-Wesley, 1978.

C. Argyris and D. A. Schon, *Theory in Practice: Increasing Professional Effectiveness*. San Francisco: Jossey-Bass, 1974.

E. Aronson, J. Turner, and J. Carlsmith, "Communicator Credibility and Communication Discrepancy as Determinents of Opinion Change," *Journal of Abnormal and Social Pyschology*, Vol. 67, July 1963, pp. 31–36.

M. Austin, *Supervisory Management in the Human Services*. Englewood Cliffs, N.J.: Prentice-Hall, 1981.

S. Bacharach and E. Lawler, *Power and Politics in Organizations*. San Francisco: Jossey-Bass, 1980.

R. F. Bales, "In Conference," in R. C. Huseman, C. M. Logue, and D. L. Freshley, *Readings in Interpersonal and Organizational Communication*. Boston: Holbrook Press, 1969.

W. Bennis, "When to Resign," *Esquire*, June 1971.

C. I. Berger and L. L. Cummings, "Organizational Structure, Attitudes, and Behaviors," in B. M. Staw, Ed., *Research in Organizational Behavior*. Greenwich, Connecticut: JAI Press, 1979.

P. Blau, *Exchange and Power in Social Life*, 1969. New York: John Wiley, 1964.

W. C. Bolman, "The Ratings of Individuals in Organizations: An Alternate Approach," *Organizational Behavior and Human Performance*," Vol. 12, 1974.

L. Bowman and T. Deal, *Modern Approaches to Understanding and Managing Organizations*. San Francisco: Jossey-Bass, 1984.

R. F. Boyatzis, *The Competent Manager*. New York: Wiley, 1982.

G. Brager and S. Holloway, *Changing Human Service Organizations: Politics and Practice*. New York: Free Press, 1978.

G. Brager, H. Specht, and J. Torcyner, *Community Organizing*, 2nd ed., New York: Columbia University Press, 1987.

R. Bucher, "Social Process and Power in a Medical School," in M. N. Zald, Ed., *Power in Organizations*. Nashville, Tenn.: Vanderbilt University Press, 1970.

T. Caplow, "A Theory of Coalitions in the Triad," *American Sociological Review*, Vol. 26, 1956, pp. 489–93.

T. Caplow, *How to Run Any Organization*. New York: Holt, Rinehart & Winston, 1976.

T. Carney, *Job Smarts*. Toronto: Methuen, 1984.

J. Cashman, F. Dansereau Jr., G. Graen, and W. Haga, "Organizational Understructure and Leadership: A Longitudinal Investigation of the Managerial Role-making Process." *Organizational Behavior and Human Performance*, Vol. 15, 1976, pp. 278–96.

J. Cheney, T. Harford, and L. Soloman, "The Effects of Communicating Threats and Promises upon the Bargaining Process," *Journal of Conflict Resolution*, Vol. 16, 1972, pp. 99–107.

T. Clark, *Community Structure and Decision Making*. San Francisco: Chandler, 1966.

N. A. Cohen and G. B. Rhodes, "Social Work Supervision: A View Toward Leadership Style and Job Orientation in Education and Practice," *Administration in Social Work*. Vol. 1, Fall 1977.

J. Coleman, *Community Conflict*. New York: Free Press, 1957.

B. E. Collins and H. Guetzkow, *A Social Psychology of Group Processes for Decision Making*. New York: Wiley, 1964.

F. Dansereau Jr., G. Graen, and W. J. Haga, "A Vertical Dyad Linkage Approach to Leadership Within Formal Organizations," *Organizational Behavior and Human Performance*, Vol. 13, 1975, pp. 46–78.

J. A. Dawson, L. A. Messe, and J. L. Phillips, "Effects of Instructor-Leader Behavior on Student Performance," *Journal of Applied Psychology*, Vol. 56, 1972.

G. Dessler, "A Test of the Path-Goal Theory of Leadership." Unpublished doctoral dissertation, Baruch College, City University of New York, 1973.

M. Deutsch, "Conflicts: Productive and Destructive," *Journal of Social Issues*, Vol 25, Jan. 1969, p. 27.

M. Deutsch, *The Resolution of Conflict*. New Haven: Yale University Press, 1973.

M. Deutsch and R. J. Lewicki, "'Locking-in' Effects During a Game of Chicken," *Journal of Conflict Resolution*, Vol. 14, 1970, pp. 367–78.

W. F. Dowling and L. R. Sayles, *How Managers Motivate: The Imperatives of Supervision*, 2nd ed. New York: McGraw-Hill, 1978.

E. A. Fleishman, "Leadership Climate, Human Relations Training and Supervisory Behavior," *Personnel Psychology*, Vol. 6, 1953.

E. A. Fleishman, "Twenty Years of Consideration and Structure," in E. A. Fleishman and J. G. Hung, Eds., *Current Developments in the Study of Leadership*. Carbondale: Southern Illinois University Press, 1973.

E. A. Fleishman and E. F. Harris, "Patterns of Leadership Behavior Related to Employee Grievances and Turnover," *Personnel Psychology*, Vol. 15, 1962.

J. French and B. Raven, "The Bases of Social Power," in D. Cartwright, Ed., *Studies in Social Power*, Ann Arbor, Mich.: Institute for Social Research, 1959.

J. Galbraith, *Organizational Design*. Reading, Mass.: Addison-Wesley, 1977.

T. L. Gibson, "The Clinical Manager," *Clinical Social Work Journal*, Vol. 11, No. 2, 1983, pp. 191–97.

A. Gitterman, "Organizational Behavior and the Social Work Clinician," paper presented at Conference on Clinical Social Work sponsored by the National Association of Social Workers, November 1982.

A. Gitterman and I. Miller, "Supervisors as Educators," in F. W. Kaslow, Ed., *Supervision, Consultation and Staff Training in the Helping Professions*. San Francisco: Jossey-Bass, 1977.

E. Goffman, *Interaction Ritual*. Chicago: Aldine, 1967.

E. Goffman, *The Presentation of Self in Everyday Life*. New York: Doubleday, Anchor Books, 1959.

H. F. Gortner, J. Mahler, and J. B. Nicholson, *Organization Theory: A Public Perspective*. Chicago: Dorsey Press, 1987.

A. Gouldner, "The Norm of Reciprocity," *American Sociological Review*, Vol. 25, April 1960, pp. 161–78.

A. W. Gouldner, *Patterns of Industrial Democracy*, New York: Free Press, 1954.

D. K. Granvold, "Supervisory Style and Educational Prepartion," *Administration in Social Work*, Spring 1977.

N. Gross, J. Giacquinta, and M. Bernstein, *Implementing Organizational Innovations*. New York: Basic Books, 1971.

B. Gummer, "The Social Administrator as Politician," in F. Perlmutter, ed., *Human Services at Risk*. Lexington, Mass.: Lexington Books, D. C. Heath, 1984.

J. R. Hackman and E. E. Lawler, "Employee Reactions to Job Characteristics," *Journal of Applied Psychology*, Vol. 55, 1971.

J. R. Hackman and R. E. Walton, "Leading Groups in Organizations," in P. S. Goodman & Associates, Eds., *Designing Effective Work Groups*. San Francisco: Jossey-Bass, 1986.

G. Hage and R. Dewar, "Elite Values Versus Organizational Structure in Predicting Innovation," *Administrative Science Quarterly*, Vol. 18, September 1973.

J. Hage and M. Aiken, *Social Change in Complex Organizations*. New York: Random House, 1970.

D. Hall and K. Nougaim, "An Examination of Maslow's Need Hierarchy in an Organizational Setting," *Organizational Behavior and Human Performance*, Vol. 3, 1968.

E. F. Harrison, *The Managerial Decision-Making Process*, 2nd ed. Boston: Houghton Mifflin, 1981.

Y. Hasenfeld, Book Review, *Administration in Social Work*, Spring 1980, p. 122.

F. Hertzberg, *Work and the Nature of Man*. Cleveland: World, 1966.

R. W. Heyns, "What Makes a Conference Tick," in R. C. Huseman, C. M. Logue, and D. W. Freshley, *Readings in Interpersonal and Organizational Communication*. Boston, Holbrook Press, 1969.

L. R. Hoffman, E. Harburg, and N. R. F. Maier, "Differences and Disagreement as Factors in Creative Group Problem Solving," *Journal of Abnormal and Social Psychology*, Vol. 64, 1962, pp. 206–14.

E. Hollander, "Leadership and Social Exchange Processes," in K. Gergen, M. Greenberg, and R. Willis, Eds., *Social Exchange: Advances in Theory and Research*. New York: Winston-Wiley, 1979.

S. Holloway and H. Hornstein, "How Good News Makes Us Good," *Psychology Today*, Dec. 1976, pp. 76–80.

S. Holloway, H. Hornstein, and L. Tucker, "The Effects of Social and Non-Social Information on Interpersonal Behavior: The News Makes News," *Journal of Personality and Social Psychology*, Vol. 35, 1977, pp. 514–22.

R. J. House, "A 1976 Theory of Charismatic Leadership," in J. G. Hunt and L. L. Larson, Eds., *Leadership: The Cutting Edge*. Carbondale: Southern Illinois University Press, 1977.

R. House and M. L. Baetz, "Leadership," in Barry M. Staw, *Research in Organizational Behavior*, Vol. 1. Greenwich, Conn.: JAI Press, 1979.

R. House, A. Filley, and S. Kerr, "Relation of Leader Consideration and Initiating Structure to R and D Subordinate's Satisfaction," *Administrative Science Quarterly*, Vol. 16, 1971.

C. I. Hovland, I. L. Janis, and H. H. Kelley, *Communication and Persuasion*. New Haven: Yale University Press, 1953.

C. I. Hovland and W. Weiss, "The Influence of Source Credibility on Communication Effectiveness," *Public Opinion Quarterly*, Vol. 15, 1951, pp. 635–50.

J. M. Ivancevich, "Effects of Goal Setting on Performance and Job Satisfaction," *Journal of Applied Psychology*, Vol. 61, 1976.

A. Jago and V. Vroom, "Hierarchical Level and Leadership Style," *Organizational Behavior and Human Performance*, Vol. 18, Feb. 1977, pp. 131–46.

A. Kadushin, *Supervision in Social Work*. New York: Columbia University Press, 1976.

R. Kahn, D. Wolfe, R. Quinn, J. Snoek, and R. Rosenthal, *Organizational Stress: Studies in Role Conflict and Ambiguity*. New York: Wiley, 1964.

J. S. Kane and E. E. Lawler III, "Performance Appraisal Effectiveness: Its Assessment and Determinents," in B. M. Staw, Ed., *Research in Organizational Behavior*, Vol. 1. Greenwich, Conn.: JAI Press, 1979.

D. Katz and R. L. Kahn, *The Social Psychology of Organizations*. New York: Wiley, 1966.

R. Katz, "Job Longevity as a Situational Factor in Job Satisfaction," *Administrative Science Quarterly*, Vol. 23, 1978, pp. 104–23.

R. Katz, "Time and Work: Toward and Integrative Perspective," in B. Straw and L. Cummings, Eds., *Research in Organizational Behavior*, Vol. 2. Greenwich, Conn.: JAI Press, 1980, p. 99.

S. Kerr, "On the Folly of Rewarding A, While Hoping for B," *Academy of Management Journal*, Vol. 18, Dec. 1975.

S. Kerr, C. A. Schriesheim, C. J. Murphy, and R. Stodgill, "Toward a Contingency Theory of Leadership Based upon the Consideration and Initiating Structure Literature." *Organizational Behavior and Human Performance*, Vol. 12, 1974.

M. Landau and R. Stout Jr., "To Manage is Not to Control: Of The Folly of Type II Errors," *Public Administration Review*, Vol. 39, 1979, pp. 148–56.

J. T. Lanzetta and T. B. Roby, "The Relationship between Certain Group Process Variables & Group Problem-Solving Efficiency," *Journal of Social Psychology*, Vol. 52, 1960.

E. J. Lawler and G. A. Youngs Jr., "Coalition Formation: An Integrative Model," *Sociometry*, Vol. 38, 1975, pp. 1–17.

P. Lawrence and J. Lorsch, *Organization and Environment*. Boston: Harvard Business School, 1967.

A. W. Lerner, *The Politics of Decision Making*. Beverly Hills, Calif.: Sage, 1976.

H. Leventhal, "Fear Appeals and Persuasion: The Differentiation of a Motivational Construct," *American Journal of Public Health*, Vol. 61, 1971.

C. Levy, "The Ethics of Supervision," in C. Munson, Ed., *Social Work Supervision*. New York: Columbia University Press, 1979, p. 220.

K. Lewin, "Frontiers in Group Dynamics," *Human Relations*, Vol. 1, 1947.

K. Lewin, "Group Decision and Social Change," in T. M. Newcomb and E. L. Hartley, Eds., *Readings in Social Psychology*. New York: Holt, Rinehart & Winston, 1958.

C. M. Lichtman, "Some Interpersonal Response Correlates of Organizational Rank," *Journal of Applied Psychology*, Vol. 54, 1970, pp. 77–80.

R. Lippitt and R. K. White, "An Experimental Study of Leadership and Group Life," in E. E. Maccoby, T. M. Newcomb, and E. L. Hartley, Eds., *Readings in Social Psychology*. New York: Holt, Rinehart & Winston, 1958.

E. A. Locke and D. M. Schweiger, "Participation in Decision-Making: One More Look," in B. M. Staw, Ed., *Research in Organizational Behavior*. Greenwich, Conn.: JAI Press, 1979.

I. MacMillan, *Strategy Formulation: Political Concepts*. St. Paul, Minneapolis: West Publishing, 1978.

D. Macarov, "Management in the Social Work Curriculum," *Administration in Social Work*, Vol. 1 (2), Summer 1977.

I. Mangham, *The Politics of Organizational Change*. Westport, Conn.: Greenwood, 1979.

A. H. Maslow, *Self-Actualizing People: A Study in Psychological Health*. New York: Grune and Stratton, 1950.

D. McClelland, *Power: the Inner Experience*. New York: Irvington, 1975.

W. J. McGuire, "The Effectiveness of Supportive and Refutational Defenses in Immunizing and Restoring Beliefs Against Persuasion," Sociometry. Vol. 24, 1961.

W. J. McGuire, "Inducing Resistance to Persuasion," in L. Berkowitz, Ed., *Advances in Experimental Social Psychology*, Vol. 1. New York: Academic Press, 1964.

W. J. McGruire, "Persuasion, Resistance and Attitude Change," in I. Pool et al., Eds., *Handbook of Communication*. Skokie, Ill.: Rand McNally, 1973.

D. Mechanic, "Sources of Power and Lower Participants in Complex Organizations," in William Cooper et al., Eds., *New Perspectives in Organizational Research*. New York: Wiley, 1964.

R. K. Merton, *Social Theory and Social Structure*, rev. ed. New York: Free Press, 1957.

R. K. Merton, *Social Theory and Social Structure*, enlarged ed. New York: Free Press, 1968.

I. Miller, "Issues and Ideas: Organization, Administration and Supervision," *Journal of Visual Impairment and Blindness*, Nov. 1982.

M. Miller and M. Burgoon, "The Relationship Between Violations of Expectations and the Induction of Resistance to Persuasion," *Human Communications Research*, Vol. 5, 1979, pp. 301–13.

R. L. Miller, P. Brickman, and D. Bolen, "Attribution Versus Persuasion as a Means for Modifying Behavior," *Journal of Personality and Social Psychology.* Vol. 31, 1975.

L. Mohr, *Explaining Organizational Behavior.* San Francisco: Jossey-Bass, 1982.

M. Mulder and H. White, "Participation and Power Equalization," *Organizational Behavior and Human Performance*, Vol. 5, 1970, pp. 430–48.

G. R. Oldham, "The Motivational Strategies Used by Supervisors: Relationships to Effectiveness Indicators," *Organizational Behavior and Human Performance*, Vol. 15, 1976.

B. Oshry, *Middle Power.* Boston: Power and Systems Training, 1980.

R. Patti, *Social Welfare Administration.* Englewood Cliffs, N.J.: Prentice-Hall, 1983.

R. Patti, E. Diedrick, D. Olson, and J. Crowell, "From Direct Service to Administrations," *Administration in Social Work*, Fall, 1979.

R. Patti and M. Austin, "Socializing the Direct Service Practitioner in the Ways of Supervisory Management," *Administration in Social Work*, Vol. 1 (3), Fall 1977.

A. Pettigrew, *The Politics of Organizational Decision Making.* London: Tavistock, 1972.

J. Pfeffer, *Organizational Design.* Arlington Heights, Ill: AHM Publishing, 1978.

J. Pfeffer, *Power in Organizations.* Cambridge, Mass.: Ballinger, 1981.

F. F. Rabinovitz, *City Policies and Planning.* New York: Atherton, 1969.

P. O. Radde, *Supervising: A Guide for All Levels.* San Diego: University Associates, 1981.

A. P. Raia, *Managing by Objectives.* New York: Scott, Foresman, 1974.

S. Ransom, B. Hinings, and R. Greenwood, "The Structuring of Organizational Structures," *Administrative Science Quarterly*, Vol. 25, 1980, pp. 1–17.

B. H. Raven and A. W. Kruglanski, "Conflict and Power," in P. Swingle, Ed., *The Structure of Conflict.* New York: Academic Press, 1970.

K. K. Reardon, *Persuasion: Theory and Context.* Beverly Hills, Calif.: Sage, 1981.

W. H. Riker, *The Theory of Political Coalitions.* New Haven: Yale University Press, 1962.

T. S. Robertson, *Innovative Behavior and Communication.* New York: Holt, Rinehart & Winston, 1971.

A. M. Rose, "Voluntary Associations Under Conditions of Competition and Conflict," *Social Forces*, Vol. 24, 1955, pp. 160–61.

J. Z. Rubin and B. R. Brown, *The Social Pychology of Bargaining and Negotiation.* New York: Academic Press, 1975.

R. P. Rumelt, *Strategy, Structure and Economic Performance*. Boston: Graduate School of Business Administration, Harvard University, 1974.

G. R. Salancik and J. Pfeffer, "The Bases and Use of Power in Organizational Decision Making," *Administrative Science Quarterly*, Vol. 19., 1974, pp. 453–73.

G. R. Salancik and J. Pfeffer, "Who Gets Power—And How They Hold on To It," *Organizational Dynamics*, Winter 1977, pp. 3–21.

D. Sanzotta, *The Manager's Guide to Interpersonal Relations*, New York: American Management Associations, 1979.

R. Sarri, "Effective Social Work Intervention in Administrative and Planning Roles: Implications for Education," in *Facing the Challenge*. New York: Council on Social Work Education, 1973.

L. Sayles, *Leadership: What Effective Managers Really Do and How They Do It*. New York: McGraw-Hill, 1979.

L. Shulman, *Skills of Supervision and Staff Management*. Ithaca, Ill.: Peacock, 1982.

W. Schutz, *The Interpersonal Underworld*. Palo Alto, Calif: Science and Behavior Books, 1970.

D. Sears and J. Freedman, "Effects of Expected Familiarity with Arguments upon Opinion Change and Selective Exposure," *Journal of Personality and Social Pyschology*, Vol. 2, 1965, pp. 420–26.

D. Silverman, *The Theory of Organizations*. New York: Basic Books, 1971.

H. Simon, *Administrative Behavior*, 3rd ed. New York: Free Press, 1976.

H. P. Sims and A. D. Szilagyi, "Leader Reward Behavior and Subordinate Satisfaction and Performance," *Organizational Behavior and Human Performance*, 1975.

H. P. Sims Jr., "The Leader as a Manager of Reinforcement Contingencies," in J. G. Hunt and L. L. Larson, Eds., *Leadership: The Cutting Edge*. Carbondale: Southern Illinois University Press, 1977.

M. Snyder, Self-monitoring of Expressive Behavior," *Journal of Personality and Social Psychology*, Vol. 30, 1974.

C. Sofer, *Organizations in Theory and Practice*. New York: Basic Books, 1972.

R. Stagner, "Corporate Decision Making," *Journal of Applied Pyschology*, Vol. 53, 1969, pp. 1–13.

A. H. Stanton and M. S. Schwartz, *The Mental Hospital*. New York: Basic Books, 1954.

L. L. Steinmetz and H. R. Todd, *First-Line Management: Approaching Supervision Effectively*. Dallas, Texas: Business Publications, 1975.

R. M. Stodgill, *Handbook of Leadership: A Survey of Theory and Leadership*. New York: Free Press, 1974.

A. Strauss, *Negotiations*. San Francisco: Jossey-Bass, 1978.

G. Strauss and L. Sayles, *Behavioral Strategies for Managers*. Englewood Cliffs, N.J.: Prentice-Hall, 1980.

G. Sykes, *The Society of Captives: A Study of a Maximum Security Prison*. Princeton, N.J.: Princeton University Press, 1958.

A. D. Szilagyi Jr. and M. J. Wallace Jr., *Organizational Behavior and Performance*, 2nd ed. Santa Monica, Calif: Goodyear Publishing Co., 1980.

J. D. Thompson, *Organizations in Action*. New York: McGraw-Hill, 1967.

V. H. Vroom, *Work and Motivation*. New York: Wiley, 1964.

E. H. Walster and L. Festinger, reported in E. E. Jones and H. B. Gerrard, *Foundations of Social Pyschology*. New York: Wiley, 1967, pp. 444–45.

J. Wax, "Power Theory and Institutional Change," *Social Service Review*, Vol. 45, Sept. 1971.

K. E. Weike, "Reduction of Cognitive Dissonance through Task Enhancement and Effort Expenditure," *Journal of Abnormal and Social Psychology*, Vol. 68, 1964, pp. 533–49.

W. Weiss, "Opinion Congruence with a Negative Source on One Issue as a Factor Influencing Agreement on Another Issue," *Journal of Personality and Social Psychology*, Vol. 54, 1957, pp. 180–86.

G. Westerlund and S. Sjostrand, *Organizational Myths*. New York: Harper & Row, 1979.

J. Whittaker, "Attitude Change and Communication-Attitude Discrepancy," *Journal of Social Psychology*, Vol. 65, Feb. 1965, pp. 141–47.

W. F. Whyte and E. L. Hamilton, *Action Research for Management*. Homewood, Ill., Irwin and Dorsey Press, 1964.

H. Wilensky, *Organizational Intelligence*. New York: Basic Books, 1967.

D. Yates Jr., *The Politics of Management*. New York: Free Press, 1985.

G. Yukl, *Leadership in Organizations*. Englewood Cliffs, N.J.: Prentice-Hall, 1981.

M. N. Zald, "Organizational Control Structures in Five Correctional Institutions," in M. N. Zald, Ed., *Social Welfare Institutions*. New York: Wiley, 1965.

A. Zaleznik, *Human Dilemmas of Leadership*. New York: Harper & Row, 1966.

A. Zaleznik, "Managers and Leaders: Are they Different?" *Harvard Business Review*, May–June 1977.

Index